CIPS Study Matters

Level 5

Advanced Diploma in Purchasing and Supply

Improving Supply Chain Performance

Ronald Wells
Business School, University of Hertfordshire

THE
CHARTERED INSTITUTE OF
PURCHASING & SUPPLY

Published by

The Chartered Institute of Purchasing and Supply
Easton House, Easton on the Hill, Stamford, Lincolnshire PE9 3NZ
Tel: +44 (0) 1780 756 777
Fax: +44 (0) 1780 751 610
Email: info@cips.org
Website: www.cips.org

While every effort has been made to ensure that references to websites are correct at time of going to press, the world wide web is a constantly changing environment and CIPS cannot accept any responsibility for any changes to addresses.

CIPS acknowledges product, service and company names referred to in this publication, many of which are trade names, service marks, trademarks or registered trademarks.

CIPS, The Chartered Institute of Purchasing & Supply and its logo are all trademarks of the Chartered Institute of Purchasing & Supply.

The right of Ronald Wells to be identified as author of this work has been asserted by him in accordance with the Copyright, Designs and Patents Act, 1988 in force or as amended from time to time.

Technical reviewer: Alan Penman, Alan Penman Associates

Instructional design and publishing project management by Wordhouse Ltd, Reading, UK

Content management system, instructional editing and pre-press by Echelon Learning Ltd, London, UK

Index prepared by Indexing Specialists (UK) Ltd, Hove, UK

ISBN 1-86124-157-7
ISBN 978-186124-157-3

Contents

Introduction

This course book has been designed to assist you in studying for the CIPS Improving Supply Chain Performance unit in the Level 5 Advanced Diploma in Purchasing and Supply. The book covers all topics in the official CIPS unit content document, as illustrated in the table beginning on page xi.

This course book is designed to enable students to use a range of techniques and strategies to develop and improve supplier performance in order to achieve competitiveness, efficiency and profitability within the supply chain.

By working through this course book students will be able to measure and evaluate the effectiveness of supply chain performance. They will be able to identify innovative development of systems to improve the performance of the supply chain, and make justifiable recommendations for implementation in order to aid the effectiveness of the supply chain.

In addition skills will be developed that will assist the CIPS professional to perform more effectively in the future.

How to use this book

The course book will take you step by step through the unit content in a series of carefully planned 'study sessions' and provides you with learning activities, self-assessment questions and revision questions to help you master the subject matter. The guide should help you organise and carry out your studies in a methodical, logical and effective way, but if you have your own study preferences you will find it a flexible resource too.

Before you begin using this course book, make sure you are familiar with any advice provided by CIPS on such things as study skills, revision techniques or support and how to handle formal assessments.

If you are on a taught course, it will be up to your tutor to explain how to use the book – when to read the study sessions, when to tackle the activities and questions, and so on.

If you are on a self-study course, or studying independently, you can use the course book in the following way:

Scan the whole book to get a feel for the nature and content of the subject matter.

Plan your overall study schedule so that you allow enough time to complete all 20 study sessions well before your examinations – in other words, leaving plenty of time for revision.

For each session, set aside enough time for reading the text, tackling all the learning activities and self-assessment questions, and the revision question at the end of the session, and for the suggested further reading. Guidance on roughly how long you should set aside for studying each session is given at the beginning of the session.

Now let's take a look at the structure and content of the individual study sessions.

Overview of the study sessions

The course book breaks the content down into 20 sessions, which vary from three to six or seven hours' duration each. However, we are not advising you to study for this sort of time without a break! The sessions are simply a convenient way of breaking the syllabus into manageable chunks. Most people would try to study one or two sessions a week, taking one or two breaks within each session. You will quickly find out what suits you best.

Each session begins with a brief **introduction** which sets out the areas of the syllabus being covered and explains, if necessary, how the session fits in with the topics that come before and after.

After the introduction there is a statement of the **session learning objectives**. The objectives are designed to help you understand exactly what you should be able to do after you've studied the session. You might find it helpful to tick them off as you progress through the session. You will also find them useful during revision. There is one session learning objective for each numbered subsection of the session.

After this, there is a brief section reproducing the learning objectives and indicative content from the official **unit content document**. This will help you to understand exactly which part of the syllabus you are studying in the current session.

Following this, there are **prior knowledge** and **resources** sections if necessary. These will let you know if there are any topics you need to be familiar with before tackling each particular session, or any special resources you might need, such as a calculator or graph paper.

Then the main part of the study session begins, with the first of the numbered main subsections. At regular intervals in each study session, we have provided you with **learning activities**, which are designed to get you actively involved in the learning process. You should always try to complete the activities – usually on a separate sheet of your own paper – before reading on. You will learn much more effectively if you are actively involved in doing something as you study, rather than just passively reading the text in front of you. The feedback or answers to the activities are provided at the end of the session. Do not be tempted to skip the activity.

We also provide a number of **self-assessment questions** in each study session. These are to help you to decide for yourself whether or not you have achieved the learning objectives set out at the beginning of the session. As with the activities, you should always tackle them – usually on a separate sheet of paper. Don't be tempted to skip them. The feedback or answers are again at the end of the session. If you still do not understand a topic having attempted the self-assessment question, always try to re-read the relevant passages in the textbook readings or session, or follow the advice on further reading at the end of the session. If this still doesn't work, you should contact the CIPS Membership and Qualification Advice team.

For most of the learning activities and self-assessment questions you will need to use separate sheets of paper for your answers or responses. Some of the activities or questions require you to complete a table or form, in which case you could write your response in the study guide itself, or photocopy the page.

At the end of the session are three final sections.

The first is the **summary**. Use it to remind yourself or check off what you have just studied, or later on during revision.

Then follows the **suggested further reading** section. This section, if it appears, contains recommendations for further reading which you can follow up if you would like to read alternative treatments of the topics. If for any reason you are having difficulty understanding the course book on a particular topic, try one of the alternative treatments recommended. If you are keen to read around and beyond the syllabus, to help you pick up extra points in the examination for example, you may like to try some of the additional readings recommended. If this section does not appear at the end of a session, it usually means that further reading for the session topics is not necessary.

At the end of the session we direct you to a **revision question**, which you will find in a separate section at the end of the course book. Feedback on the questions is also given.

Reading lists

CIPS produces an official reading list, which recommends essential and desirable texts for augmenting your studies. This reading list is available on the CIPS website or from the CIPS Bookshop. This course book is one of the essential texts for this unit. In this section we describe the main characteristics of the other essential text for this unit, which you are strongly urged to buy and use throughout your course.

The other essential text is:

Purchasing and Supply Chain Management 7th edition, by Kenneth Lysons and Brian Farrington, published by FT Prentice Hall in 2006.

Clearly written and covering a wide range of information, models and definitions, this book is an ideal overall resource for this course. The contents clearly cover a wide range of purchasing topics and the text will provide a quick source of reference for practitioners on many aspects of purchasing and supply. This new seventh edition has been fully revised and chapters on storage, transport and human resources have been replaced by new chapters on supplier relationships, product innovation and supplier involvement. This new edition contains: an emphasis on purchasing strategy; the inclusion of public sector purchasing; coverage of topics such as e-procurement, RFID, value management and fraud. The book contains a comprehensive bibliography, index and glossary as well as case studies and discussion questions in every chapter and sample past examination questions from CIPS.

Unit content coverage

In this section we reproduce the whole of the official CIPS unit content document for this unit. The overall unit characteristics and learning outcomes for the unit are given first. Then, in the table that follows, the learning objectives and indicative content are given in the left hand column. In the right hand column are the study sessions, or subsections, in which you will find coverage of the various topics.

Unit Characteristics

Achieving success within the supply chain involves a complex range of variables, which can frequently be dependent on one another for the success of the supply chain.

This unit is designed to enable students to use a range of techniques and strategies to develop and improve supplier performance in order to achieve competitiveness, efficiency and profitability within the supply chain.

By the end of this unit, students will be able to measure and evaluate the effectiveness of supply chain performance. They will be able to identify innovative development of systems to improve the performance of the supply chain, and make justifiable recommendations for implementation in order to aid the effectiveness of the supply chain.

Learning Outcomes

On completion of this unit, students will be able to:

- Understand the contribution technology can make to supply chain performance management
- Evaluate the organisational procedures and techniques that can be used in developing and improving supplier performance, including the reduction of risk and the introduction of supplier innovations
- Set performance standards to which supply chain strategies should aspire
- Develop an integrated approach to the implementation of supply chain activities which are designed to maximise competitive advantage and reduce risk exposures
- Propose systems and techniques to achieve best practice and enhance customer service for all stakeholders
- Contrast different negotiation strategies and styles and their effectiveness in a given range of situations
- Use a variety of support tools available and apply them in complex and high-level negotiations
- Understand the critical elements of supplier development and techniques to foster supply chain innovation
- Work together to support cross-functional key performance indicators and objectives (KPIs) and to measure performance

Learning objectives and indicative content

1   **Developing and improving supplier performance
    (Weighting 30%)**

1.1   Develop source-related activities so as to inform and provide   Study session 1
      value to other functional areas in the organisation, and in ways
      that support the overall objectives of the organisation.
      •   The business requirements for supply, and document in
          an appropriate way (specification, service level agreement
          (SLA) etc
      •   Cross-functional team-working skills to determine business
          requirements through appropriate stakeholder consultations
      •   The need to align supply chain activities to the
          organisational strategy, while maintaining a degree of
          flexibility to respond to changing needs
      •   The need for purchasing to provide customer service to
          other functional areas and identify appropriate tools and
          techniques to implement such service (e.g. engagement
          and consultation, regular management reporting, helpdesk
          solutions, consultative style)
      •   How purchasing, as a function, can add demonstrable value
          to the business, including cost reduction, risk mitigation,
          security of supply, enhanced service, improved quality and
          supplier innovations
      •   How purchasing can use its supply-market knowledge
          to assess and report risks, threats and/or supply chain
          vulnerabilities in an accurate and timely manner
      •   An appropriate communications programme that keeps
          other functional areas informed about purchasing-related
          activities and adds value to their own areas of responsibility

1.2 Employ appropriate key performance measures.   Study session 3
- The purpose of supplier key performance indicators (KPIs) in the improvement of supplier performance
- How a supplier KPI is developed and measured
- The need for base-lining existing performance prior to the development of supplier KPIs
- A range of potential supplier KPIs, including price effectiveness, cost savings, service enhancements, quality measures and improvements, innovation and risk/compliance
- The implications of a supplier failing to meet KPIs and outline appropriate management controls that can be used to assist compliance (e.g. service credit/debit regimes, incentivisation and gainshare models)
- Penalty clauses, liquidated damages, increased/decreased share of business etc
- How a supplier's performance can be audited to ensure KPIs are accurately reported
- The various processes of benchmarking and explain how benchmarking can be used to generate stretching KPIs
- The term Balance Business Scorecard (Kaplan & Norton) and describe how this could be used in the purchasing environment
- How to draft a prospective balance business scorecard (BBS) to measure an on-going supply situation

1.3 Manage purchasing activities to influence the ability of an   Study session 4
organisation to achieve its objectives.
- The benefits to the organisation of robust supplier selection and evaluation
- The range of appropriate supplier selection and evaluation techniques designed to achieve business requirements
- The methods of monitoring and measuring supplier performance
- Information on how purchasing can influence the quality delivered from suppliers
- How purchasing can contribute to an organisation's approach to total quality management
- Process improvement models, such as 6-Sigma, and how they can be used in a purchasing context to bring benefit to an organisation
- A typical purchasing planning cycle and how purchasing activities need to be aligned to plans adopted by the rest of the organisation
- How purchasing can contribute to fiscal planning activities
- Ways in which purchasing assists research and development by third party suppliers and collaborators
- How should vendors be rated to demonstrate a positive contribution to the business' performance?
- How cross-functional teams can help purchasing deliver better results for a business

1.4 Develop and manage external contacts with the supply market to gain important information about new technologies, potential new materials and services, new sources of supply and/or changes in market conditions (specifically emerging risks and opportunities).

- Define the terms: innovation, market research, supplier analysis, market intelligence, competitive intelligence (and others)
- Define the term reverse engineering
- The process of supply market research/analysis
- How to develop an appropriate relationship with third party research and analysis organisations
- Business reasons to conduct supply market research
- Appropriate processes for testing and evaluating supply innovations
- The processes of benchmarking and how they can be used to gain market information
- The ways in which purchasing can contribute to production forecasts

1.5 Identify, evaluate and develop new and existing suppliers and use appropriate techniques to develop and improve supplier performance including:

- The processes and benefits of supplier appraisal and selection
- The processes and benefits of vendor rating and feedback
- The terms value analysis, value management and value engineering
- The ways in which suppliers can work with an organisation to improve productivity, efficiency and quality. The role of purchasing in facilitating these processes
- The meaning of supplier adoption. The process for adopting a new supplier and the key stages in implementation needed to switch supply
- The meaning of sunk and switching costs. Practical reasons why some organisations will not switch supply, despite potential benefits
- The process of trialling and piloting new innovations
- The follow-on processes required to implement a new supply innovation (including user acceptance and controlled roll-outs)
- How suppliers can be managed and developed to contain supply-related risks and reduce supply chain vulnerability

1.6 Devise appropriate supplier management organisational models   Study session 2
in both the centralised and decentralised purchasing function,
and demonstrate how other functional areas might interact in
these models:
- The meaning of single point of contact, and the benefits
- The relative merits of single point of contact versus multiple
  touch-points for managing supplier relationships effectively
- The prospective number of touch-points that a supplier
  might have within a client organisation and evaluation of
  the relative merits of a diverse supply relationship
- The role of purchasing as a facilitator of supplier
  relationships
- The purpose and potential benefits of a cross-functional
  approach to managing supplier relationships
- The role of executive sponsors of supplier relationships, and
  their responsibilities
- The decentralised purchasing function. The concept of a
  lead buyer and how this might operate for different types of
  supply

1.7 Describe appropriate leadership styles to support supplier   Study session 2
development:
- Key driving factors that will encourage a supplier to develop
  and improve the delivery of goods and services
- The relative merits of selling and telling
- Various types of supplier incentive and their relative merits
- How a gainshare model works and potential problems with
  the concept
- Appropriate circumstances for purchasing to take a directive
  approach to supplier development and, similarly, those
  required for a facilitative approach
- The need for consistent measures of progress when
  developing suppliers
- The need for purchasing to communicate supplier
  development internally within an organisation

2 **Maximising competitiveness (Weighting 30%)**

2.1 Propose and manage systematic organisational efforts to create   Study session 7
and maintain networks of competent suppliers, and to improve
various supplier capabilities necessary for an organisation to
meet increasingly competitive challenges:
- Why and how suppliers are segmented (e.g. ABC)
- The key characteristics of each segment of the supply base
  (e.g. Tier 1: strategic, high value-add, high risk, innovative;
  Tier 2: regular purchases, medium-high value, framework
  agreements; Tier 3: commodity items, one-off purchases,
  little relationship or value-add
- The need for a consistent supplier management process and
  some of the key components it might contain
- The benefits of supplier rationalisation

XV

2.2 Develop, manage and maintain effective communications between an organisation and its suppliers to ensure that correct quality specifications are given to suppliers and subsequently delivered back to the business in measurable terms. To include early supplier involvement and risk transfer techniques: Study session 8
- The process of cross-functional involvement in the development of a specification and the specific role for purchasing
- The meaning of the term early supplier involvement and the key benefits and potential drawbacks to an organisation
- Some of the key principles of communicating effectively to suppliers
- The benefits of supplier forums and supplier associations

2.3 Manage cost reduction for organisational efficiency and provide added value to customers: Study session 9
- A typical purchase cost reduction programme and how such a programme is developed
- The benefits of volume (time and/or quantity) contracts and systems contracts
- The relative merits of stockless purchasing and just-in-time (J-I-T)
- How customer-driven supply chain innovations can be developed and the role of purchasing in creating and establishing effective supply
- The balance between cost efficiency and quality/risk issues

2.4 Plan and develop a well-structured approach to measuring the performance of suppliers including: Study session 10
- The development of joint performance appraisal systems
- Use of cross-functional teams from both organisations to monitor, review and analyse results on a periodic basis
- The use of both quantitative and qualitative measures
- Use of 360-degree feedback
- Supplier business continuity plans

2.5 Compare and contrast – through purchasing research – different supply markets and conditions, and liaise closely with logistics/suppliers to co-ordinate inbound logistics and associated materials flows: Study session 11
- Benchmarking (as described in 1.2 and 1.4)
- The benefits of documenting the key steps in a supply chain process flow and typical ways in which this is achieved (e.g. iDEF)
- The role of business process re-engineering in improving the supply chain for inbound logistics and materials flow
- The process of lean supply and the arguments for and against (Lamming/Cox)

2.6 Appraise the benefits of automated processes and information   Study session 12
flows and their impact on the supply chain in terms of
efficiency, productivity, quality improvement, cost reduction,
payments and materials flow management:
- The benefits of automated supply chain processes (reduced
  cost, improved communication, reduced error, reduced
  lead time, higher accuracy, greater quality, improved
  supplier relations, real-time information, reduced fraud,
  management information and feedback)
- The benefits of automated processes and the information
  gained from them for suppliers and their businesses
- How and why suppliers might choose to invest jointly with
  the purchaser in automation of the supply chain
- Extranets and how in practice they work with a supply base
- The benefits of automated purchase-to-pay systems

3.0 Advanced negotiations in the supply chain (Weighting 15%)
3.1 Compare, contrast and evaluate different negotiation strategies,   Study session 13
styles and levels in different supply chain contexts. (e.g. open
and closed-book negotiation). Formulate appropriate strategies
for negotiation within and across the supply chain and to
manage risk and reward in the negotiation process:
- The basic tenets of the negotiation process and the key
  behaviours required to negotiate effectively in a variety of
  purchasing contexts
- The need for teamwork in negotiation
- The role of trust in negotiation for both new and
  long-standing supplier relationships
- Open-book negotiations and their relative merits
3.2 Manage the negotiation process in line with organisational   Study session 14
objectives and its relation to policy, general strategy and internal
strategy for the purchasing and supply process:
- How a negotiation campaign is designed and developed and
  the key considerations required in doing so
- How the business requirements for supply need to be
  reflected in the detailed negotiation plan
- How corporate policy and/or organisational objectives may
  affect the negotiation plan in terms of behaviour, targets,
  timescales and/or scope
- Key ethical considerations when leading a negotiation
3.3 Plan and develop appropriate techniques for managing effective   Study session 16
supplier relationships so as to foster trust and commitment in
the negotiation process, including:
- The three definitions of trust (Sako)
- Development of inter-organisation relationships
- Buyer-supplier partnership agreements
- Development of a relationship charter
- The importance of ethics, integrity and values
- Escalation routes to resolve issues effectively
- The human factor within relationships

4.2 Identify the critical elements of supplier development:　　　Study session 19
- Respective roles and responsibilities of those involved in supplier development including those of executive sponsors
- The need for continuous improvement (Kaizen) and methods for achieving it (e.g. quality circles)
- The need for creating and fostering a team-working collaborative environment both internally and externally with the suppliers
- The role of innovation councils
- The relative merits of joint problem solving with suppliers
- Process improvement techniques such as quality circles, 6-Sigma and business process re-engineering
- Gainshare models for innovation and process improvement
- The meaning of breakthrough value creation and how this can be achieved in a supply chain context
- The need for policy creation and compliance

4.3 Appraise the application of technology to automate and　　Study session 20
streamline key operational processes within the supply chain (both internal and external to the organisation), including:
- Information flow and use of supply-side extranets
- E-sourcing and electronic ordering/payments: on-line catalogues, electronic point of sale (EPOS), electronic fund transfer (EFT)
- Automated purchase-to-pay systems
- Automated payments, accounting and reconciliation
- Use of an extranet to include cross-functional representatives both internally and externally
- Reduction of fraud and payment error risks

Aligning procurement activities with business objectives

Introduction

The purchasing function is an important part of the organisation and must operate with the business objectives in mind. There has to be clear understanding of the strategic direction of the business, a willingness to respond quickly to changing market conditions and a communication strategy that ensures the buyers are in tune with customers and suppliers inside and outside of the organisation.

The purchasing function must demonstrate that it can add value to the business operations by an inherent culture of customer service and a responsive structure that is flexible in the light of environmental changes.

'Corporate strategy is the pattern of major objectives, purposes or goals and essential policies or plans for achieving those goals, stated in such a way as to define what business the company is in or is to be in and the kind of company it is or is to be.'

Andrews (1971)

Session learning objectives

After completing this session you should be able to:

1.1 Explain the importance of linking the procurement function with business objectives.
1.2 Describe how the purchasing function can add value to the business.
1.3 Explain how strategic alignment must contain an element of flexibility.
1.4 Evaluate the importance of customer service within the supply chain function.

Unit content coverage

Learning objective

1.1 Develop source-related activities so as to inform and provide value to other functional areas in the organisation, and in ways that support the overall objectives of the organisation.

Prior knowledge

An understanding of the essentials of corporate strategy.

Resources

Access to organisational strategic plans.

Timing

You should set aside about 4 hours to read and complete this session, including learning activities, self-assessment questions, the suggested further reading (if any) and the revision question.

1.1 Aligning procurement activities with business objectives

Strategic management

There are many definitions by academic writers, but essentially strategic management is concerned with the overall direction of an organisation. As businesses have developed, strategic management has been introduced into other layers of the organisation, as a result of the move towards leaner structures, the increasing division of the business into strategic business units, and a sense in some organisations that it is too important a subject to be left entirely in the hands of a few managers.

Businesses are increasingly complex, with the requirement to digest large amounts of information drawn from the macro and micro environments. This needs a balance between carrying out the immediate needs of the business, and the future demands of that same business. Decisions have to be made as to who becomes responsible for the overall strategic management so that all business objectives are achieved. In addition, any attempt to plan formally must take into account the potential for change as environmental factors interfere with those plans (Mintzberg's emergent strategy).

Life cycle analysis

The product life cycle is a concept that states that all products in their original unmodified form have a definite life cycle. It plots the potential sales of a product over its lifetime as it goes through periods of introduction, growth, maturity, decline and withdrawal. The *length* of the product life cycle can of course vary with the success of the product, innovative adjustments and the impact of competition and substitutes. Also the product can vary according to whether the product is the whole *class* of products, a *form* of this product or a particular *brand*.

Learning activity 1.1

The alignment of the purchasing function will be dependent upon the position of the organisation within the life cycle of that industry. Its strategy will be one of:

1　growth if it is successful selling its product and its strategy will involve looking at new markets, new products, product development and innovation
2　stability and combination strategy – involves looking at strategies that maintain the current position, including some growth in certain divisions

(continued on next page)

Learning activity 1.1 *(continued)*

3   retrenchment – defensive strategies seeking to get the best from the situation.

In addition, irrespective of whether the organisation is in a growth, mature or declining position, there will be strategies adopted to maintain and sustain the best cashflow and level of profitability.

Your task is to examine the existing strategic and life cycle position of the organisation at which you work.

Outline how the purchasing function is asked to respond to the current and future position. Are there plans to grow the supply base? If so, why?

Are there strategies to integrate vertically or horizontally? What are the reasons behind such a move?

Comment on how changes in the supply base impact on your current technological support systems – can they cope?

To what extent is the organisation pursuing a long-term relationship with suppliers, and to what extent does this give a satisfactory return?

Does the organisation seek supplies from overseas? Are the reasons based only on cost? How does this increased logistical exercise reflect on the structure of the purchasing function?

Are some parts of the business to be sold or outsourced? How does this affect the operational plans of the purchasing function?

Feedback on page 11

Strategists will need to build into their planning:

1   The **stage of its life cycle** that any product has reached.
2   The **product's remaining life**, i.e. how much longer the product will be able to contribute significantly to profits.
3   How **urgent is the need to innovate**, to develop new and improved products in time?

However, not all products conform to the classic life cycle and can be changed and influenced by internal and external factors. Organisations also have to take into account whether or not a specific product is declining or the whole product class is seeing the end of its useful life.

The life cycle has become important for businesses because of the many changes that can affect its performance. Lysons (2006) states the following reasons:

- environmental factors – such as the impact of packaging on waste management
- durability factors – such as competition between substitute materials
- obsolescence – as with capital equipment that may lead to an outsourcing strategy

1

- changing demand – purchasing managers have to liaise with other business functions so that orders in the future can be planned with some accuracy.

The product life cycle and market dynamics

There needs to be some form of assessment for planning purposes as to the speed at which new ideas and product innovations will spread or be diffused through the marketplace. This will depend upon the marketing and communications efforts as to the benefits to the potential consumer, plus the degree of complexity in the product, and the degree to which it fits into existing or future needs.

Organisations will then have to decide on the basis of estimates in terms of both sales revenue and profits whether or not to continue to invest in the products or to look to take them out of circulation. These strategic decisions will inform and direct the purchasing function's activities, which must be integrated and aligned with the planning process so that the organisation's goals are achieved.

Self-assessment question 1.1

Jaeger

Recently Jaeger has been attempting to emulate Burberry in continuing to transform the business into a dynamic and recognisable world-wide brand. It has a clothing range which emphasises style and elegance, and a brand with aspirations for cross-border recognition.

Examine the website of the company Jaeger home page: http://www.jaeger.com. Where does this company sit in the product life cycle?

- If you were a buyer at this company where would you be looking to source materials?
- What would be the particular challenges facing the purchasing function in order to fulfil corporate objectives?
- How would their strategy differ from that of the Swedish fashion retailer Hennes and Mauritz (H&M)?

Feedback on page 11

1.2 How the purchasing function can add value to the business

Adding value

All the functions in a business have to contribute some value in order to sustain that business's competitive advantage. The value chain concept was developed by Michael Porter in the 1980s.

His suggested primary activities of the business – inbound logistics, operations, outbound logistics, marketing and sales, and service – are supported by services such as technology development and of course procurement.

All of these various components to the business should add value. Value is the amount that buyers will pay for the product or service and the extent of this value will be dependent upon the cost of delivering the final product or service.

The value chain also details the number of competitive areas involved from the first transformation of a basic product through to a final distributor to the end users. It is 'the chain of conversion processes from the initial raw thing or concept through to final consumption of the associated product or service' (Finlay, 2000).

Porter (1985) identified the 'value chain' (see figure 1.1) as a means of analysing an organisation's strategically relevant activities in order to understand the behaviour of costs. Competitive advantage comes from carrying out those activities in a more cost-effective way than one's competitors.

Figure 1.1: Porter's value chain

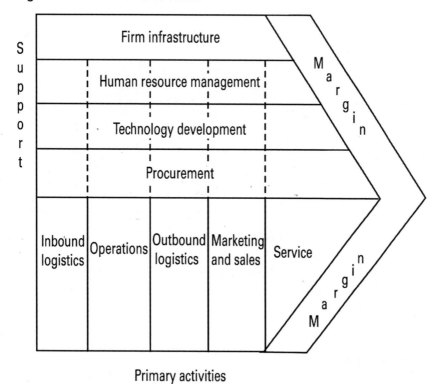

Primary activities

Source: Porter (1985)

Porter's work has contributed to the raising of the value of the purchasing function in the eyes of the senior management, although there has been some criticism (Hines, 1993) that it does not deal sufficiently with the requirements of integration of the different units of the business, nor is there sufficient emphasis on the position of the customer. In a world where the customer's expectations are rising and there is an ever-increasing complexity

1

of suppliers to the customer, it is important that a more sophisticated model is adopted. Hines's model involves a greater emphasis on integration, examining costs, improving quality, implementing technical data systems and training and development. Instead of the emphasis in the Porter model on a group of chains pointing from raw material to customer, this is reversed in the Hines model and emphasises a large pull from the customer to the raw material.

Learning activity 1.2

1 As a means of showing how the purchasing function has contributed to the success of the business and added value, include examples of business improvement from your own organisation over the last 12 months.

Table 1.1

Purchasing activity	Example of value contribution
Quality improvement	
Innovative introduction	
Administrative improvements	
Supplier improvement	
Technology improvement	

2 To what extent are the improvements planned or systematically developed?

Feedback on page 12

Added value and the purchasing function

The ability to add value within the supply chain is often a critical measure of performance. Value can be added in a number of different ways including:

- cost reduction
- effective new product design
- supply performance improvement, using a range of methods including supplier development, supplier motivational programmes, or spend aggregation target costing
- risk avoidance and management, using a mix of contract strategy, contract performance management, and supplier risk profiling and supply chain optimisation methods
- managing internal interfaces which include the creation of policies and procedures, the provision of internal consultancy services or the provision of internal services supported by a service quality programme.

Feedback on page 12

Self-assessment question 1.2

It is well documented that, in the last year, the price of oil has risen considerably as a result of a combination of economic, political and natural events. How can the procurement function respond to these world 'shocks', minimise the impact and still add value?

Feedback on page 12

1.3 Strategic alignment and the need for flexibility

A flexible planning process

If the organisation develops a prescriptive strategy, then it should result in clear, well-defined objectives being promulgated. There are a number of professed advantages to this approach, namely that it involves a complete overview of the direction of the business, and can be linked to detailed resource demands to fulfil the objectives, and that it provides a discussion for which choices the organisation should make as to the way forward. In addition there is a plan which can be measured, benchmarked and evaluated.

The prescriptive strategy is based on the early economic theory of Adam Smith which relies on the rational decision-making individual. A prescriptive business strategy is seen 'as being similar to sending the troops (employees) into battle (against competitors) with a clear plan that has been drawn up by the generals (directors) and implemented by launching new products and innovations etc' (Lynch, 2000).

Learning activity 1.3

Imagine that your organisation has over the last 12 months been subjected to the following pressures:

* Two major suppliers of key components have announced a merger. In the past you have been able to use your stronger bargaining position to secure a good discount on the price of the supplies. The merger has changed the bargaining position. Will you still be able to keep prices at old levels?
* The rising price of fuel has added to your transportation and packaging costs. As it affects all competitors in some way, would the price upgrades be something that is accepted or would other steps be taken to change the cost base?

Feedback on page 12

Emergent strategy

Mintzberg and others have challenged the assumptions of the prescriptive mode, suggesting barriers to the fulfilment of planned objectives.

For example it is increasingly difficult to forecast the future in the business world, and long-term plans may lead to the sacrifice of short-term and beneficial aspects. Strategic plans also sometimes fail to look at the problems surrounding choice and implementation.

An emergent strategic process is one that is gaining favour amongst several academics. This approach concentrates on the formulation of a strategy rather than its prediction and planning. Managers making small decisions as the environment changes will have a closer impact on the performance of the organisation and will enable realignment of direction without too great a shift.

However, this does not absolve managers from being prepared to adjust, even react quickly and flexibly if the organisation is affected by a larger 'shock' from the economy, the political scene and especially competitor activity. In addition there needs to be strategic planning that takes the organisation forward into new markets and develops new products while at the same time allowing it to respond to other external pressures.

The contribution from all key persons within the organisation is essential if this multidimensional approach is to be successful. Strategies need to be proactive if they are to be able to respond to environmental factors and competitor activity.

Hamel and Prahalad (1994) suggest that some organisations fail because of an inability to escape the past – for example, a general contentment with the organisations' achievements and position, and an inability to change. Perhaps the structure is too embedded to allow for a new form of leadership.

Self-assessment question 1.3

Examine the traditional model of 'lean' supply chains with a just-in-time philosophy and comment on whether that fits with the increasing sophistication of modern customers plus the increasing fragmentation of markets.

Feedback on page 12

1.4 The importance of customer service within the supply chain function

Customer relationships

The importance of customer service has grown considerably over the last 20 years as changes in demand patterns, customer expectations, technology and the business environment have occurred.

Berry (Vollman et al, 2004) coined the term 'relationship marketing' and defined it as 'the process of identifying and establishing, maintaining and where necessary terminating relationships with customers and other stakeholders, at a profit so that the objectives of all parties involved are met, where this is done by a mutual giving and fulfilment of promises'.

This 'customer first' philosophy of the organisation means that the purchasing function also responds to individualised demands. Today's economy is no longer straightforward but increasingly characterised by customisation and fragmentation. Getting goods to the marketplace as quickly as possible is now a priority, along with keeping costs to a minimum so that the final price is as low as possible.

Learning activity 1.4

You have been asked by your manager to write a report setting out some key steps in how internal relationships within the organisation could be improved. You are asked to initially consider how the work of the department could be further integrated with the other key functions for the overall benefit of the business.

Feedback on page 13

Palmer and Brookes (2004) identify five drivers in the need for improved customer relationships. Although specifically aimed at the marketing department, can this have implications for the supply chain:

- increased financial accountability and customer value management
- increasing emphasis on service elements of all products
- organisational transformation to reduce costs and increase service
- increasing retailer power and greater systematic relationships within networks
- the rise of interactive media and greater customisation.

Improved customer service links to the need for businesses to maintain profitability, and this can only be done if the objectives of all the parties involved are met.

We have already discussed the importance of organisations scanning the environment to ensure a realistic strategy. Competition is extremely important when assessing strategic direction. One particular model that incorporates customer needs is the concept of a *value proposition* in which the notion of what customers get from an organisation is related to how much they pay relative to alternatives from competitors.

Reliability is a factor in the value proposition, in that customers will evaluate the performance of the product purchased as against competitive products, linking it to the price they paid. Consumer goods have become increasingly reliable over the years, and with reducing prices. This makes it difficult for

1

manufacturers to position high quality products in the market with so much price competition and customers reluctant to pay for expensive models.

It is imperative therefore that the purchasing department develop a successful and sound professional relationship with all those customers that they engage with, external and internal. Those that make up the procurement function should be well qualified with demonstrable expertise. It is an essential management requirement that if leadership and direction is to be successful then correct use of the power within the function is demonstrated.

French and Raven in their definitive discussion on sources of power within the organisation state that *expert power* is based on the perception that someone is competent and has special knowledge in a given area. This will apply to all managers and professionals within the purchasing function.

Those dealing with the purchasing function can then feel confident that they can deal with a function that delivers results. They know how to select the right suppliers, research the supply markets, produce contracts and deal with the effective implementation of IT to support the business aspects. They have good administration and above all are in a position to discuss and consult with others around the organisation to get best results.

The purchasing department has the skills to manage and sustain the internal supply chain that makes up the hierarchies and bureaucracies within the organisation. Like the external supply chain, customer relationships need to be developed and sustained. Research has demonstrated that the most integrative businesses are likely to perform better (Lawrence and Lorsch, 1967). They argued against the elimination of differences between organisations but recognised that different departments could have their own distinctive structure according to their outlooks. Success was based on the degree of cooperation and mediation that took place.

The function sets standards through techniques such as tendering that demonstrate to the business that value for money is a prerequisite.

Success is based on knowing the customers, so procurement functions need to establish networks and systems that get to their market, building relationships and sustaining the relationships through change and turbulence.

Self-assessment question 1.4

With reference to key suppliers to the organisation, construct a checklist showing the points of contact and how relationships are maintained and sustained. Included in your checklist should be style of communications, response times, dealing with problems and issues, changes to contractual terms, transfer of information relating to alterations to supply, technical changes and responses to pricing matters.

Feedback on page 13

Revision question

Now try the revision question for this session on page 341.

Summary

To be successful the purchasing function needs to add value as part of the supply chain. This requires an integrative and responsive organisational approach and activities that pursue relentlessly the objectives and goals of the organisation. Communications are also key to developing positive relationships within and outside of the organisation.

Suggested further reading

Read the chapter on corporate strategy in Lysons and Farrington (2006).

Feedback on learning activities and self-assessment questions

Feedback on learning activity 1.1

A review of the priorities of an organisation in terms of costs, volumes, growth strategies and quality issues will need to be discussed. Is the organisation looking to expand? What are the implications for sourcing of products and services? Is it a market leader or follower? How does it intend to sustain its competitive position? Does it outsource aspects of production? Does it source from overseas? Does it have good relationships with suppliers? How is the added value of the purchasing function measured?

The strategic planning of a business is usually a formal process driven by the senior management team, and is complex and detailed. However, it is at the operational stage that the various functions play a major part in that detailed operational plans will ensure the organisational strategy is implemented.

Feedback on self-assessment question 1.1

An awareness of the differing strategies in differing products is essential for buyers, including a need for breadth of view on world markets. As well as the need to source high quality textiles, cost is a big driver if it is to improve margins, and many developing countries now have the expertise to provide a good range of finished supplies at low cost. The need to have an international strategy is important as quality materials and textiles will not be available within the domestic market. Buyers should be aware of the competitive influences in the marketplace which are forcing the pace of change. The global environment gives greater access to new sources of supplies and materials, and the technological revolution enables greater access to those markets. There are many examples of organisations sourcing overseas from the quality clothing and footwear businesses, e.g. Nike, and this has led to a restructuring of the whole business. The UK, for example, has a much diminished textile business when once it was a world leader.

Feedback on learning activity 1.2

An opportunity to explore the capturing of improvement processes within the organisation and the extent to which they have been delivered by the purchasing strategic focus. Cost reduction, improvements in waste management, and improvements to systems, organisational restructuring, and examples of changes in supply policy – a reduction of the supply base?

What are the driving forces in the organisation that contribute to success? How is the organisation set up to implement improvements? How is innovation encouraged and developed? The need for continuous improvement within the purchasing function is important if the organisation is to continue to maintain a competitive position and achieve satisfactory margins. The function must continue to add value as indicated in Porter's value chain model.

Feedback on self-assessment question 1.2

This involves consideration of how the organisation deals with contingencies in terms of process, pricing and market strategies. How wide and diverse is the supply base? Does the organisation have a number of first tier suppliers who can continue to source efficiently in difficult times? Are there strategies in place to consider alternative product combinations? Does the organisation buy in bulk? Is hedging used to avoid fluctuations? Does it use intermediary sources for essential material purchasing?

It would seem that the increasing demand for scarce resources will put increasing pressure on existing suppliers to maintain supplies by themselves prospecting for new sources, but it is also putting pressure on the buyer to become more innovative on resource usage.

Feedback on learning activity 1.3

It is important to understand that whatever new position is undertaken by the organisation, a rigid adherence to a strategy would not be correct. It may mean that the organisation must think about changing its cost base if prices increase as a result of the increased strength of the suppliers. Does the organisation have an approach that deals with negotiating complexity? How quickly does it respond and who are the drivers within the organisation? It may also mean that the buyer must look for alternative sources, but only if similar pricing structures can be obtained.

New sources of supply and logistics may, therefore, emerge. Alternative packaging methods may be examined. The product itself may be redesigned. How does the organisation respond to threats?

Feedback on self-assessment question 1.3

The obsession with achieving a differential to meet the increasingly sophisticated customer requires organisations to have flexibility of response to rapid changes in the market. In particular, the need to keep costs down so that prices can remain keen is now an essential ingredient in any product strategy. A competitive position can also be built around a constant supply of new consumer products, a strategy which forces buyers to consider closer alliances with the supply chain.

How lean and mean are your own organisation's operations?

Does it apply strict just-in-time? If not, what are the reasons?

Certainly there will probably be a culture of cost and waste reduction, and movement towards real-time delivery if margins are to be maintained. Leanness and an agile response to market changes are important but there may be barriers and costs in achieving this responsiveness.

Feedback on learning activity 1.4

The use of effective communication strategies plus involvement in cross-functional teams will enhance the profile of the purchasing function. Integration is essential if the buying function is to comprehend the shifting market position, implications on design and the advent of a material strategy. It is only by constant communication and networking that the purchasing function will remain in touch with other functions and deliver value.

Examining the organisational structure of departments and functions will give information on the interrelationships between the organisations. What formal and informal communications occur? How does purchasing and operations communicate? Is there awareness of the different communication models or is it all done on email? How proactive is the purchasing function in ensuring that the rest of the organisation is aware of its activities, philosophies and link to the overall objectives of the business?

Feedback on self-assessment question 1.4

An examination of the supplier database and any supporting software will provide the process of maintaining contact and relationships. How often is contact made with suppliers and how much time is spent on developing rapport? What steps are taken to fully understand the concerns and pressures of the suppliers? How are communications conducted? Face-to-face is a good source of communication but expensive. How often does this occur and what are the procedures?

1

Management of the supplier

'The real challenge of management is to manage change by leading and inspiring people.'
Hannagan (2005)

Introduction

It is very important that the supplier is managed effectively by the buyer if the relationship is to bring the desired benefits. Management of the supplier is a skill which is based on clear objective focus and the need to establish a trusting and long-term relationship that benefits both parties. Managing the purchasing function needs management and leadership skills if effective relationships are to be built and sustained.

Session learning objectives

After completing this session you should be able to:

2.1 Explain the role of the purchasing function in managing supplier relationships.
2.2 Assess the potential for improving the management of supplier relationships.
2.3 Evaluate how leadership style can contribute to improved supplier development.

Unit content coverage

Learning objectives

1.6 Devise appropriate supplier management organisational models in both the centralised and decentralised purchasing function, and demonstrate how other functional areas might interact in these models.
1.7 Describe appropriate leadership styles to support supplier development.

Prior knowledge

Knowledge of the role of managers.

Timing

You should set aside about 4 hours to read and complete this session, including learning activities, self-assessment questions, the suggested further reading (if any) and the revision question.

2.1 The role of the purchasing function in managing supplier relationships

Introduction

Choosing and managing the suppliers is a key factor to obtaining quality, performance and price. This is in itself not sufficient and it is essential for the long-term success of the relationship that the supplier is monitored, maintained and improved. The management of the supplier will involve supplier appraisal and assessment, procedures for monitoring and the development of the most suitable relationships between the parties. That relationship will vary according to the specific qualities and strengths of the supplier – e.g. how many are in the market and how specialised are the supplies. Differentiated supplies mean a shift in the balance of power between buyer and supplier.

Supplier relations

One of the most important aspects for the buyer in assuring supplies is the maintenance of good supplier relationships. Good supplier relationships can be a major asset to the buyer, not only in assuring supplies, but also in maintaining quality levels and good prices. Good supplier relations have always been an important factor in the maintenance of supplies, particularly during periods of shortage, but over recent years attitudes towards supplier relationships have gradually changed from an adversarial to a 'partnership' approach, with an element of 'shared destiny'. This change has been brought about by the increasing use made by buyers of techniques such as quality assurance, zero defect policies, statistical process control (SPC) and just-in-time (JIT), all of which place additional responsibilities on suppliers, who will only be willing to accept them if they see some long-term benefit for themselves in the relationship. So, in return for accepting these additional responsibilities, it has become common to offer the supplier a long-term prospect of business in what is referred to as a 'partnership' relationship, with both parties offering and accepting complementary responsibilities and helping to solve problems to their mutual benefit.

The partnership approach, or 'co-makership', clearly influences the nature of the relationship between buyer and sellers. However, it also influences the selection criteria for new suppliers. The criteria for the selection of a supplier in the long-term relationship may differ from the competitive criteria apparent in the adversarial approach.

Supply chain management role

The partnership approach to supplies is part of the concept of supply chain management. This approach is broader than the simple relationship between the suppliers and buyers of separate organisations. It deals with the total concept of managing materials in a positive way; all aspects, from the suppliers and subcontractors through purchasing, stock control, production and distribution, to the final customer. It is concerned with achieving the lowest cost in the whole manufacturing and supply process by identifying and balancing the relationship between the separate links in the supply chain and ensuring that the whole chain operates at the lowest total cost and the maximum efficiency.

The point we are considering here is the link in the chain between the buyer's organisation and the supplier, as this is a vital element in ensuring continuity of supply, particularly where a JIT system is in operation and there is no margin of error on supplies.

The supply chain assumes a flow of value to the customer and pressure for low prices on the supplier. In reality the relationship is complex, as figure 2.1 illustrates.

Figure 2.1: Value flow to customer

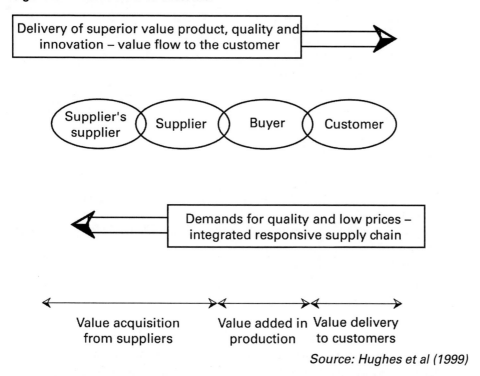

Source: Hughes et al (1999)

Supplier relationships are an integral part of the any organisation's operations with the potential for cost reduction and increased revenues. These relationships are often not coherent with other policies of the organisation if the purchasing function is viewed elsewhere as a function that merely responds to other functional requests including specific technical requirements, and if there is a lack of integration into the supply strategy

Supplier selection role

It is pertinent here to discuss some developments in supplier selection and supply chain management and to consider the selection of suppliers for a service or activity which is contracted out.

Supplier selection has traditionally been described as being based on the 5 Rs (right price, right quality, right quantity, right time and right place). However, greater emphasis is now placed on the management of the buyer/supplier relationship in a non-adversarial, longer-term perspective and it may mean that the 5 Rs are no longer sufficient when compared with the qualitative aspects of the relationship and the longer-term perspective. An article by Ray Carter entitled 'The 7 Cs of Effective Supplier Evaluation' advocated a more comprehensive approach to supplier selection (Carter, 1995). However, the approach has subsequently been developed and extended by Carter and now consists of the 10 Cs. Acceptance of this approach does not actually make the 5 Rs any less important.

They are still there, but the supplier selection approach is broader.

Carter's original 7 Cs for supplier selection were:

- Competency: all staff, all the time (requires evidence)
- Capacity: sufficient and flexible
- Commitment: to quality (quality systems)
- Control: control of process
- Cash: sufficient funds for the business
- Cost: cost/price relationships and total cost of ownership
- Consistency: consistent production of goods or services (ISO 9000).

More recently, Carter has added three more Cs, which are:

- Culture: compatible with similar values
- Clean: environmentally sound (conforming with legislative requirements)
- Communications: the supplier is fully integrated with information and communication technology (ICT).

Hence the selection criteria have now become Carter's 10 Cs of supplier selection.

When contracting out work as discussed above, the selection of a supplier takes on a special dimension. Contracting out can be in the form of a 'make-or-buy' decision; for example, contracting out a subassembly ready-assembled rather than buying in components and assembling them in-house.

This process provides:

- tighter control over quality
- reduced supplier base
- taking advantage of suppliers' distinctive competencies and building them into our own. Again it facilitates focused operations.

Contracting out services requires special attention, bearing in mind the special problems of managing service quality.

Early supplier involvement (ESI)

The best suppliers are an important source of information; the purchasing function is in a strong position to gather this information and make use of it. This can be a *collaborative arrangement* where a partnership arrangement exists or simply a *good working relationship* where there can be collaboration at an early stage over the design and specification aspects and the establishment of quality standards.

Learning activity 2.1

The traditional adversarial approach to commercial supplier relationships was one built around a competitive supply base, managed using short-term contracts and win–lose negotiations. The objective was to obtain the best possible price, safeguarding budgets and maximising revenues. Using examples from your own knowledge of the supply chain, identify why such an approach is now heavily criticised. In particular, draw examples from the role of the supplier in modern-day transactions, the use of JIT, the expectations of customers and the types of product life cycle with which you are familiar.

Feedback on page 35

Supplier appraisal

The management of any new supplier starts with an assessment of their capabilities.

The process is one that should be based on experience. It is important that organisations develop procurement strategies that gather and retain knowledge of supplier selection and management. This is a process that in order to be successful needs to be developed, reflected upon and refined over a period of time. The procurement function should be able to take advantage of signal learning that is carried out by the organisation itself. These are learning activities such as environmental scanning that will signal changes to markets, customers, products and services.

Organisational structures may involve the development of a learning organisation as described by Peter Senge (2006): 'an organisation that is continuously expanding its capacity to create its future'. A procurement department's ability to mange the supply chain will be more effective if there is some shared vision of the objectives of the function and a learning climate that builds on experience and knowledge. The increased availability of computer-based information permits the establishment of systems that make supplier selection and management a more consistent process.

Any firm with limited visibility will fail to adapt to the ever-increasing change caused by competitive action.

An analysis of:

- the macro environment
- the industry and market
- the supplier base and potential

will assist the organisation to develop knowledge that can be used strategically.

These drivers have clearly changed over time. In some industries, notably automotive and construction, customer pressure on performance engendered a growing understanding of the nature of organisational networks. As these networks of organisations began to appear, the customer organisation tended to keep the suppliers at arm's length. The buyer had the controlling hand in setting up supplier contracts and was constantly on the lookout for price reductions or cheaper sources. The stressful economic climate of the 1970s led to increasingly adversarial relationships between the buyer and supplier. Competition continued to increase, and the adversarial relationships were shown not to work effectively in complex industries and uncertain environments.

The Japanese were doing things differently, and the early 1990s saw many studies attempting to understand these differences. But after years of adversarial relationships and aggressive business practices, many organisations have struggled to build partnership-style relationships and have found it very difficult to adopt a truly collaborative approach, despite beginning to understand the benefits of such a strategy.

Other factors that impact on relationships are the role of the parties involved in the relationship, the nature of the transaction process itself and the task environment in which the relationship takes place. In some ways, commercial relationships are the easiest element to manage, as changes in role can be much more difficult to achieve. Although we might use the word 'role' casually to describe a set of behaviours, the concept of role is much more complicated.

The concept of role

Erwin Goffman, an eminent sociologist, brought the word 'role' into current scientific thinking when he suggested that social life could be perceived as a drama, during which the expressiveness of an individual can be seen as performance (Goffman, 1981). Goffman uses the term 'performance' to refer to all the activities of an individual that occur during a period marked by her/his continuous presence before a particular set of observers and that have some influence on the said observers/audience.

This idea of 'role' is a very powerful one, and indeed can lead to other, less desirable constructs or concepts. These include the idea of stereotyping where a supplier may be considered to have certain characteristics, such as greed, obstructive behaviour or untrustworthiness, simply because they are a supplier. It is, therefore, important to remember that roles can be flexible and that people within an organisation can take on multiple roles.

This is seen within some approaches to the role of the supplier in new product development. In the past, suppliers weren't involved early in the process. The activities of the product development process were carried out in series, and suppliers were only involved towards the end of the process. This meant that in a manufacturing industry, a typical product could involve many stages, and many different stakeholders. Such a product might be 'born' in the marketing department, and then go through conceptual design, engineering design and failure mode effect analysis, testing, detailed design, manufacturing engineering, process planning, tooling, NC programming, production planning, purchasing, machining, assembly, testing, packaging, and even installation and maintenance in some cases.

Often, supplier involvement would be limited to manufacturing some of the parts. They wouldn't be involved at the design stage, and often their work only started when they received the released design documentation. Usually, they would raise good questions about some aspect of the design. The resulting change process wasted time, led to the introduction of new problems, and often resulted in the product getting to market late.

As well as having an impact on performance, this approach didn't take advantage of supplier knowledge and experience. Despite being a world-class producer of a particular component, suppliers might not be consulted on initial specifications and design, and instead be expected to produce to a plan developed by individuals with much less experience.

In addition, traditional roles often meant that suppliers were only brought into the process to compete against each other on pricing. As a result, the company finished up working with a large number of suppliers, and even with different suppliers on similar products.

Often the product development process needs to be reorganised to get products to market faster, reduce the cost of product development and to make sure the product provides customer satisfaction – leading to repeat buying behaviour. There are many possible approaches to reorganisation; many of them will increase the reliance on suppliers and enhance and develop supplier roles.

However, as some manufacturers learned to involve suppliers in the product development process and were attempting to introduce them in the new product programme as early as possible, there were both practitioners and academics who saw this as too high risk an approach. Instead they suggested that, due to the subjective and iterative nature of the design process, the degree of confidential information that may be generated, and the inability to measure and monitor technical capability, early supplier involvement would only lead to opportunistic behaviour and, ultimately, competitive disadvantage.

This balance of risk and performance is, of course, at the heart of the purchasing task.

Developing roles

In many industries, however, organisations do engage in a certain level of collaboration with their first tier suppliers. Companies that focus on upstream product specification and design activities, where they can best use their resources, will want to outsource downstream activities where they are not cost-effective (for example, in detailed drafting) or are less competent than specialised organisations (for example, in parts manufacture), so suppliers will have a greater role to play in these areas.

2

In some literature, 'partnership' is seen as a preferred role for suppliers. Here we might see the roles as involving a range of factors that might include:

1   cost management in the same way that QS 9000 defines such a role for suppliers to large automotive assemblers
2   innovative suggestions
3   longer-term planning and early supplier involvement in product or service design
4   sharing of information, including cost information and transparency, facilitating planning.

However, roles, like relationships, are subject to change, and we often need a more dynamic model that explains how these change. In order to identify how a supplier can, and should, act to maximise the value creation for the customer, it is often useful to consider learning processes between the buyer and supplier. This may involve looking at the link between a supplier's offerings and learning processes and a customer's various learning processes, some of which were considered in study session 1.

When we consider roles, however, it is also essential to consider the environment of the industry in which the role is being practised.

The environment

As we have already seen, the management of relationships is complex and difficult. Many factors impact upon relationships and these factors often also impact upon role. In fast-changing, volatile trading environments, the role of the supplier may involve setting up (and breaking off) new partnerships fairly quickly.

Market fluctuations, and therefore roles and relationships, can be driven by rapidly changing customer preferences, rather than supplier strategy. In many industries, better-informed customers are becoming less loyal and more demanding about what they buy. The effects of market volatility are both worsened and helped by information and communication technology, which allows organisations to make use of information embedded within enterprise systems as a key factor in business relationships.

It is, therefore, important to take the environment into account, and achieve the right balance of control and risk management in developing suppliers into new roles. We cannot force partnership or transactional roles and relationships where such roles and relationships are not matched with the environment in which the business operates.

Supplier roles, in many industries and markets, have changed considerably over the past two decades. These changes can be seen in many areas. One of these is quality, where the receiving inspection process used places much of the cost and responsibility on the purchaser. This responsibility has largely shifted to suppliers, requiring them to provide evidence of product quality, often through reporting of process stability and capability. Elsewhere, the involvement of suppliers in new product development has become critical in many industries.

It should be noted, though, that shifts in roles, and relationships, must be sensitive to changes in the nature of the trading and operating environment, and to changes in the nature of the transaction processes used.

Self-assessment question 2.1

List examples of how customers have become less loyal and more demanding in today's world. How does that impact on supplier management and relationships?

Feedback on page 35

2.2 Supplier development

Introduction

After having considered the nature of supplier relationships the next step is to consider how to maintain them – the management and development of suppliers.

What is supplier development?

As with so much else in the field of supply chain management, supplier development means different things to different people. Some people refer to competitive tendering as 'supplier development' as it helps the supplier develop tendering skills. For other buyers, supplier development may consist of statistical process control workshops.

For the purposes of this section we can suggest that supplier development consists of a range of activities integrated into a relatively seamless whole to ensure effective supply chain management. These activities may include:

- sourcing strategy
- vendor assessment (surveys, site visits)
- supplier rating and qualification
- supplier award programmes
- use of new technology (for example, computer-supported collaborative working, advanced planning and scheduling)
- cross- or multi-disciplinary team working
- supply base reduction
- joint supplier problem-solving team
- supplier development 1 (Kaizen teams)
- supplier development 2 (redesign of internal processes)
- electronic data interchange
- supplier associations (Kyoryoku Kai)
- longer-term contracts
- partnership (win–win negotiation, partnering agreements)
- lean supply (JIT for example)
- standards development
- supplier tiering
- cost analysis methods

2

- cost management (VE, gain sharing, inventory management and re-engineering).

Using supplier development

Because of the different meanings of supplier development, this subsection will consider an integrated framework of suppler development, which includes seven elements. This is not to say that all these elements need to be in place in every case, but this framework demonstrates how the elements of a supplier development strategy interlock. These elements are:

- sourcing strategy
- analysis strategy
- communication strategy
- infrastructure strategy
- motivation strategy
- standards strategy
- development strategy.

Learning activity 2.2

Identify a potential source of 'economic shock' from one of your supply chain products, components or raw materials, for example price rises, shortages caused by world demand, other preferred customers taking the bulk of supplies and so on. Write a report outlining how your existing supply base would respond to pressures to continue to supply. Comment on how you manage suppliers to ensure that you remain a preferred supplier.

Feedback on page 36

1 Sourcing strategy for supplier development

Objectives

The objectives of a sourcing strategy should be in keeping with the philosophy of the extended enterprise, which is to ensure that suppliers have the capacity and capability to match systems and policies with the enterprise's current and changing needs. The costs and benefits of a relationship to an organisation will vary according to how that relationship relates to portfolio of other suppliers. There may be less of an expectation to be innovative, for instance, with some suppliers than with others. The organisation will also have to have some judgement of the different expectations of both parties and the perceptions of value from the relationship.

Processes

Many organisations that are global in scope base sourcing policy upon raw materials and labour costs. This can be mitigated by the need for technical innovation. Enterprises that work in technically sophisticated markets may need to consider a range of issues when sourcing. Environmental pressure groups, ethical issues, plant and distribution hub locations all contribute to make sourcing decisions politically based, as well as price sensitive.

In addition, an emphasis on early supplier involvement in the design process and supplier innovation will impact on sourcing decisions, as will the need to ensure continuity of supply. This can also have an effect on sourcing policies, as an enterprise may prefer, in some cases, supply assurance over part price. In some industries, the majority of an enterprise's suppliers will be situated in areas contiguous with their plants.

Supply base reduction or rationalisation also has an impact on sourcing. Suppliers may be brought into an extended enterprise to act as first-tier supply team leaders. An enterprise may assign a particular supplier to act as team leader for particular platform groups.

Potential pitfalls

As we have seen, in reducing supplier numbers and increasing the complexity of sub-operations, enormous savings can be created and the risk of obsolescent stockholding reduced. However, it is also necessary to achieve a balance between autonomy as an enterprise and dependency on the supply base. This involves the strategic use of the make-or-buy decision. In some cases, this balance can be exceeded, and enterprises can become too dependent on some suppliers. This can also have an impact on labour relations.

In addition, this closeness can also cause problems for suppliers. Examples exist where closeness between an enterprise and supplier has an impact on the supplier's relationship with other customers. One of these relates to a supplier refusing an audit from another major customer because they felt that the audit was designed to uncover process improvements developed jointly by themselves and a major customer.

2 Analysis strategy for supplier development

Objectives

Supplier development is expensive. This means that it is important to target efforts carefully. There is little point in carrying out supplier development with a first tier supplier if the problems lie in the second or even third tier. This means using an analysis strategy to identify the capabilities and competences of different suppliers within different supply categories or platform groupings. These capacity profiles can be used to match suppliers to particular projects and issues within the product development and manufacturing process.

Processes

It can require considerable effort to identify suppliers in both first and lower tiers. This, in the case of manufacturing enterprises, may be carried out on a platform-specific basis. 'Platform' in this case refers to a specific group of manufacturing processes carried out to produce a particular product.

One way of analysing data is to develop supplier capability profiles. These profiles can be used to identify suppliers with complementary skills and capacity to carry out specific projects.

2

As well as looking at individual suppliers, analysis also needs to look at the relationships between suppliers. In this way an understanding of the complexity of the supply chain becomes clear and the supplier development task can be broken down into manageable chunks. A manager within one large automotive supplier stated, 'In the old days we didn't even know where the bolts came from!' Mapping out the chains can help identify significant opportunities for cost reduction. One automotive assembler discovered, for instance, that even a simple-looking item like a roller lifter – a £30 engine part – required 35 separate suppliers.

Analysis enables purchasing and supply to identify opportunities for cost savings and innovation by eliminating gaps and overlaps within the extended enterprise and enabling better distribution of work tasks across business processes. Examples of improved task distribution here are:

- The aggregation of operations within one supplier that had previously been carried out in 12 separate suppliers.
- The strategic use of vendor managed inventory within one supplier, who fed other key suppliers from stock.

Carrying out an analysis might involve a range of actions including supply chain mapping and business process analysis workshops.

Potential pitfalls

The cost of mapping supply chains and identifying cost reduction and aggregation opportunities can be high. The scale of the task has also had some effect on the credibility of the process within an enterprise as a whole. Establishing cost management opportunities often shows how much more opportunity there is, but also how difficult it is to reach these opportunities. This means that budgets for analysis of supplier development can be difficult to find.

3 Communication strategy for supplier development

Objectives

Communication is perhaps perceived as the major tool in supplier development. Communication is the way in which trust can be developed, information acquired and shared and business opportunities identified. The objectives of a communication strategy may be to create seamless relationships across an extended enterprise, which will involve and motivate suppliers to identify opportunities for improvement.

Processes

There are a number of elements within any communication strategy which contribute to its overall effectiveness. Perhaps the most important of these is to introduce and maintain a strong, unambiguous message that both staff and suppliers within an extended enterprise can understand and then subscribe to. In many organisations this message has been about price or total quality. Increasingly, we can see organisations turning to the fulfilment of customer needs as a message. Some enterprises in technically complex sectors, such as aircraft assembly or semiconductor manufacture, may flag innovation as a way of avoiding future costs. The quality and credibility of the message is a key factor in supplier development.

Once the key message has been designed, it needs to be supported by an internal programme of education and training. Effective internal communication is supported by extensive use of cross-functional teams (CFTs). These may, in turn, be supported by trained facilitators to help avoid some of the problems CFTs face in their initial stages. This is also assisted by the use of a range of information and communication technologies.

Communication for the purposes of supplier development means that everyone needs to hear the same message and buy in to the same key objectives. Everyone needs to work to manage costs, improve quality, ensure delivery, improve customer satisfaction or capitalise on existing technological advances. One critical element of communication is also about the future. This may involve committing to existing suppliers when developing a new technology or process.

Message effectiveness can be improved by ensuring that it is repeated by the buying enterprise, and also by other enterprises and trade associations. In this sense, communication is marketing. Multiple communication channels increase message credibility and effectiveness where messages from one customer may be ignored. One way in which external communication infrastructure can be developed is through supplier conferences. Conference areas may be dedicated to specific issues: cross-platform issues or strategic issues.

The purpose of these conferences is to improve the business relationship with the suppliers through a bi-directional communication channel and provide recognition for their efforts and work in achieving preferred supplier status (if supplier awards and tiering are used). Strategic conferences may address the accomplishments of suppliers as a group and recognise their achievements through a supplier certification process. Platform-specific conferences may look at suppliers for a given programme and discuss current platform plans and future marketing strategies with the specific suppliers.

In addition to the conferences, transactional and relational communication can take place using a variety of EDI and intranet/extranet functions. Communication also takes place through supplier development programmes and supplier award programmes.

4 Infrastructure strategy for supplier development

Objectives

In order to communicate effectively, there is a need for a simple, powerful and consistent message that can be easily communicated, and also for a range of tools that will support that message. We can identify two types of communication, which rely on different tools. These are:

- relational communication: which may require frequent face-to-face communication supported by phone/email, for example

- transactional communication: which may involve EDI, electronic procurement systems, for example.

This involves developing a broad-based information and communication technology (ICT) infrastructure that will enable the message to be transmitted both internally and externally. This can involve heavy expenditure on both EDI technologies and communication technologies, such as dedicated extranets and e-marketplaces.

Processes

Communication tools need to extend along the chain, but also through the enterprise itself. Where enterprise resource planning (ERP) systems are employed, these may assist in lateral intra-enterprise communication, but within large enterprises this still requires a great deal of investment.

Some enterprises are historically fragmented.

This is not, however, to suggest that even with ERP implementation there is always a total enterprise-wide information infrastructure in place. Again, a lack of strategic planning can mean that more than one corporate intranet exists and that ERP fails to include some functions.

Potential pitfalls

Although comprehensive information infrastructure may be in place, this does not necessarily mean that information is used to its fullest extent. Information can still too often be filed rather than being used, and the very complexity of the information systems used means that there is little cross-referencing between different information systems. In addition, information is not introduced systematically into an overall risk management framework.

5 Motivation strategy for supplier development

When employing supplier development programmes, the common assumption is that suppliers that need developing will be grateful for development activity. This is often far from true. More often than not, supplier development programmes need to include a motivational element. There are often two key components of a motivation strategy which are:

- gain sharing
- supplier award programmes.

Gain-sharing programmes are used in a number of industries. They enable the pursuit of quality, efficiency and affordability without eroding suppliers' profit margins.

Supplier award programmes

Award programmes are common in a number of industries. Generally such programmes offer a number of award levels. Awards should, in order to work, be linked to targets or processes in a specific area. Awards should also not be easy to obtain.

Awards may be given in a number of categories including:

- cost reduction
- customer support
- delivery
- price
- quality
- technology
- warranty.

Potential pitfalls

Potential pitfalls for motivation are about failing to maintain the vision and energy within the process and suppliers beginning to see the system's awards as 'just another event'.

6 Standards strategy for supplier development

Objectives

One of the main problems in supplier development is effective communication. We have seen that communication at a strategic level needs to be clear and powerful. However, communication at an operational or tactical level also needs to be effective. One of the ways of improving communication effectiveness across organisational boundaries is to use process-based standards. Cross-company standards are obviously more powerful than company-specific standards. Standards are used to give suppliers a clear and unambiguous message with regard to minimum standards of quality performance. ISO 9000 is one such standard and others have been developed in manufacturing to improve or enhance it.

7 Development strategy for supplier development

Objectives

The combination of sourcing, analysis, standards, communication and motivational strategies can all be integrated into a relatively seamless whole to ensure that the supply base is managed effectively. There is, however, a clear need to ensure that the system is not only managed but improved. Kaizen is a technique that could be used and will be discussed in another unit.

Self-assessment question 2.2

What is the state of relationship with key suppliers in terms of

- competition in the supply market
- your sourcing decision-making
- administration and data transfer
- the attitude to capacity planning
- delivery practices
- the manner of adjusting prices

(continued on next page)

2

Feedback on page 36

2.3 How leadership style can contribute to improved supplier development

Introduction

We have seen in the above section the variety of techniques that can be applied to obtain improved supplier performance. Procurement managers need to possess certain qualities if they are to be effective in dealing with the issues and problems arising from the supplier relationship. The function has many complex facets so a combination of sound management and innovative leadership is a strong prerequisite for successful relationships. The performance of an organisation is closely connected to the performance of its suppliers.

Influencing people

A key function of managers is to influence through their leadership. It is impossible to consider leadership as a type of influence without considering the position of power in the manager's status and role. In other words a manager of authority will have a degree of power as a result of their position. The first step is to instil in others the need for performance improvement. Some of the power for these initiatives will come from the allocation of the purchasing spends. This may not always be a strong basis so other techniques must be used.

Power involves the ability to influence people, although there is no guarantee that it will be used well. Often the power that a manager possesses is seen as a negative power. It can be used to intimidate or browbeat others such as in adversarial style negotiating.

Today's problems seem to surround the inability of a leader to use power effectively such as in situations where the complexity of the world is too much.

Types and sources of power

French and Raven identify a number of power sources for managers.

- Positional power: A person's position power can be broken down into other categories. Sometimes it is known as legitimate power, whereby subordinates comply with the reasonable instructions of the manager. This role has changed as society and its norms have changed. Also, the perception of the manager's credibility will have an effect on the degree of power use. It is characterised by the need for the relationship to continue.
- Expert power: This is a growing and useful power influence for managers. It is based upon specialised knowledge not readily available

to other people. It is imperative for most managers to have some form of expertise if they are to have some influencing ability. Expertise can be in the form of information and so on that others do not have. Jack Welch of General Electric required senior managers to reach down in the organisation for expertise.

- Referent power: When a person admires or is attached to another. This is when someone wants to please another. It is not easy to decide how it can be developed. Certain personal attributes help such as honesty and integrity.
- Reward power: The ability to reward another is a feature of supplier negotiations in terms of continuing and future contracts.
- Coercive power: This is about the power to punish for failure to behave in a desired fashion

How much power should be used?

Enough to achieve objectives. Managers often flinch from using power when too little will lead to inaction. Obviously excessive use will lead to negative actions.

Which type of power to use?

Referent and expertise has low costs, otherwise position or reward power is used which can lead to negative responses.

Can it be put to use?

Power influences. It needs influence tactics to persuade and convince people. There are many techniques which also have to be used in context. For example, skills in rational persuasion are important, as are exchange of favours. Charismatic leaders might use inspirational appeal, and those without charisma might try simple pressure. Also, in the relationship world the use of informal networks should not be underestimated.

Using the power as a leader

Leaders bring traits to their roles. This is a relatively enduring characteristic of that person. Although some people look for some 'great man' as leader it is now recognised that it is a combination of traits that will make an effective leader, including:

- drive
- motivation to lead
- honesty and integrity
- self-confidence
- emotional maturity.

Most current research has concentrated on men so any gender differences have not yet been identified. In addition, this has been linked to Western culture and work environments.

As managers climb the ranks, their ability to manage will be dependent upon the skills and competences they exert: *technical* skills, *interpersonal* skills and *conceptual* skills (the latter may become more important as the manager rises through the organisation).

Emotional intelligence and *social intelligence* have become important in recent years. In addition the leader needs the ability to perform, so *task behaviours* and *people behaviours* also have to be strong.

Learning activity 2.3

Assess the dealings you have with a range of suppliers.

1 Identify and evaluate the power that you bring to bear to achieve desired outcomes.
2 Outline examples when this power is most effective and situations when it fails in its objectives.

Feedback on page 36

Managers or leaders?

With a combination of power, managing and leading, and influencing tactics it is possible for managers to influence others for desirable outcomes. This is particularly important for the purchasing function, where considerable influencing and negotiating is with outside suppliers, and increasingly across cultures.

People continue to influence each other (modify another's behaviour) continuously throughout the organisation. 'Manager' and 'leader' are interchangeable words which lead to some confusion. Managers are sometimes referred to as 'someone who gets things done' to ensure order and continuity. They maintain a steady state with incremental improvements. Effective leaders are people who bring innovation, move activities out of trouble and make a worthwhile difference. They see opportunities to do new things. It is this combination of the two roles that is important to ensure stability but also innovative changes as the external environment alters.

Drucker (1985) writes of the leader's ability to generate unusual or exceptional commitment to a vision – 'the lifting of people's vision to a higher sight'.

The effectiveness of senior managers in influencing others has the most impact on the business, but they will also require others lower down the organisation to influence and help implement changes. That is particularly pertinent within the purchasing function, where often considerable responsibility is delegated down the chain of command.

Effective managers and leaders often influence people who are equally powerful.

Traits of leaders

Early research concentrated on the traits that prominent leaders possessed on the assumption that some people had attributes which made it more likely that they would be effective. People inherit aspects of temperament such as energy and personal drive, while experience shapes their values.

Stogdill (1974) identifies the qualities of a successful leader (see table 2.1).

Table 2.1

Traits	Skills
Adaptable to situations	Clever intelligent
Alert to social environment	Creative
Ambitious and achievement oriented	Conceptually skilled
Assertive	Diplomatic
Cooperative	Fluent in speaking
Decisive	Knowledgeable about group tasks
Dependable	Persuasive
Dominant	Socially skilled
Energetic	Well organised
Persistent	
Self-confident	
Tolerant of stress	
Willing to assume responsibility	

It has been said that these traits are too complex and are rarely all present in individuals. However, research by Yuki (2001) suggests that some of these traits do appear in people that achieve influence.

Behaviour of managers

- Ohio State University Model (1953): This work was on effective managers and the extent to which their behaviour was demonstrated on two levels:
  (a) initiating structure (defining and organising the role of followers)
  (b) consideration (help and support to others and praise of jobs well done).
- University of Michigan Model (1967): They found that two types of behaviours distinguished effective from ineffective managers:
  (a) job-centred supervisors (driven by the tasks and planning coordinating)
  (b) employee-centred supervisors (added in human resource skills and were judged to be the more effective managers).
- The Blake and Mouton Grid (1969) has also been used to identify styles of manager/leader and extends the earlier models, and is a reminder of the importance of developing skills in both task and people.

In addition leadership models such as Hersey and Blanchard's model of situational leadership behaviour (see figure 2.2) attempt to identify the contextual factors that affect one or more styles of leadership. On occasions managers must tell or sell their decisions, in others a more delegated decision-making process is in place. This combination of styles could lead to effective team and individual performance.

Figure 2.2: The situational leadership behaviour model

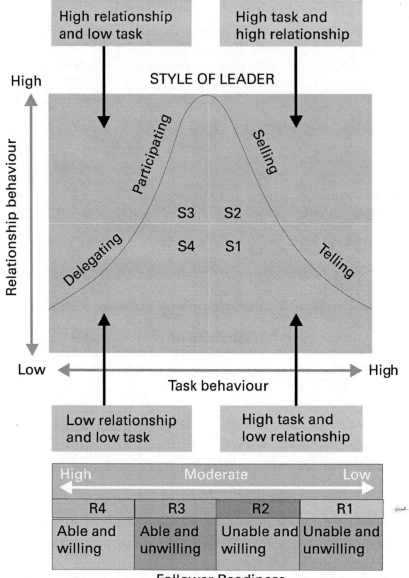

From an internal perspective, House's path-goal models (House and Mitchell, 1974) suggest that the most effective managers are ones who clarify their objectives, helping and supporting subordinates to learn and develop – characteristics include:

- being directive
- supportive behaviour
- achievement oriented
- participative decision making.

John Adair and his well-known *action-centred leadership* reinforces the need for an effective manager to combine the elements of task, team and individual.

Self-assessment question 2.3

What type of leader are you? Are you concerned more with people or the task?

Feedback on page 36

Revision question

Now try the revision question for this session on page 341.

Summary

Effective leadership and management skills are essential in this competitive world where relationships between employees, other departments and suppliers is so important if the management is to deliver the desired competitive edge.

The need to develop suppliers in line with management objectives, and the need to communicate, inspire and influence all those key players within the supply chain, requires people with effective skills.

Suggested further reading

Read the chapter on models of management in Boddy (2005).

Feedback on learning activities and self-assessment questions

Feedback on learning activity 2.1

Adversarial styles of procurement may obtain early wins, but a long-term and hopefully stable relationship will deliver more in a competitive world. 5 Rs (right price, right quality, right quantity, right time and right place) are still relevant but Carter's 10 Cs have extended the role.

The move towards world-class operations requires high standards of performance from all functions. This is not sustainable without the close cooperation of suppliers. An adversarial approach may bring short-term compliance but it is purely commercial and there is no incentive for the supplier to develop long-term commitment. Good supplier relationships can be a major asset to the buyer, not only in assuring supplies, but also in maintaining quality levels and good prices. Most organisations have introduced techniques that involve such supplier commitment.

Feedback on self-assessment question 2.1

Basic secondary research will indicate the extent of customer turnover or 'churn' as it is known in some sectors. Even those organisations with successful brands will experience customer loss as the choice and availability of a wide range of products grows. Loyalty is less prevalent in our increasingly materialistic and fast-paced world where the latest innovation, price reduction or bargain will lead to customers switching allegiance. Organisations can only keep customers over a longer period of time if they are delivering products to their satisfaction and expectations. Suppliers therefore have to be part of that drive to keep the customer satisfied, and must be managed to ensure that the organisational objectives are achieved, and the customer base maintained.

Feedback on learning activity 2.2

The building of long-term relationships in which the profitability and concerns of both sides is important may help in protecting supplies in times of difficulty. Markets have become increasingly volatile. What would the first tier suppliers do, for example, if raw material prices increase significantly? How much of the costs are passed on? How quickly would they assist in the sourcing of materials from new areas? What priority do they give the organisation in terms of shortage? How do they manage the pricing if supplies are short and demand is high? The supplier response will be a gauge to the effectiveness of the supplier relationships.

Feedback on self-assessment question 2.2

An analysis of the supply base will reveal the buying style and its effectiveness. The above checklist allows for some analysis of the depth of relationship between the two parties. How, for example, is product quality viewed by the suppliers? How responsive are suppliers to delivery schedules? How integrated are the administrative systems? How competitive is the supply base? What quality measures are in place within the supply organisations? A few paragraphs on each point should be sufficient.

Feedback on learning activity 2.3

Buyer power is possible if they have developed profitable relationships with key suppliers who value the contract to supply. The spend will be significant, plus there is the tie-up of capital equipment for the implementation of the purchase orders to consider. In addition, the planned longevity of the relationship will be important in creating an atmosphere of dependency.

Power comes from the importance of the relationship to the supplier and the desire to continue to be a customer. Power can be exercised in a more coercive fashion, but the long-term relationship may be damaged. Suppliers will not respond to pressure from the buyer if it is impossible for them to achieve a suitable margin.

Feedback on self-assessment question 2.3

A concern for both task and people is important for successful management of the relationship. Leadership requires attention to both task and people.

Driving the task will achieve results, but may damage future relationships. The Blake and Mouton Grid plus research from Ohio State and the University of Michigan suggest that good leaders work hard to deliver task compliance but also address concerns of teams and individuals. Without strong people skills it is difficult to obtain the necessary commitment for the working relations that benefit the organisation.

2

Getting results through performance measures

Introduction

This unit is to consider the importance of performance measures and controls in order to achieve organisational objectives. Without some form of direction and measurability, business success is harder to achieve. Setting standards through measurable objectives brings focus to the business.

'Business metrics such as share added value and balanced scorecards are forcing business leaders to re-examine tired business behaviours.'
McDonald and Christopher (2003)

Session learning objectives

After completing this session you should be able to:

3.1 Summarise the importance of establishing key performance indicators for supplier improvement.
3.2 Describe the function of benchmarking internally and externally and its relationship to KPI setting.
3.3 Demonstrate systematically how auditing applies to the procurement function.
3.4 To demonstrate analytically the value of the Kaplan and Norton balanced scorecard model.
3.5 Summarise the consequences of a supplier failing to meet KPI standards.

Unit content coverage

Learning objective

1.2 Employ appropriate key performance measures.

Prior knowledge

A knowledge of setting targets and other performance measures.

Timing

You should set aside about 5 hours to read and complete this session, including learning activities, self-assessment questions, the suggested further reading (if any) and the revision question.

3.1 Establishing key performance indicators for supplier improvement

Measuring suppliers

Measurements are a key part of the purchasing function. They drive and inform decision making regarding supplier performance, as well as providing data for the measurement of the purchasing function itself. Measurement also allows comparison of actual results with planned performance and provides data and analytical material to relate back to strategic initiatives.

Many measurements, or key performance indicators (KPIs), may be captured and recorded routinely. Other softer issues may require a different approach.

Assessment may be *quantitative* or *qualitative*. The former is objective whereas the latter is largely subjective. Quantitative measurements are possible in all purchasing functions irrespective of size and range and can deal with a number of key performance issues:

- orders placed
- reduction in lead times
- price savings
- reduction in administration costs.

Qualitative measurement will tend to be more strategic and involve many facets of the purchasing function, for example:

- the process of supplier development, and long-term collaborative relationships
- the introduction of JIT systems
- the observance of quality standards
- implementation of e-procurement systems
- financial performance from a total sales perspective.

The methods of establishing KPIs should take into account the following:

- *Acceptability* – to all parties involved
- *Achievability* – realistic standards of performance must be set
- *Appropriateness* – relevant to the current work role and ethos
- *Flexibility* – methods can be changed as circumstances change
- *Continuity* – sustainable periods of measurement so that comparisons can be made
- *Comprehension* – are they understood by the parties?
- *Credibility*
- *Cost* – should be proportionate.

KPIs should reflect the goals of the purchasing function within a particular enterprise. Traditional measures include:

- savings on cost of purchased supplies
- inventory levels
- incoming defects and reworking
- on-time deliveries
- total cycle time from requisition to delivery
- costs of placing purchase orders.

Once the criteria have been established some form of *monitoring* role needs to be in place. Integrating the measurement model into the supplier relationship is not without problems.

Feedback on page 55

Learning activity 3.1

1 Explain how you would implement a series of KPIs with a major supplier in response to an increasingly competitive market.
2 How do you ensure that the supplier's targets are realistic and achievable?
3 How do you implement a KPI strategy where there is reluctance or resistance?

A model based on a simple control cycle (see figure 3.1) outlines how this might be possible.

Figure 3.1: The control cycle

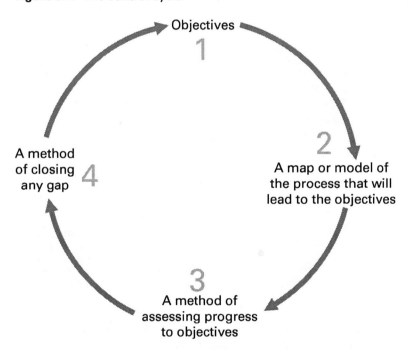

In order for any process to be controlled there need to be four elements in place. If any of these elements are missing, the process will not be controlled.

These four elements are:

1 Objectives need to be in place because, without objectives, control is meaningless.
2 A 'map' or 'model' of the process being controlled in order to show how objectives will be reached.
3 A method of assessing how the process corresponds with the model.
4 A method of closing the gap between the model and the process.

Setting supplier relationship objectives

When setting objectives for the relationship, there are a number of approaches that can be taken. Objectives can be set:

- unilaterally by the buyer or the supplier
- jointly by both the buyer and the supplier
- openly with no hidden objectives
- covertly with many hidden objectives.

There are a number of ways in which joint, open objectives can be defined and set. These may include supplier workshops in which objectives can be defined and negotiated, or this may be carried out using survey methods and techniques.

Some common objectives for a relationship involve the generic outcomes, which may include:

- cost
- flexibility/agility
- delivery
- level of service
- quality as reliability
- innovation
- quality as consistency.

By selecting objectives and performance indicators on the basis of the importance to the respective parties within the relationship, and the contribution that the objectives are likely to make, both buyers and suppliers are likely to reach agreement about the overall objectives in a timely manner.

Relationship maps or models

Once objectives and metrics are decided, the next step is to develop the relationship map or model. There are a number of relationship models. Everyone should be familiar with the supplier positioning model whereby purchasing and relational strategies can be decided according to the degree of risk and expenditure involved.

Another view of the positioning matrix was developed at the University of Bath, whereby relationships were positioned according to the strategic or tactical contribution that the supplier makes and the nature of the economic relationship. This gives four forms of supply relationship:

1 traditional relationships: where the adversarial approach is still key and purchasing power is used to achieve lower prices in a competitive market
2 stress relationships: describe even more adversarial relationships where buyers drive suppliers to the wall by demanding lower prices and increasing product complexity
3 resolved relationships: have hidden some of the problems faced in the first two forms and may involve the introduction of SPC training, TQM methods and some supplier or customer involvement in solving joint problems

4   partnership relationships: as we have seen, are characterised by information/risk/reward sharing, the setting of joint goals and openness in dispute avoidance and resolution.

Models such as the supplier positioning matrix or the above relationship positioning model are interesting but less than useful in the real world when we are involved in managing relationships. There are many more variables than spend value or length of relationship.

If we consider a range of models, there are a number of common factors which impact upon the nature of the relationship (see table 3.1). It is important to remember, when considering these factors, that information with regard to their impact is often difficult to obtain. Transaction value may be an important factor but value is perceived and depends on the overall market share which an organisation's purchase represents compared to the market share achieved by the supplier.

This means that customer and supplier perceptions may differ. In addition, circumstances may change, leading to changes in these factors. Also some of these changes may be beyond the control of the purchasing and supply function, and when considering the contribution of these factors it is important to consider the degree to which these factors will vary over the course of the relationship.

Table 3.1

Factors impacting on relationships	Customer perception	Supplier perception	Variability
Transaction value – the amount of expenditure within the transaction as a proportion of overall customer spend/purchasing revenue	Low – High	Low – High	Low – High
Transaction risk – the likelihood that a supplier will fail in terms of price, quality, delivery, reliability, flexibility, innovation, service, etc	Low – High	Low – High	Low – High
Transaction contribution – the degree to which the transaction contributes to the goals of the department, another department or the organisation	Low – High	Low – High	Low – High
Transaction complexity – the type, mix, range of contracts, activities and sub-projects	Low – High	Low – High	Low – High
Transaction volume – the number of items	Low – High	Low – High	Low – High
Transaction replicability – the degree to which other transactions can be substituted	Low – High	Low – High	Low – High
Transaction predictability – the impact of demand in terms of both quantity and type on both supplier and customer	Low – High	Low – High	Low – High
Transaction longevity – the length of time that the contract lasts or the likely number of repeat contracts	Low – High	Low – High	Low – High
Transaction profile – the trade-offs between price, quality, flexibility, innovation and service required by the contract	Low – High	Low – High	Low – High
Transaction intensity – the amount of time and other resource the management of the contract will entail	Low – High	Low – High	Low – High

It is possible to then plot these factors onto a graph. When plotting these estimates, it should be remembered that there is a relationship with some of the factors and by considering the different graph shapes, purchasing professionals can obtain an idea of the way in which different levels of value, volume, intensity and so on impact upon relationships in their own industry. This will help in looking at the appropriateness of the performance indicators in place and the likelihood of achievement of the agreed targets and standards.

Assessing process-model correspondence

In understanding how the process and the model correspond we are forced to rely on metrics. Without reliable and agreed measures it will be impossible to measure how people reach these objectives.

Selecting metrics is often challenging. Reasons for this include:

1   The effort involved in measuring: although some enterprises may carry out inbound quality inspection, delivery accuracy assessment and so on, many do not. In addition, in multisite, multinational enterprises, consistent measurement does not take place within organisations. Inventory recording practices often vary within Europe and are even more different from continent to continent. This means that data is often simply unavailable or the way in which it is interpreted is different. This is changing under the influence of advanced planning, scheduling and supply chain optimisation tools, but many enterprises in non-manufacturing sectors do not see the need to expend this effort.
2   The use to which measures are put: suppliers are often concerned about the fact that broader measures may be used as a way of leveraging price (cost). This means that they may be reluctant to measure. In addition, assessment data is rarely used to improve joint performance. Instead, the measuring party uses it to suggest improvements in the other party. This can lead to conflict.
3   Measure variations over time: relationship needs will change over time, as will relationships. Measurement changes need to be recorded, validated and communicated.
4   The perceived need for measurement: buyer–supplier relationships do not take place in isolation. When entering into any relationship we look at our prospective partner's other relationships. The assumption is that if a supplier can supply a number of other buyers, the supplier will also be able to supply us. In this sense we trust other people's judgement, although this does not necessarily offer the optimum solution.

Nonetheless, the metrics chosen will have a major impact on the relationship. Relationship assessment can be validated against the same criteria that are used in vendor assessment. Common metrics for relationship assessment might include:

- price against target or against market assessment
- rejected parts per thousands/tens of thousands/hundreds of thousands delivered
- scrap and rework costs
- number of deliveries arriving within an agreed time window
- order lead times
- administration costs

3

- levels of service expressed in terms of accessibility, courtesy, competence, for example
- number of innovative suggestions per time period
- range of stock-keeping units (SKUs)
- mix of SKUs.

These outcome metrics can also be supported by process metrics. In many industries, customers have implemented target costing across the board. In the oil and gas industry, for instance, some customers have advised their suppliers that they require 15% cuts across the board on prices within a set period of time. The problem with this strategy is that the buyer has no idea of the cost structure within the supplier. Suppliers do not use activity-based costing, and there is therefore no way of knowing how cost reductions of this scale will impact upon product quality. In hostile environments, such as drilling in the North Sea, such cost reductions can have a major health and safety implication.

The logic for using process metrics is that the buyer can see the impact of changes in price – delivery, for example – on quality or innovation. By understanding the relationship between supplier processes and the outcomes the buyer needs, it is possible to obtain a finer degree of understanding about the relationship, and use the right approaches to influence the relationship in useful ways.

Closing the gap

Closing the gap between the expected and desired state and the actual state relies on the use of strategies and tactics which range from contract management, through to supplier development and interpersonal skills.

Self-assessment question 3.1

A number of suppliers have failed:

- to achieve agreed delivery times
- to deliver the right quantities
- to maintain acceptable quality standards.

Would you reassess the KPIs or impose performance penalties?

Feedback on page 55

3.2 The use of benchmarking internally and externally and its relationship to KPI setting

Benchmarking

Benchmarking is where an organisation measures its performance against industry leaders in a number of areas such as performance, quality control and procedures.

'Measuring your performance against that of best-in-class companies, determining how the best-in-class achieve these performance levels and using information as a basis for your company's targets, strategies and implementation'

Pryor (1989)

Benchmarking analysis can yield results that inform an organisation's own KPIs which could be used to transform supplier performance.

Harrison (1994) identifies three types of benchmarking which can be used at different times:

- *internal* benchmarking – enabling the organisation to learn from the best practices within the organisation
- *competitive* benchmarking – a systematic check against key competitors
- *best practice* benchmarking – where comparisons are made against world-class organisations.

The importance of benchmarking

- It provides information on what standards create or contribute to a competitive advantage. All organisations need to seek methods by which a competitive advantage is secured.
- It enables the establishment of standards and targets that have to be achieved.
- It motivates employees and overcomes resistance if achievable and improving goals become possible.
- It prevents the organisation from stagnating and becoming insular.

David et al (1999) identify a number of benchmarks that are attributable to purchasing organisations within the US. The list is extensive but it also shows how it might be possible to segment the market in more detail, and against virtually any criteria:

- purchase dollars as a percentage of sales dollars
- purchasing operating expenses as a percentage of sales dollars
- cost to spend a dollar
- purchasing employees as a percentage of company employees
- sales dollars per purchasing employee
- active suppliers per employee
- active suppliers per professional purchasing employee
- purchasing dollars spent per active supplier
- purchasing operating expense dollars per active supplier
- change in purchase dollars spent with minority-owned suppliers
- percentage of dollars spent with women-owned suppliers
- percentage of suppliers accounting for 90% of purchase dollars
- purchase order cycle time
- percentage of purchasing transactions transacted through electronic commerce
- percentage of service purchasers handled by the purchasing department
- percentage of total purchases handled by the purchasing department
- average annual training hours per professional purchasing department

- percentage of purchase transaction processed via procurement card.

Learning activity 3.2

1 Undertake some preliminary research on a few major competitors. Prepare an outline for further research of areas that appear in these organisations to have a competitive advantage.
2 List the problems you see in obtaining appropriate information for comparative purposes.

Feedback on page 55

Approaches to benchmarking

There are a number of approaches to benchmarking. The DTI broke down the approach into a number of stages (DTI, 1991):

Stage 1 Decide what aspects of purchasing or logistics to benchmark

This should happen where there are perceived differences between the company and competitors in current policies and procedures. Costs are always a benchmarking matter, as is the need to improve competitive advantage.

Stage 2 Plan the benchmarking project

A leader and a skilled team must be put together.

Stage 3 Create a baseline for benchmarking comparisons

A quantitative statement has to be prepared which shows the current position.

Stage 4 Decide who to benchmark against

The process of gathering information will be dependant upon relationships between suppliers and customers, and the possibility of restraints due to confidentiality.

Stage 5 How we will collect the information?

As stated, there are problems in information gathering. High-level contacts may have to be used to extract the more pertinent information.

Stage 6 Analyse the information obtained

This is about making judgements of the appropriateness of the information and also putting it into a quantitative format.

Stage 7 Use the findings

The final report will include implementation strategies which embed the better practices into the functions, and provide monitoring and evaluative tools.

The value of benchmarking

- Benchmarking is not industrial spying but the open gathering of information with the full cooperation of the company against which the benchmark is undertaken. Any confidential information should not be asked for.
- Benchmarking should consider all factors that make another organisation successful, including the training and skills base. Resources in terms of investment in capital and people are obviously a major contributor to success. People skills and the accumulation of knowledge are often the most difficult to identify and imitate.
- It also has to be remembered that benchmarking is not a static activity but is part of the overall strategy to be the best supplier.

Self-assessment question 3.2

Examine your own organisation and identify and list the internal standards that would be suitable benchmarks for improvement in the purchasing function.

Feedback on page 56

3.3 Auditing the procurement function

The importance of auditing

We have seen in the first part of this unit the need to monitor supplier performance.

Purchasing management audits add a layer of controls in that they:

- police the extent to which the purchasing policies laid down by the strategic plan and senior management are adhered to
- help ensure that the organisation is using techniques, procedures and methods which conform to best working methods and best practice
- monitor and measure the extent to which resources are used effectively
- assist in the prevention and detection of fraud and malpractice.

If the internal processes and procedures are operating at the highest standard this provides a suitable framework for improving the supplier network and performance.

The purchasing function is particularly vulnerable to fraudulent action and auditing can assist the organisation establish vigorous procedures for detecting and eliminating potential fraud.

Standard controls involve:

- ensuring a separation between recording and custodian practices
- controls on employees' requisition and spend limits
- a check on all requisitions

- specially designed and controlled goods inward areas
- a random check on invoices
- a mixture of systems and organisational controls that act as gatekeepers to unacceptable procedures
- a control system that makes it difficult for individuals to undertake fraudulent activity.

3

Learning activity 3.3

Imagine that your organisation has not recently carried out a procurement audit.

1   How would your organisation establish an audit team?
2   What would be its brief and how would it report?
3   What are the mechanisms in your organisation for feedback and implementation of any changes?

Feedback on page 56

The responsibility for the audit

The audit is usually carried out by senior personnel within the organisation or by external auditors selected by the company. External auditors are often used as they carry greater authority. To be effective it is important that those selected to carry out the audit have a detailed knowledge of the purchasing perspective and problems.

Areas for the audit include

- *purchasing procedures:* there is scope to examine the whole of the administrative process including the use made of technology as well as the speed and efficiency of the documentation and how it is effective in different purchasing scenarios
- *reporting processes:* the extent to which reports are used, costs, internals and value of the reports
- *the supply process:* an examination of the budget in terms of quantities and spend, a breakdown of the supplier base, relationships with suppliers and style of management, pricing strategies, savings and costs
- *inventory:* there is substantial scope to look at the inventory level and how it is analysed by the organisation, with efficiency, cost and wastage all specific items for attention.

Reporting to management

Senior management will be the recipient of any audit reports. Recommendations will address the extent to which efficiency and effectiveness can be improved. Also, a good report will highlight current good practice and strengths within the purchasing environment.

Constructive proposals based on a wider projection of the impact of the findings can provide substantial ideas for new courses of action.

3

Self-assessment question 3.3

1 What supplier audit would you undertake within the organisation?
2 What would be the data sources?
3 How would the audit relate to any genuine supplier problems?

Feedback on page 56

3.4 The value of the Kaplan and Norton balanced scorecard model

What is the balanced scorecard?

A new approach to strategic management was developed in 1992 by Kaplan and Norton. They named this system the 'balanced scorecard'. Recognising some of the weaknesses and vagueness of previous management approaches, the balanced scorecard approach provides a clear prescription as to what organisations should measure in order to 'balance' their operational perspective.

The balanced scorecard is a *management system* (not only a measurement system) that enables organisations to clarify their vision and strategy, and translate it into action. It provides feedback around both the internal business processes and external outcomes in order to continuously improve strategic performance and results. When fully deployed, the balanced scorecard transforms strategic planning from an academic exercise into the nerve centre of an enterprise. The balanced scorecard is a technique designed to ensure that the different functions of the business are integrated together in order that they work to achieve the corporate goals.

Kaplan and Norton describe the innovation of the balanced scorecard as follows:

> 'The balanced scorecard retains traditional financial measures. But financial measures tell the story of past events, an adequate story for industrial age companies for which investments in long-term capabilities and customer relationships were not critical for success. These financial measures are inadequate, however, for guiding and evaluating the journey that information age companies must make to create future value through investment in customers, suppliers, employees, processes, technology, and innovation.'

The balanced scorecard suggests that we view the organization from *four* perspectives, and to develop metrics, collect data and analyse it relative to each of these perspectives:

1 *The innovation and learning perspective:* Organisations should also attempt to identify and question their quest for improvements to value creation. This means an analysis of the product base and the skills and competences of the staff.

2   *The internal perspective:* Continuous improvement measures might also
    be relevant here and some measurement of the organisations' distinctive
    competences and the critical technologies they need to ensure continued
    leadership. Which processes should they excel at?

To achieve these goals, *performance measures must relate to employee
behaviour, to tie in the strategic direction with employee action.* An
information system is necessary to enable executives to measure
performance. Information will also be required to deliver this analysis.

3   *The customer perspective:* Focus on issues such as lead time, quality
    performance, the performance of the product and service response can
    be used to set benchmarks form the supply chain.
4   The *financial perspective:* From the financial perspective, the question to
    be asked is: 'How do we appear to shareholders?' Financial performance
    indicators indicate 'whether the company's strategies, implementation
    and execution are contributing to bottom line management'.

Figure 3.2: The balanced scorecard

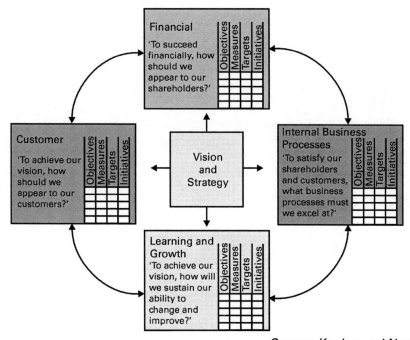

Source: Kaplan and Norton (1992)

The model helps organisations approach the development of a range of
objectives in a systematic way and to relate them to relevant performance
measures. It forces organisations to look at the interrelationship of the
various stakeholders in the business and address gaps in the corporate
performance.

Learning activity 3.4

The balanced scorecard was developed as a measurement tool to be used in
strategic and marketing planning. With reference to the key indicators in
your own purchasing function, evaluate how it may be applied to improving

(continued on next page)

3

Learning activity 3.4 *(continued)*

supplier performance. As a model, how easy is it to use in the supply chain environment?

Feedback on page 56

Kaplan and Norton suggest the balanced scorecard is best used to:

- clarify and update strategy
- communicate strategy throughout the company
- align goals with the strategy
- link strategic objectives to long-term targets and budgets
- identify and align strategic initiatives
- conduct periodic performance reviews and improve strategy.

It does have its limitations if it is not related closely to the contributions made by suppliers. It is a measurement tool and does not provide all the answers to strategic direction. If results do not occur it may be because the measures have not been fully explored.

Self-assessment question 3.4

Your line manager has recently been reading of the value of the balanced scorecard as a strategic tool. He asks you to provide a list of measurable aspects of the strategic plan that could be incorporated into the model. Construct a suitable list from those areas of the purchasing function that would enable realistic measurement.

Feedback on page 57

3.5 The consequences of a supplier failing to meet KPI standards

The impact of performance standards

The establishment of standards within the organisation is essential if the organisation is to match best practice standards elsewhere and obtain and sustain a competitive advantage.

The difference in performance of different organisations within the same industry is often difficult to explain. Certainly the way that the resources are deployed to create competences in the organisation's individual functions is a potential source of competitive advantage.

Procurement as one of the fundamental parts of an organisation contributes to the value chain analysis of the organisation's competitive strength. Johnson and Scholes (2002) refer to a number of competence bases that inform the efficiency of the organisation:

- cost efficiency
- value added

- managing linkages
- robustness.

As we have seen, Porter's value chain model has procurement as a support activity, referring to the process for acquiring the various resource inputs to the primary activities. Its impact on various areas of the business raises the importance of supplier performance.

Learning activity 3.5

With reference to your organisational contracts, identify and evaluate the impact of contract clauses in the supply agreements.

- What is the purpose of such clauses within the supply relationship?
- To what extent do you think they ensure compliance with performance standards?
- To what extent are they used as remedial action when performance slips?

Feedback on page 57

If we examine the core competences that underpin the organisation's competitive advantage, it is obvious that threshold competences have to be developed in the servicing of a particular industry. However, unless core competences that are different to the other competitors are established, there will be no competitive advantage achieved for similar or other substitute businesses.

The importance of quality and competences in defect-free manufacture underpins the need for suppliers to conform to quality specifications. The increasing need for agile and flexible production also links to supplier performance and their responsiveness.

Supply costs are another important performance indicator which contributes directly to an organisation's overall cost position. Organisations should expect their real unit costs to decline over a period of time through a combination of innovation, experience and the management of the internal and external linkages within the business. Failure to do so will mean threats from competitors.

The management and coordination of the supply chain function will improve efficiency and assist the organisation to grow and develop. Most organisational strategies will have a growth plan, as failure to grow also leads to competitive pressures as larger organisations take advantage of cost improvements.

Improving supply chain performance is part of the transformation that has occurred within the purchasing function, from being mere order placers to having an important effect on business strategy.

Using Pareto's 80/20 rule and having systems in place that track suppliers as a group can lead to better decision making for the business.

3

For example, mapping the spends of suppliers into a matrix of value and risk to the operations raises the debate on the consequences of poor supplier performance.

Such analysis will also indicate whether or not the efforts of the purchasing function is directed in inverse proportion to the value of suppliers to the business.

Those suppliers that are in abundance can be targeted with more pressure to achieve targets. If there is a scarcity of supply then the bottlenecks that might apply will trigger a number of possible outcomes – more sourcing or alternative design, for example. Those groups of supplies who are seen as strategically important can be at the centre of the relationship pattern in the future.

Therefore it is not just the individual performance of suppliers that is key to business success, but the need to manage the KPIs within the differentiated supply base in which sub-groups of suppliers are managed differently. That requires management techniques that ensure both parties are aware of their obligations. Monitoring and constant evaluation will reflect the changing world, the initiation of remedial action and if necessary the replacement of some suppliers.

Self-assessment question 3.5

List the principal reasons for supplier performance failure. To what extent are the failures an issue of management or force majeure? What action is normally taken by the organisation?

Feedback on page 57

Revision question

Now try the revision question for this session on page 341.

Summary

Failing supplier performance has to be minimised. The use of techniques and procedures that build in measurements of success and comparative data will assist the management of the procurement function to deliver business success. This involves setting appropriate standards within the function that will be achievable and, more importantly, link to the overall objectives of the organisation.

Suggested further reading

Read the chapter on logistics and supply chains in Lysons and Farrington (2006).

Feedback on learning activities and self-assessment questions

Feedback on learning activity 3.1

Implementation will be determined to a degree by the existing relationship between the two parties, but the KPIs will be a reflection of what the organisation wishes to achieve in terms of its performance with end users and a reasonable link with metrics. There will be a number of factors that the organisation wishes to achieve such as improved quality, price reduction, faster lead times and so on.

This involves a discussion with the supplier with joint agreement rather than unilateral imposition. Targets like objectives within the organisation should be SMART. Issues of power and strength of relationship will determine the outcomes. KPIs that are not realistic will lead to problems.

Again the relationship will be a determinant and the power of the two parties, but negotiating skills, influencing skills and rational argument will be important approaches.

Feedback on self-assessment question 3.1

There will have to be an analysis of the severity of the breach; a look at the history, reasons and circumstances behind the poor performance; the validity of the metrics; the impact and the capability for correction – all will be considerations. Most suppliers will prefer the use of logical and persuasive techniques in the first instance rather than threats of contractual action. Ultimately a review of the failing performance may lead to a switch of suppliers.

Feedback on learning activity 3.2

This activity is essentially research and requires the examination of a range of secondary sources of competitor organisations to see the scope for more in-depth research of their resource base and competitive advantage. Buyers will be familiar with internet research, and this will give an opportunity to explore the amount of secondary information available from this valuable resource. Sources will include corporate publications, research papers and the wealth of material in newspaper archives, some of which, such as *The Times*, is downloadable. Evidence of the success of organisations can be found, although the reasons behind the success can be more difficult. Use of technology by a competitor will have measurable benefits, but the skills of people are a different matter.

Problems occur in collecting secondary information about confidential aspects of an organisation's performance. Buyers are not in the business of espionage, so only information that can be gleaned from public sources can be used. What is difficult to analyse are the people skills within an organisation that make a difference between organisations in the same industry. Investment in technology may be detectable, but not how it is employed. Relationships with customers by competitors can be identified through contacts from the buyer's own supply base, although there will be some aspects of involvement and communication that will not be disclosed.

Feedback on self-assessment question 3.2

All organisations have good examples of successful performance, in terms of systems, people, resource allocation and usage. These should be the basis of benchmarks which can be used to raise the performance of all functions. What benchmarks or good practice does the organisation have and how is this communicated and shared? What is the process of identifying high performance teams and functions? Why do some teams perform better than others – is it because of the successful management and culture within the function, or perhaps there is a heavier investment in skilled people?

Feedback on learning activity 3.3

1   All organisations should engage in regular and professional audits of the purchasing function. The selection of the audit team would depend upon resources but they should wherever possible be independent or detached auditors, with proven skills and ability to seek out problem areas. Selection will be based on availability, strong experience and an appropriate CV.
2   The organisation should establish the criteria, which essentially focus on the factors which are important to the success of the organisation, including costs savings spend ratios, savings and fraud. Some audits, although more time-consuming, look at a full range of activities. KPIs will be the benchmark by which an audit is designed, although other important areas such as fraud detection will usually be added.
3   The feedback process by the audit team through the hierarchy of management should be explained. Statistical analysis of issues is important, but so is feedback and correction. How is feedback given? What is the tone and style and how is change to be implemented?

Feedback on self-assessment question 3.3

Supplier audits are an opportunity for the independent and in-depth appraisal of aspects of supplier performance. Secondary information from systems and records, including vendor rating systems, will provide the basis of the audit. Audits are more successful if conducted on a regular basis and with prior knowledge and agreement from the supplier. There is usually substantial material within the organisation for supply audits, which are linked to the KPI measures. Organisations have to be clear as to the extent of audit in terms of depth and cost.

Feedback on learning activity 3.4

The balanced scorecard is about measurement and targets from four perspectives that are relevant for all functions within the organisation. There is scope here to look at the measurement criteria that is used to assess organisational performance and to link it into a more comprehensive evaluation of that performance. Even if it is not used as an interrelated model the metrics should be there to ensure improvement in individual functions. The importance is that several areas of the organisation are assessed using KPIs which are essential for improved performance.

Feedback on self-assessment question 3.4

Financial indicators will be the easiest to identify, as they relate to competitive edge, but the question also requires a look at end users, stakeholders, customers and internal processes and systems. The normal metrics linked to performance errors, lateness, defects, wrong quantities should be identified. There is also an opportunity to review how improvements are built into the purchasing function through training and development, and also how the function relates to the overall organisational performance. There is a focus on questions such as: Who is the customer? What efficiencies can regularly be gained and how?

Feedback on learning activity 3.5

All organisations have procurement contracts that in most cases will provide scope for remedies if there is a breach of agreed specification, targets or standards. It is assumed that most agreements will be agreed on typical industry terms, but whose? It makes sense to be familiar with contractual clauses dealing with delivery, pricing, quality and so on, but also to have some awareness as to their impact within the organisation and the supply base. Is the contract a standard form one? Is it an active contract in that breaches are referred to and used to support remedial action, or is it down to the buyer to negotiate improvements through the relationship model?

Feedback on self-assessment question 3.5

Buyers should be aware of the causes of supply failure and the extent to which it is manageable and within the control of the supplier. Vendor rating systems plus the impact of the poor performance will be determinants of the course of action. This is an opportunity to examine whether the control mechanisms in place are sufficient to prevent the majority of non-force majeure events. If performance failure regularly occurs, then it may mean that the systems are inadequate or perhaps a more fundamental issue of supplier selection. There is an opportunity to review procedures in dealing with failing performance. How quickly are problems picked up and dealt with? Who actions remedial activity? How are supplier problems communicated?

3

Developing a competitive approach

Introduction

This unit focuses on a number of techniques that aids competitiveness. The importance of having the right supply base is stressed, along with the need to plan for the future. Internal quality systems are also explored as a reminder of the value in reaching the highest possible standards of quality.

'Constant improvement in the quality and reliability of an organisation's products or services can result in a competitive advantage others cannot steal.'
Robbins and DeCenzo (2005)

4

Session learning objectives

After completing this session you should be able to:

4.1 Assess the value of supplier selection and performance systems within the organisation.
4.2 Critically assess the impact on business competitiveness of supplier performance systems.
4.3 Give examples from TQM of its contribution to the achievement of business objectives within a competitive world.
4.4 Apply the concept of 6-Sigma to organisational improvement.
4.5 Explain how procurement planning might improve competitiveness.

Unit content coverage

Learning objective

1.3 Manage purchasing activities to influence the ability of an organisation to achieve its objectives.

Prior knowledge

Awareness of competitive forces and the responses of organisations to changes in the macro environment. Understanding of the importance of quality systems in raising the quality profile within the organisation.

Resources

Access to information on quality systems.

Timing

You should set aside about 5 hours to read and complete this session, including learning activities, self-assessment questions, the suggested further reading (if any) and the revision question.

4.1 The value of effective supplier selection and performance systems within the organisation

Introduction

Supplier selection should be undertaken at the strategic and tactical levels of the business.

Organisations should have a strategic and higher level view as to the decision making over a longer term about the many issues concerning the supply base: as to where are the risks, especially high ones, and bottlenecks. Policies need to be developed to assess core competences required of suppliers, strategic make-or-buy decisions, the size of the supplier base, partnership sourcing, reciprocal and intra-company sourcing, the impact of globalisation, the part that countertrade may play, capital equipment purchasing and ethical issues.

Strategic sourcing involves the creation of *value added* to provide a competitive advantage.

At a lower level tactical sourcing will concentrate on some of the lower risk issues, and the short-term solutions to supply issues.

Supplier selection focuses on identifying alternative and new sources of supply from within an increasingly complex and competitive market.

Purchasing managers should have some understanding of the general economic conditions relating to the supply of goods and services applying at a particular time:

- It helps the forecasting of the long-term demand for the product of which the brought-out materials, compensates, sub-assemblies and so on are a part.
- It assists in forecasting price trends.
- It indicates the alternative goods and services available within the market.
- Where appropriate it gives information and guidance on the security of supplies sources.

Market intelligence regarding the supply chain will help capture a number of potential suppliers.

Typical sources of information for new and potential suppliers include:

- *Catalogues* both paper and electronic. These are often a good source of material as they often provide easy information that is also technical.
- *Trade directories* such as Kompass, Rylands, and Buyer's Guide are especially useful for new items or unusual products. Often used in an emergency.
- *Yellow Pages*.
- *Databases*: These have superseded the need for large paper-based reference sections. There are a number of commercial databases dealing with different supply items, such as Reuters, Kompass and Pergamon Infolin. In addition, the business support agencies such as Business Link and the Chambers of Commerce have information that may be valuable.

However, there are a number of potential limitations of databases. The potential duplication and referencing may make it difficult to easily identify the full range of potential suppliers. It is also generally a time-consuming matter. The online databases vary in flexibility of usage. Information rapidly goes out of date.

Thompson and Homer (2001) have developed a number of approaches to overcome some of the shortcomings:

- use sales staff more extensively for their specialist product and organisational knowledge
- attend exhibitions as these have representatives and literature that provides unavailable information
- look through trade journals – they are good sources of gossip
- look at trade association websites
- capitalise on informal exchanges of information between purchasing professionals
- make use of information provided by prospective suppliers in response to questionnaires
- use e-marketplaces – these have developed in the larger markets where costs to find suppliers are high as there are a large number of potential suppliers. They are useful where buyers have difficulty in making suitable comparisons. Such sites are evolving and can take several formats which may specialise in supplying one industry or a range of industries with common suppliers.

Adding value to the enterprise requires the delivery of high standards of performance from suppliers. Added value inside the business is an important KPI, but securing performance improvements from the supply chain will also greatly enhance the competitive advantage of the business.

As we have seen in study session 3, establishing specific KPIs for suppliers will drive improvements throughout the business, especially the need to reduce costs, assisting in the integration of a variety of channels of distribution and reaching the market faster with new products and services.

Learning activity 4.1

With reference to your own sourcing of suppliers prepare a report of around 1,000 words which compares the effectiveness of using e-catalogues as a sourcing aid.

Feedback on page 82

Measurement of suppliers

It is important that the performance of the suppliers is measured in a credible way.

An effective performance system can measure desirable outcomes of the suppliers, which are critical to the business, notably cost and price, delivery reliability, consistency, service, innovation and flexibility.

4

In terms of measurement the system needs to be:

- efficient
- effective
- valid
- benchmarked where appropriate.

Establishing a system of metrics is perhaps the hardest part of any performance assessment. There is no common measurement system for suppliers or theoretical basis. Whatever method is chosen, a successful performance system will include the following criteria as suggested by Gower:

- accurate
- complete
- augmentative
- timely
- credible
- relevant
- usable
- scalable
- predictive
- cost-effective.

Implementation is also a potential barrier, the collection and effective use of the information. Therefore, in relation to the KPIs, the purchasing function needs to identify what information is required to make strategic or shorter-term decisions. The impact of the measurement should then be drawn from the information, preferably linked to some comparable measure.

For example, a specific area is one of risk management. Do suppliers have the capacity or the agility to respond to changes? What is the impact of technology or new material design having on the business and industry?

The data itself needs to be in a presentable format. Key external measures will include:

- the impact of costs, how it has changed from previous contracts, and other competing bidders
- delivery accuracy and lead time performance
- conformance to specification
- number of defective parts
- agility in the response to product changes
- service quality and customer satisfaction
- the number of innovative suggestions.

In addition, the use of performance ratios is often appropriate for strategic assessments and provides easy and presentable outcomes, for example:

- purchasing spend v sales revenue
- purchasing operating expenses v sales revenue
- number of suppliers v total spend.

4

Some of the more moveable or intangible aspects of service quality might provide useful information. It is a difficult area to measure because of many variable factors, the perceptions of different people within the organisation and the extent that it might vary at different times.

The Servequal scale devised by Parasuraman, Zethami and Berry (1990) identifies a range of service dimensions:

- *reliability:* delivery of the service on time and to promise?
- *responsiveness:* adaptation to user's needs
- *competence*
- *empathy:* to the needs of the user
- *accessibility:* can the service be reached when required?
- *courtesy:* are the users valued?
- *communication:* are the users kept informed of the service?
- *credibility:* do they know their job?
- *security:* is the risk managed effectively?
- *tangibles:* do the premises and staff appearance communicate the desired effect?

Self-assessment question 4.1

What are the benefits of buyers using e-marketplaces?

Feedback on page 82

4.2 The importance to business competitiveness of supplier performance systems

The contribution of appropriate relationships to supplier performance

Introduction

'Good' relationships offer a number of advantages to buyers and suppliers. They can reduce costs, raise service quality, improve information and communication quality, solve joint problems, identify opportunities and generally improve flexibility in commercial activities. Relying on self-interest is not enough in global markets that are populated by increasing levels of technological breakthrough and characterised by increasing competition. The formalising of the relationship with agreed KPIs will assist the process towards buyer/supplier success.

However, defining and developing the right type of relationship is often difficult. Limited models of relationship lead to, or at least imply, limited strategies for managing within those relationships. In addition, as we have already seen, the tools used to manage within those relationships do not always clearly correspond to the relationships we require. Some KPIs may have been unrealistic or accepted reluctantly. Some aspects of poor performance are attributable to events beyond the control of the supplier.

However, it is still pertinent for buyers to seek to provide some measurement of their supplier relationships. As we saw in study session 3,

4

it is important to ensure that performance is measured against a balanced range of stakeholder goals and perspectives: many organisations turn to the balanced scorecard. Standards should be set and constantly reviewed and fed back. Mechanisms for corrective action should be in place.

Trading environments are increasingly characterised by rapidly escalating competition based on:

- price–quality positioning
- competition to create new know-how and establish first-mover advantage
- competition to protect or invade established product or geographic markets
- competition based on deep pockets and the creation of alliances with even larger war chests
- the growing expectations of customers and the need to improve service and quality.

In such environments, the frequency, boldness and aggressiveness of movement by the players can lead to even more market instability. This, in turn, is made even worse by short product life cycles, short product design cycles, new technologies, frequent entry by unexpected outsiders, repositioning by existing competitors and radical redefinitions of market boundaries as diverse industries merge. In other words, environments escalate towards higher and higher levels of uncertainty, dynamism, differences between players and hostility.

The traditional sources of advantage no longer provide long-term security. Multinational corporations still have economies of scale, massive advertising budgets, the best distribution systems in their industries, cutting-edge R&D, deep pockets and many other features that give them power over buyers and suppliers and that raise barriers to entry that seem impregnable. But these are not enough any more. Leadership in price and quality is also not enough to assure success. Being first is not always the same as being best. Entry barriers are destroyed or circumvented using new ideas and technologies.

As enterprises struggle to sustain advantage, it becomes increasingly evident that no single organisation can build a sustainable competitive advantage. Every advantage erodes. So in this changing environment companies must actively work to improve their own advantages and disrupt the advantages of their competitors. One way in which enterprises can do this is through the management of the supply chain.

Risk assessment and evaluation in relationship decisions

Introduction

Risks are endemic in any business transaction. These risks can become even more problematic when we consider the commercial area of enterprise-wide activities on which our decisions can have a major impact. Product recalls, for example, can have a serious impact on reputation and the bottom line. Organisations will have to investigate whether the fault was a supplier risk, a purchasing risk or a production risk. Choosing one supplier over another, choosing one type of contract and choosing a particular negotiating position are all risk-laden activities. However, risks are necessary for ultimate profitability. The organisation has to adopt a systematic approach to the setting up and evaluation of these risks.

Assessing risk

There are a number of approaches to assessing risk. Broadly these fall into two groups. The first rests upon the belief that events in the past can be quantified (numbered) in such a way as to offer a platform upon which we can predict the future. The second rests upon a belief that the past cannot be quantified. It is just too complex, and therefore presents no safe platform for predicting the likelihood of future events. In the first of these views, risk assessment is a science. In the second it is an art.

If we are going to assess risk, we must agree that certain predictions can be made on the basis of past events. Assessing risk on the basis of this belief involves a set of steps. These steps are:

1   Understanding the nature of the risk involved by creating a set of possible risks from each activity carried out.
2   Calculating the probability of the risk occurring by looking at the frequency of an event happening in the past and the reasons for its happening.

A key aspect of managing risk is risk analysis – identifying and evaluating the sources of risk. Microsoft has a program of risk analysis based on a 'universe of risk'. This identifies 12 primary sources of risk which are:

1   business partners
2   competitive
3   customer
4   distribution
5   financial
6   operations
7   people
8   political
9   regulatory and legislative
10   reputational
11   strategic
12   technological.

The critical task for purchasing and supply is to manage risk appropriately. In many cases, there is little time for anything else but a snap decision based on minimal information and a gut feeling. In other cases, such as preparing an outsourcing contract, purchasing will need to invest time and effort before making a particularly risky choice that could have a major impact on company profitability.

When assessing risk, it is important here to think about the differences between risk avoidance, risk shifting and risk taking.

- *Risk avoidance* allows one party to assess the risk and avoid it. If we can assess the likelihood of a supplier failing to deliver to quality standards or on time, we could probably reduce our risk by choosing another supplier.

- *Risk shifting* means passing the risk on to another person or organisation. Risk can be shifted to insurance companies who will assess the risk on our behalf and charge a premium for remedying the damage done. Risks can also be shifted on to suppliers. Inventory holding is a good case in point. In an industry with short product life cycles, inventory may become obsolete. Some organisations pass risk down the chain to suppliers who are forced to hold stocks on their behalf.
- *Risk taking* means assessing the risk and taking it because the value of the potential pay-off outweighs the risk. It is always useful to remember that although human beings as a whole are generally risk-averse (they do not like taking risks), profit and risk are closely linked. Once it has been decided to take a risk, it is important that this risk is properly allocated. Joint venture agreements are often a way of allocating risk across two separate organisations. Within organisations it is equally important to recognise the risk and allocate it fairly between the individuals and groups involved.

When considering risks, it is possible to say that risk, as a whole, cannot be eliminated. There will always be factors beyond the control of governments, enterprises and individuals. It is a question of assessing and managing risk so as to optimise benefits against potential losses.

Types of risk

Because many risks are unforeseeable, it is impossible to categorise them all in a study guide. People and enterprises develop experience about risk over time. In commercial relationships risks may include:

- failure to obtain the optimum price so that a competitor can deliver the same, or a similar product, much more cheaply to the end user
- failure to deliver or complete a project on time when other projects, as part of a major programme, are contingent upon completion
- physical risks to plant, machinery and other assets such as theft, fire or other loss
- bad faith risks where a supplier or a buyer may have no intention of fulfilling the contract
- risks from shifts in national or transactional policy which cause cost increases in a core business activity or lead to it being banned
- intellectual property risks when a supplier may use trade secrets in developing a relationship with another customer
- risks from contract misinterpretation caused by poorly drafted specifications or poorly drafted agreements
- significant design or manufacturing shortcuts in the face of delivery or cost pressure leading to a serious health and safety problem causing injury or loss of life
- ethical risks which may become shareholder or customer risks when enterprises employ transnational low-cost labour in poor conditions.

Some organisations do in fact keep a register of risks, which guides staff in making risk decisions, and such registers can be useful. However, to be able to make rational, informed decisions about risks, it is important to understand some basic concepts of risk, risk evaluation and decision making.

Learning activity 4.2

With reference to your own organisation, show diagrammatically how failure to perform by a key supplier affects the performance of the organisation itself.

Feedback on page 82

Risk and decision making

Risk is inextricably linked with decision making. Decision making is becoming more complex for many purchasing professionals. Increasingly purchasers are being asked to move away from decisions that are based purely on lower costs and higher quality, and to make comprehensive assessments of supply organisations. One of the most valuable attributes of a purchasing professional is their analytical ability. The capacity to perform value analysis, cost analysis, supplier finance and performance, and business process analysis is increasingly a key to success in the profession.

Commercial relationships and organisational success

There are many views about the contribution that commercial relationships make to organisational success. Perhaps the first is the need for both enterprises, and the supply chains that support them, to become more flexible. A number of authorities have noted that the manufacturing function within the United Kingdom has moved from manufacturing to 'design, sourcing and assembly'. Such strategies maximise organisational flexibility and shift the traditional role of purchasing.

The second of these drivers includes the need to secure competitive advantage through reduction of waste, and thus cost minimisation. The need to minimise cost dictates increases in process visibility and efficiency. Increases in process visibility facilitate the process and also the performance measurement. Performance measurement is a necessary component of cost minimisation.

Although the logical extension of this lean philosophy may have a number of drawbacks, it is firmly embedded within many organisations in the form of JIT systems and continuous improvement programmes.

The third driver is the need to deal with increasing complexity within the purchasing process. We can identify increases in complexity both in product/service specification and assembly in items ranging from manufactured goods to construction projects. Appropriate relationships are an important way of managing these drivers, and developing these relationships sometimes requires a shift in focus or 'mindset'.

Self-assessment question 4.2

Explain the measures against which first tier suppliers are assessed in your own organisation.

Feedback on page 83

4.3 TQM and its contribution to the achievement of business objectives within a competitive world

The importance of quality

Buyers must make sure that they know exactly what quality they want and ensure this is understood by the supplier. The buyer achieves the first of these through good liaison with the other departments involved in quality determination and the second through the comprehensive compilation and communication of specifications to the supplier(s).

The meaning of quality

Buyers need to be absolutely sure what is meant by quality. Quality from the purchasing point of view means simply 'that which is suitable for the purpose intended' – no more and no less. Note that it does not mean the 'best available' or 'most superior'. If buyers purchase a better quality than is required for the purpose, then they are wasting money unnecessarily.

Specifications

Quality requirements are communicated internally and externally by means of a specification – *it is* in fact a statement which provides a description or list of the characteristics required in an item.

It can be thought of as a detailed description of what is required. Buyers should always take the greatest care with specifications, particularly in purchase orders, because if an incorrect specification is stated on a purchase order and the suppliers supply what has been stated, then they have fulfilled their contractual obligations and the responsibility rests entirely with the buyer.

Some methods which may be used as a basis to specify requirements to a supplier – in different situations – include:

- brand name
- dimensions
- physical or chemical properties
- specify and use
- market grade
- production to standards: British (BS), European (EN) or international (ISO)

- method/materials of manufacture
- blueprint
- samples.

Reliability

Reliability is an important element in cost and is something which the buyer pays for and is entitled to receive. Reliability is defined in BS 4778 as 'the ability of an item to perform a required function under stated conditions for a stated period of time'. It should be an integral aspect of any specification.

Purchasing as a profit centre

Purchasing is now seen as an important generator of profit. This ability to generate profits comes about through the *profit leverage effect*. On average, purchased goods and services account for approximately 60% of the cost of sales (sales £), with the balance being the costs of overheads. A good quality system and a supplier chain that responds to the quality standards will be a direct contributor to ultimate cost savings.

The processes for improving quality

Quality assurance

Quality assurance comprises a series of planned and systematic activities implemented within the framework of a quality system, and demonstrated as needed to provide adequate confidence that an entity will fulfil requirements for quality. Quality assurance is concerned with defect prevention – unlike *quality control*, which is concerned with defect detection and correction – and is often based on an appropriate standard published by BSI or ISO.

In order for quality assurance to be effective, clear agreement has to be developed with suppliers for the assurance of items supplied in matters such as inspection, testing, evaluation and implementation of the quality systems.

Quality systems

Note that it is not necessary for you to learn in detail all of the content of the specific standards – just a general familiarisation with the approach they take is sufficient. Compare the approach taken in ISO 9000 with that in the new standard ISO 9001 2000.

The purpose of a quality system is to establish a framework of reference points to ensure that, every time a process is performed, the same information, methods, skills and controls are used and applied in a consistent manner. Documentation providing an 'audit trail' is the central feature of any quality system. The three levels of documentation required in a quality system are:

- Level 1: company quality manual
- Level 2: procedures manual
- Level 3: work instructions, specifications and methods.

4

A quality system should also:

- have a database containing all other reference documents
- cover all aspects of an organisation's activities
- incorporate good management practice
- be developed against a reference base – 'a quality system standard'.

Standards such as ISO 9000 provide an effective managerial framework on which to build a company-wide approach to continuous quality improvement.

Consistency and control

It is *variability* in a process which is the cause of bad quality. Variability means that sometimes the output of the goods or services will be satisfactory and sometimes it will not. Unless variability in a process is eliminated, then it will not be possible to achieve desired quality standards. The requirement, therefore, is to achieve **consistency of output**.

The elimination of variability and the achievement of consistency of output is obtained through improving process control; this is true of both goods and services.

Process control is achieved through techniques such as:

- standard operating procedures (SOPs)
- statistical process control (SPC).

The elimination of variability also requires consistency of quality systems and inputs. With variability of inputs, quality will still be inconsistent despite internal processes being under control. Purchasing has an important contribution to make here. This aspect of consistency can be achieved by the use of systems and methods including:

- selection of quality capable suppliers through effective vendor auditing
- maintaining supplier performance through vendor rating and development
- supplier quality assurance schemes
- well-designed specifications and 'early supplier involvement' (ESI).

When consistency of inputs and outputs has been achieved and random variability eliminated, then it should be possible to achieve desired quality standards, and subsequently move towards continuous quality improvement.

Standard operating procedures

A strategy for quality needs to be implemented at operational levels within the organisation to have a real and significant impact. The term '**standard operating procedures**' encompasses any set of sequential techniques which outline the order and methods to be followed to accomplish any given task.

The use of SOPs emphasises the importance of consistency, and is consistent with other techniques to reduce process variation.

A European approach to quality

The European Foundation for Quality Management (EFQM) was set up in 1988 to encourage organisations to achieve success through total quality management. The EFQM model, commonly known in the UK as the 'business excellence model', is a non-prescriptive tool designed to help organisations assess their own strengths and weaknesses, and to stimulate improvement activities.

Studies by International Survey Research in employee opinions, between EFQM and non-EFQM companies, suggest that those adopting the model outperform their competitors in several areas. In particular, employees gave EFQM companies higher scores for quality, innovation and customer orientation. They were also rated highly in relation to teamwork.

The EFQM's (European Foundation for Quality Management: http://www.efqm.org) partner in the UK is the British Quality Foundation (British Quality Foundation: http://www.quality-foundation.co.uk), a not-for-profit company founded in 1992 to provide support on business excellence matters. Other possible sources of information on quality matters are:

- BSI Quality Assurance (BSI Quality Assurance: http://www.bsi.org.uk)
- Institute of Quality Assurance (Institute of Quality Assurance: http://www.iqa.org).

Learning activity 4.3

To what extent is TQM embedded within the organisation? How has this been achieved? How has this improved the quality position of the business?

Feedback on page 83

TQM and continuous improvement

TQM emphasises the idea of 'getting it right first time', resulting in zero defects; and also seeking continuous improvements (Kaizen). These approaches to quality are examined in detail below.

Continuous improvement

The concept of continuous improvement, or 'Kaizen', has been increasingly influential in recent years. The key principle is that all members constantly seek small improvements in all aspects of the organisation's activities.

Kaizen is the Japanese for 'continuing improvement' – in personal life, home life and working life. When applied to the workplace, Kaizen means continuing improvement involving everyone – managers and workers alike.

Kaizen is therefore the Japanese philosophy of the continuous improvement of all employees in an organisation, such that they perform their tasks a little better, all the time. This is viewed as a never-ending journey, which is centred on the concept of starting each day with the principle that it is always possible to improve methods of working.

Hence Kaizen is small, but continuous, improvement. It should be implemented by workers and middle management, with the encouragement and direction of the top. The top management's responsibility is to cultivate the appropriate working climate and culture in the organisation.

The most common way in which Kaizen is implemented is through Kaizen teams, or 'quality circles', also referred to as 'quality improvement teams'. Quality circles are groups of workers doing similar work, who meet voluntarily at regular times in normal working time. They are under the leadership of their supervisor with the objective of identifying, analysing and solving any work-related issues and recommending solutions to management. Whenever possible, the quality circle members should be responsible for the implementation of the solutions themselves. This gives the team ownership over the solution, reduces resistance and is a form of empowerment.

As Kaizen is almost exclusively based on people solving problems themselves in teams in the workplace, there is a high emphasis on training so that people have the necessary skills to solve the problems with which they are faced. Typical training for Kaizen or quality circles is in eight stages:

- the concept of quality circles
- brainstorming techniques
- data gathering and histograms
- cause and effect analysis
- Pareto analysis
- sampling and stratification
- statistical control charts
- presentation skills and techniques.

The benefits of this approach are that people are motivated and empowered, and quality problems are solved without great capital investment.

Zero defects

The concept of zero defects encompasses a strategy for supplying products that cannot be faulted. This requires firms to have confidence in their product quality; this can facilitate long-term supply contracts, as buyers minimise their inspections of components or products supplied. Clearly the pursuit of perfection is not without difficulties, and, as Womack et al (1990) remind us, the pursuit of the unattainable can often provide inspiration and direction towards a desired future state.

The notion of zero defects is rooted in the idea that it is easier to design and build quality into a product than attempt to ensure quality through inspection alone.

Avoiding defects – failure mode and effect analysis

Failure mode and effect analysis (FMEA) is a method of predicting what can go wrong with a product or service. FMEA attempts to identify all the possible ways in which failures may occur and analyses their root causes; this 'grades' the risks involved. Unacceptable risk levels are selected for corrective action and the final risk level reduced to acceptable proportions.

FMEA is divided into two categories:

- design FMEA
- process FMEA.

Both require a team approach in order to analyse them. A specialised form is used to record the findings of the team of analysts. The team members start by defining customer expectations; they ask the customer what he expects and then drive the production or service process into failure mode by dreaming up all the things which could go wrong and deprive the customer of his or her just expectations. After prioritising the possible failures, they are systematically prevented from happening. The failure modes are recorded on the specialised form in terms of severity, effect, frequency and detection in order to obtain risk priority numbers.

This team-based analysis is conducted for both design FMEA and process FMEA.

Taguchi methods

The Taguchi definition of quality is: 'Quality is the (minimum) loss imparted to society from the time the product is shipped.'

This loss includes the loss of customer satisfaction that leads to the loss of market standing by the company in addition to the usual costs of quality, such as scrap and rework.

Customer satisfaction is deemed to be the most important part of a process. It is the total financial loss to society which is the true cost – a very broad view of cost which also incorporates factors such as environmental costs. This methodology suggests that traditional measures of quality underestimate the costs of poor quality. In particular, it suggests that the zero defects approach is not a sufficiently tight criterion.

The Taguchi approach requires that quality be built in to the product from the design stage and quality is measured by the *quadratic loss function*. According to Taguchi, performance begins to deteriorate as soon as the design parameters deviate from their target values. Hence the loss function is measured by the deviation from the ideal or target value.

Quality function deployment and 'the house of quality'

This is a technique which attempts to produce robust designs while at the same time putting the customer at the forefront of the design process (in other words, 'deploying the voice of the customer').

The customer's requirements are identified by researching the market and are then built into the design by use of a system of matrices known as the 'house of quality' (so called because its outline has the shape of a house). The technique incorporates the technical, manufacturing, benchmark and customer requirements into the 'house of quality' matrix, which should produce a product which incorporates the best design features and customer preferences.

Much design work now utilises computer-aided design (CAD), and manufacturing techniques are improved in the degree of precision and finish by the use of computer-aided manufacturing (CAM); these assist in the attainment of quality and consistency in techniques such as quality function deployment (QFD).

The benefits of QFD can be summarised as:

- improved quality
- increased customer satisfaction
- improved company performance
- improved time to market
- lower cost in design and manufacture
- reduction in design changes/problems
- improved product reliability.

Simultaneous engineering and cross-functional teams

Simultaneous engineering refers to the practice of involving all relevant functions right from the outset of the design stage; such *cross-functional teams* include representatives from engineering, design, purchasing, production, marketing and suppliers. The idea is to get the product right from the start of the design stage. Where it has been used, the technique has been remarkably effective in reducing both the time to market for new products and the performance of new products during assembly and in the field.

By using cross-functional teams and ESI, all of the issues are resolved simultaneously. In this process, design is not seen as being the sole preserve of technicians.

The value of total quality management

Rather than looking at quality from an isolated perspective, an organisation should have a strategic plan for quality, which is referred to as *total quality management* (TQM). TQM requires a quality-conscious attitude throughout the organisation and for a commitment to the objective of achieving quality to exist at all levels. This approach is essential if organisations are to survive in the face of international competition, where there is an ever-increasing emphasis on quality. Quality must be seen as an essential aspect of management and one to which the purchasing function must be committed alongside the other management functions. Evans (1993) defined TQM as 'an integrative management concept of continually improving the quality of delivered goods and services through the participation of all levels and functions of the organisation'.

The following points are integral to all TQM schemes:

- company-wide commitment to quality
- the need for a quality programme

- the need for a system of quality
- measurement of quality
- quality targets and measurement of performance
- appropriate training in the required technology for assessment of quality
- an integrated approach to problem solving
- involvement of everybody
- continuity.

The importance of focusing on customers (both internal and external) has already been illustrated. If everybody within the organisation attempts to 'delight' their customers, then performance should improve significantly.

An improvement or innovation that takes the organisation to another level is termed 'breakthrough'. These types of improvement concentrate on major variations within the business performance and seek to find solutions to such variability.

The concept of *continuous improvement*, or Kaizen, has been very influential over recent years. The guiding principle is one of constantly seeking small improvements in all aspects of the organisation's activities. It affects everyone at all levels of the organisation and requires the effective performance of teams rather than individuals.

Once a culture of safety has been established, employees will self-manage their tasks and seek voluntarily to take responsibility for improvements.

For TQM to be successful there must be clear implementation of the philosophy:

- provision of leadership from the top
- creation of a quality culture
- teamwork
- adequate resource allocation
- quality training of employees
- measurement and use of statistical concepts
- quality feedback
- employee recognition
- supplier involvement.

TQM and measurement techniques

It is a precondition of improvement that *what we do is measured*. Measurement is necessary for identifying and solving problems and for monitoring improvements. JS Oakland has identified seven *tools of quality management* – simple but effective statistical tools which you should be familiar with from your foundation studies. The seven tools are:

- statistical process control (SPC)
- Pareto analysis
- bar charts
- histograms
- fishbone technique
- flow charts
- scatter diagrams.

It is important to consider how these techniques can be applied to improvement in the purchasing function.

TQM and suppliers

One of the buyer's essential contributions to TQM is the development of the same commitment to quality in suppliers as in the buyer's own organisation. High standards of quality cannot be attained and maintained unless suppliers of components are willing to share that commitment; systems such as SPC and QA are useful tools.

But just as important is attitude and commitment. It is the buyer's task to ensure that suppliers develop the correct attitude towards quality.

Self-assessment question 4.3

Outline an example of an organisational success with a quality standard and how it has benefited the business.

Feedback on page 83

4.4 The value of 6-Sigma to organisational improvement

6-Sigma

6-Sigma is a process improvement methodology using data and statistical analysis to identify and fix problem/opportunity areas.

Over the past ten years, 6-Sigma has delivered a variety of benefits to companies, such as reducing costs, increasing revenues, improving process speed, raising quality levels and deepening customer relationships. In addition, 6-Sigma has been used across a variety of industries and business models, from manufacturing to services. It is argued that it has the capability of:

- improving gross margins
- enhanced relationships with customers
- efficient processes and discipline within an organisation
- sustained benefits (not just one-off improvements disappearing with time)
- enduring change, as employees continue executing projects years after initial deployment.

Deployed correctly, 6-Sigma has the ability to generate *breakthrough* value in a business. If used correctly it can be integrated with other quality processes such as TQM and Kaizen.

What is it?

6-Sigma is a process system for improving quality performance by means of aiming for a failure rate of just 3.4 parts per million, or 99.9997% perfect.

However, the term in practice is used to denote more than simply counting defects. 6-Sigma can now imply a whole culture of strategies, tools and statistical methodologies to improve the bottom line of companies. In all, it is a rigorous analytical process for anticipating and solving problems and one which concentrates on achieving high levels of production performance.

Why is it important?

World-class companies typically operate at about 99% perfection. To get to the 6-Sigma level requires a considerable effort of improvement in the operations teams with an emphasis on cost cutting and wastage.

The popularity of 6-Sigma has been growing. Companies such as Motorola (1987), Texas Instruments (1988), IBM (1990), Asea Brown Boveri (1993), Allied Signal/Kodak (1994), GE (1995), Whirlpool, Invensys and Polaroid (1996/98), and many other companies worldwide have successfully implemented 6-Sigma. Recently Ford, DuPont, Dow Chemical, Microsoft and American Express have started working on instituting 6-Sigma processes.

Learning activity 4.4

Undertake online research into organisations that use 6-Sigma, identifying and critically assessing whether organisational benefits claimed are transferable to other similar industries and cultures, including your own organisation.

Feedback on page 84

When to use it?

Bottom line drives management action. What is your Cost of (poor) Quality? First you need to determine that. Properly implemented, 6-Sigma implementation can become a profit centre for the company. Jack Welch at GE claimed that the returns on 6-Sigma implementation amounted to about $500 million during 1998. It should be remembered that 6-Sigma is complementary to other initiatives such as ISO 9000 (which is mainly procedural), total quality management (which is mainly cultural) and statistical process control (which is primarily statistical process monitoring).

How to use it?

6-Sigma focuses on process quality. As such, it falls into the category of a process capability technique. Traditionally, a process is considered capable if the natural spread of error was plus and minus *three* sigma (a yield of 99.73%), less than the engineering tolerance. A later refinement considered the process location as well as its spread, and tightened the minimum acceptable so that the process was at least four sigma from the nearest engineering requirement. 6-Sigma requires that processes operate such that the nearest engineering requirement is at least plus or minus

6-Sigma from the process mean. This requires considerable scientific and testing actions – often thousands of tests are run on multiple variables to get an understanding of what's going on. Once the process variables have been determined, and using the other process analysis techniques, the organisation needs to consider the ones causing the major losses and work on making them more capable. It is a system that insists on a search through testing and evaluation for near perfection – leading to a justified claim for world-class status. In seeking this status it enables the organisation to:

- understand clearly who are the customers and the value of the product to them and the organisation
- review consumer surveys, concession reports, and other data and in so doing contribute useful feedback into the organisation
- screen and prioritise issues by severity, frequency/likelihood of occurrence, and so on
- determine the internal processes causing the most errors and wastage
- find out why and where the defects are occurring
- devise ways to address these defects effectively
- set up a good metrics (6-Sigma places a lot of emphasis on measurement).

Who or what is a Green Belt?

The quality system uses a number of terminologies and approaches to embed good practice. 6-Sigma uses role such as Green Belt and Black Belt as part of the establishment of a culture geared to solving problems and raising standards to a level of excellence. It also sends signals around the organisation that this is a serious quality system with defined operational parameters. For example, a Green Belt is a person trained in the 6-Sigma methodology who is a team member of 6-Sigma process improvement action teams.

Who or what is a Black Belt?

People that are part of the leadership structure for process improvement teams are called 'Black Belts' (just as TQM utilised 'quality improvement team leaders' to provide structure). Black Belts are highly-regarded, technically-oriented product or line personnel who have an ability to lead teams as well as to advise management.

Who or what is a Master Black Belt?

A Master Black Belt is a person trained in the 6-Sigma methodology who acts as the organisation-wide 6-Sigma director or a programme manager. He oversees Black Belts and process improvement projects and provides guidance to Black Belts as required. A Master Black Belt teaches other 6-Sigma students and helps them achieve Green Belt and Black Belt status.

Driving the process

The process is usually driven by a top executive or senior manager who is the sponsor, a catalyst and the driving force behind the organisation's 6-Sigma implementation.

4

The impact on the purchasing function

The above outline of the 6-Sigma function illustrates that, as with all systems and processes surrounding quality, it is possible to raise the stakes and seek higher performance. The continuous improvement philosophy and quality circles introduced by Japanese industry, for example, is similar in that it works if it can become embedded into the operational processes and culture of the organisation.

This in turn will require the purchasing function to work more closely with the supply chain to deliver and achieve a higher quality specification. The purchasing processes will also have to be revisited in terms of supplier assessment, capability and risk. It may also involve a closer examination of the approaches to preferred suppliers, collaborative partnerships, early involvement in design issues and perhaps the whole approach to cost-cutting and negotiation.

Self-assessment question 4.4

Prepare a diagram or flow chart to show how 6-Sigma might fit into your organisational life.

Feedback on page 84

4.5 The importance of procurement planning to business competitiveness

The planning process

We have already seen in study session 1 that strategically an organisation has to plan for the long term. Planning is also essential for the supply chain if the organisation is to be assured of the right volume and mix of materials, parts and sub-assemblies at the right cost and the right time. There is now an additional shift in the integration of the planning process to create dramatic improvements in cycle time, lead time and cost.

Learning activity 4.5

It is important that managers plan. Consider how your own organisation formally plans. To what extent is planning also informal? How does the planning inform the decision making? Is it effective?

Feedback on page 84

Senior management in response to shareholder demands often seek to drive the whole planning process of the supply chain in the direction of cutting costs, reducing costs and the sharing of data with established trading partners. Contributions from the growing e-commerce technology have been seen as a way to gain these efficiencies.

Other organisations are looking for responsiveness from the supply chain so that they can deliver products and services much more speedily. Amazon and Dell's internet-enabled systems are examples of this approach.

Meeting these needs without increasing inventory levels to the point where the business is unprofitable requires bringing the traditional planning aspects of the supply chain closer to the actual real-time execution, and closing the gap between traditional supply chain issues and the customer. It also means that the planning process needs to be a lateral one across the various related functions, for example connecting the supply chain processes with customer relationship management software.

The increased complexity of operations in many organisations requires more monitoring and evaluation of the plan and changes to it. This requires greater analysis of data information to extract the true drivers of customer demand. This might involve access to data systems that are based at point-of-sale locations.

Such drivers may include:

- environment, such as weather, calendar, demographics and econometrics
- marketing mix such as advertising levels, consumer awareness, price, display, distribution and promotion activities
- competition such as advertising, price difference and new products.

The procurement function will require different types of information for effective planning (Baily et al, 2004):

- The external environment – technical developments, competition for available supplies, withdrawal of suppliers from a falling market?
- The extent of supply-market research.
- Is there a corporate supply strategy?
- Can procurement deal with rapid changes?
- How are the supply interests being protected in a competitive environment of scarce supplies?
- What is the position regarding power supplies?
- What are the supply-cost trends over the next few years?
- How does the supply function link to product development?
- What information is in hand regarding the capacity and mix of suppliers? Does the mix have to be reviewed?
- What make-or-buy decisions will be made?

The marketing function will usually be responsible for forecasting customer demand and to adjust marketing mix to increase demand. Marketing will perform detailed analysis of historical data to determine price sensitivity, media responsiveness, marketing event effectiveness and current and future product mix.

Information from the marketing function will be directly involved in:

- planning the marketing mix
- the planning of new product introductions

- identifying those products reaching maturity
- building promotional calendars
- determining prices
- identifying and determining cannibalisation effects of new products and promotions
- evaluating and monitoring marketing plans.

The sales function uses demand projections to set targets. This function will also be fully involved in the understanding of the drivers of demand. The sales organisation provides input to the plan and uses the output of the plan to:

- review accounts and adjust account-level forecast
- plan and execute account-specific events and promotions
- evaluate and monitor category performance by account
- measure projected sales versus actual plan/account
- evaluate and monitor marketing plans.

The link between the *operations* function and *procurement* is key to the planning process if there is to be effective decision making on plant and material levels, the sourcing of manufacturing replenishment request, distribution logistics and inventory levels.

Finally the involvement of *finance* is important as it needs information for demand projections to fix budgets, manage cashflows and guide investor expectations.

Each organisation's planning needs will be varied according to its strategic focus. This will impact on the planning cycle (daily, weekly, monthly), the volume of explicit information required for forecasts, the level of detail, the number of products and the time horizon of the forecasts.

Self-assessment question 4.5

Examine a typical purchasing decision within your own organisation. Identify how it links to business objectives. Is it carefully aligned to the planning process?

Feedback on page 84

Revision question

Now try the revision question for this session on page 341.

Summary

Measurement is a feature here of the supply chain management. Efficient selection of suppliers is essential for the reduction of risk to the organisation. The management of the supply base in terms of importance and tiers plus sound systems for measuring performance will ensure performance standards are met and risks minimised. Internally, the organisation will also have to consider strategies for raising the quality of products to enhance competitiveness and meet customer expectations.

Suggested further reading

Read the chapter on purchasing and supply chain strategy in Lysons and Farrington (2006).

Feedback on learning activities and self-assessment questions

Feedback on learning activity 4.1

Increasingly the internet is providing access to a wider range of potential suppliers by the use of e-catalogues and cybermediary websites that permit quick and useful access without the need for extensive secondary research. Has this form of supplier sourcing become the norm, replacing traditional secondary searches? How are suppliers identified within your own organisation? What are the advantages of electronic sourcing approaches? Is there evidence that a wider supply base is reached and how useful is the information of the potential supply as a possible future source?

Feedback on self-assessment question 4.1

Advantages of joining an e-marketplace include:

- greater opportunities for suppliers and buyers to make new trading partnerships, either within their supply chain or across supply chains
- the potential to lower the costs of negotiating and making transactions with automation of standard business procedures
- the potential for more transparent pricing as buyers and sellers take the opportunity to trade in a more open environment
- the opportunity to access value-added services such as inventory control and management of dispatch and distribution processes using electronic systems
- the potential to access global markets.

Feedback on learning activity 4.2

This is an opportunity to look at aspects of failure such as late delivery, defects, price increases, and how there is a knock-on effect on the quality and performance of the product and the resulting impact on the end user. The supply chain is being increasingly managed more tightly to ensure, for example, delivery of business objectives of leanness, speed of response or high quality. Failure to perform can have a major impact on costs, incomes and future customer confidence. Supply-chain disruptions are on the rise in many industries, partly because of the growing reliance on overseas suppliers for components. For example, when Motorola introduced its first camera phone in late 2003, the company couldn't acquire enough lenses and chipsets to meet demand for the fast-selling product. Sony, Boeing,

Hershey, Nike and Cisco are just a handful of other big companies hurt by disruptions in recent years. Small businesses are particularly vulnerable to the ill effects of disruptions because they're focused on fewer products and wield less clout with supply-chain partners.

What are the typical failures? Why do they occur? Is it because of initial poor selection criteria or is it other micro and macro events? Have costs been cut too drastically?

Feedback on self-assessment question 4.2

First tier suppliers are the most important in the supply chain. There should be some understanding of the concept of first tier suppliers, who because of their importance are closely involved in the performance of the business. First tier suppliers should be in close relationship with the buyer and communications ongoing to ensure awareness of changing business situations and also to act as an early warning system if performance begins to falter. Consequently assessment of their performance should be vigorous, and action taken to establish remedial and corrective measures if performance is below what is expected.

- As well as the traditional measures, financial reports of the supplier should be monitored, as well as any press comments about the organisation.
- Periodic site visits might be planned.
- Monitor delivery performance: Signs of trouble can also be found through the supplier's delivery and performance (or lack thereof). These signs can include late deliveries, increased use of expedited freight, requests for technical support, delay in response to production issues, requests by the supplier for price increases or accelerated payment terms, or changes in product quality.
- Draft strong purchase orders and contracts.
- Establish and maintain tooling ownership to avoid disruptions.
- Determine the ability to resource to an alternative supplier.

Feedback on learning activity 4.3

TQM is an important approach to improving the quality of the business and the improvements can be tracked quantitatively. However, it does require management impetus and embedding in the culture, which in turn requires systems, controls, monitoring and evaluation. There should be evidence of the process of TQM, including managerial, administrative and statistical controls that can help develop the culture of quality. Also to be considered is the process by which it is communicated to the whole workforce. Does everyone within the function understand what TQM is about? Are targets set for groups and individuals on quality performance? How are quality improvements measured?

Feedback on self-assessment question 4.3

There should be many examples of quality improvements within the business. This should be linked to a clear measurable improvement which has improved performance of the product, simplified manufacturing, reduced stock levels or reduced waste. Costs and processes should be identified.

Feedback on learning activity 4.4

6-Sigma is a useful quality system if quality is a key indicator for organisational performance. It is a system that does require significant management and training investment plus processes to ensure sustainability and a return on that investment. There should be some indication from the research as to the type of organisations that have adopted the process, plus some indication of accrued benefits. The question is whether such a system benefits all organisations. It requires considerable planning and expertise to embed such a system within the whole organisation, although the benefits in the raising of quality standards will be measurable. Not all organisations, however, have a strategy that focuses on quality enhancement to this degree.

Feedback on self-assessment question 4.4

This exercise show what additional resources and organisational changes are required to make the implementation of such a system work. An implementation structure must be efficient and effective if the process is to be sustained. Does the system run alongside or supplant the existing quality assurance system, and how? Would it require a new division, extra staff? Who would be responsible in the chain of command?

Feedback on learning activity 4.5

All organisations plan, but in what detail and for how long? What processes are in place to deal with the intervening impact of external issues and the need to change direction? What level of detail informs the planning? Who is involved? What feedback, monitoring and evaluative techniques are used? You should be able to obtain copies of organisational plans and be able to match them with the reality. Why might they be changed or altered?

Feedback on self-assessment question 4.5

It should be possible to assess the formal decision-making process on matters of importance and examine the extent of linkage to broader organisational goals. Standards within the business will inform the decision-making process and limit the amount of discretion without approval. Examples might be from the area of supplier selection, spending levels, targets based on costs reduction, the reduction of the supply base and so forth.

Selecting and sustaining effective suppliers

Introduction

Systems that effectively select and assess the performance of suppliers are now an essential part of the procurement function. The strategy of a business is informed by its operational effectiveness, and tactical and operational sourcing holds the key to successfully achieving organisational objectives. A formal approach to the management of the supply chain will ensure that standards are maintained and sustained, and if necessary changes to the supply base can be made.

'Sourcing of suppliers is both strategic and tactical.'
Lysons and Farrington (2006)

5

Session learning objectives

After completing this session you should be able to:

5.1 Evaluate essential criteria for supplier selection and appraisal.
5.2 Assess the contribution to the function of vendor rating systems.
5.3 Give examples of how vendor rating systems can contribute to overall value of the function.
5.4 Demonstrate the circumstances when supplier switching will be considered.
5.5 Describe the process of new supplier adoption.

Unit content coverage

Learning objectives

1.4 Develop and manage external contacts with the supply market to gain important information about new technologies, potential new materials and services, new sources of supply and/or changes in market conditions (specifically emerging risks and opportunities).
1.5 Identify, evaluate and develop new and existing suppliers and use appropriate techniques to develop and improve supplier performance.

Prior knowledge

Awareness of the concept of supplier selection.

Resources

Access to supplier performance systems.

Timing

You should set aside about 5 hours to read and complete this session, including learning activities, self-assessment questions, the suggested further reading (if any) and the revision question.

5.1 Criteria for supplier selection and appraisal

Supplier selection and appraisal

In this section we consider the essential issue of supplier selection and management. If quality and other performance requirements are to be optimised, then selection of the most suitable supplier in the first instance is vital. This requires the selection of the most suitable criteria for a valid comparison and also a systematic approach to the selection process itself.

The concept of supply chain management has naturally influenced the way in which this process is conducted as well as the requirement sought in a supplier. Finally, having selected a supplier it is important to manage their performance and to develop them so that they continue to match our exact requirements over the long term.

Choosing the right supplier is frequently the key to obtaining quality, performance and price, therefore the sourcing of suppliers is critical to optimal purchasing performance.

This obviously requires consideration of issues such as supplier appraisal and assessment, procedures for monitoring and the development of the most suitable relationship between the parties. Effective decisions will only be made when all the relevant decisions have been considered and weighed against the risks and opportunities. It is not just a question of picking the right supplier but of developing continuing relationships.

Supplier relations

One of the most important aspects for the buyer in assuring supplies is the maintenance of good supplier relationships. Good supplier relationships can be a major asset to the buyer, not only in assuring supplies, but also in maintaining quality levels and good prices. Good supplier relations have always been an important factor in the maintenance of supplies, particularly during periods of shortage, but over recent years attitudes towards supplier relationships have gradually changed from an adversarial to a 'partnership' approach. This change has been brought about by the increasing use made by buyers of techniques such as quality assurance, zero defect policies, statistical process control (SPC) and just-in-time (JIT), all of which place additional responsibilities on suppliers, who will only be willing to accept them if they see some long-term benefit for themselves in the relationship. So, in return for accepting these additional responsibilities, it has become common to offer the supplier a long-term prospect of business in what is referred to as a 'partnership' relationship, with both parties offering and accepting complementary responsibilities and helping to solve problems to their mutual benefit.

The partnership approach, or 'co-makership', clearly influences the nature of the relationship between buyer and sellers. However, it also influences the selection criteria for new suppliers. The criteria for the selection of a supplier in the long-term relationship may differ from the competitive criteria apparent in the adversarial approach.

Supply chain management

The partnership approach to supplies is part of the concept of supply chain management. This approach is broader than the simple relationship between the suppliers and buyers of separate organisations. It deals with the total concept of managing materials in a positive way, all aspects from the suppliers and subcontractors through purchasing, stock control, production and distribution, to the final customer. It is concerned with achieving the lowest cost in the whole manufacturing and supply process by identifying and balancing the relationship between the separate links in the supply chain and ensuring that the whole chain operates at the lowest total cost and the maximum efficiency.

The point we are considering here is the link in the chain between the buyer's organisation and the supplier, as this is a vital element in ensuring continuity of supply, particularly where a JIT system is in operation and there is no margin of error on supplies.

The supply chain assumes a flow of value to the customer and pressure for low prices on the supplier. In reality the relationship is complex, as figure 5.1 illustrates.

Figure 5.1: Value flow to customer

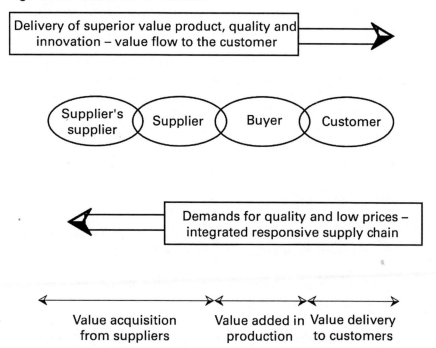

Supplier selection

Supplier selection has traditionally been described as being based on the 5 Rs (right price, right quality, right quantity, right time and right place).

However, greater emphasis is now placed on the management of the buyer/supplier relationship in a non-adversarial, longer-term perspective and it may mean that the 5 Rs are no longer sufficient when compared with the qualitative aspects of the relationship and the longer-term perspective. Carter's 'The 7 Cs of Effective Supplier Evaluation' (1995) advocated a more comprehensive approach to supplier selection, and it is worth repeating them again. However, the approach has subsequently been developed and extended by Carter himself and now consists of the 10 Cs. Acceptance of this approach does not actually make the 5 Rs any less important.

They are still there, but the supplier selection approach is broader.

Carter's original 7 Cs for supplier selection were:

1   *competency:* all staff, all the time (requires evidence)
2   *capacity:* sufficient and flexible
3   *commitment:* to quality (quality systems)
4   *control:* control of process
5   *cash:* sufficient funds for the business
6   *cost:* cost/price relationships and total cost of ownership
7   *consistency:* consistent production of goods or services (ISO 9000).

More recently, Carter has added three more 'Cs', which are:

* *culture:* compatible with similar values
* *clean:* environmentally sound (conforming with legislative requirements)
* *communications:* the supplier is fully integrated with information and communication technology (ICT).

When contracting out work as discussed above, the selection of a supplier takes on a special dimension. Contracting out can be in the form of a 'make-or-buy' decision; for example, contracting out a subassembly ready-assembled rather than buying in components and assembling them in-house.

This process provides:

* tighter control over quality
* reduced supplier base
* for taking advantage of suppliers' distinctive competencies and building them into our own. Again, it facilitates focused operations.

Contracting out services requires special attention, bearing in mind the special problems of managing service quality.

The correct supplier selection decision should be made alongside support from supply market research. The approach will vary according to the type of purchases being made – consumable supplies, production materials, capital purchases and so on.

What are the attributes of a good supplier?

Baily et al (2004) suggest the following:

- delivers on time
- provides consistent quality
- gives a good price
- has a stable background
- provides a good service backup
- is responsive to needs
- keeps promise
- provides technical support
- keeps the buyer informed on progress.

Learning activity 5.1

International sourcing

Organisations have to develop an international strategy for the sourcing of suppliers, mainly to achieve flexibility and cost reduction. However, the sourcing of new suppliers is hampered by the increasing complexity of supplies, plus the scarcity of suppliers to meet new demands. Construct an action plan showing how you might extend the choice of suppliers into different geographical areas. Highlight the differences from a traditional domestic sourcing approach.

Feedback on page 105

Early supplier involvement (ESI)

The best suppliers are an important source of information; the purchasing function is in a strong position to gather this information and make use of it. This can be a *collaborative arrangement* where a partnership arrangement exists or simply a *good working relationship* where there can be collaboration at an early stage over the design and specification aspects and the establishment of quality standards.

This collaborative approach can also utilise supplier management teams where teams of specialists from the buying and selling organisation meet to undertake joint problem solving. In essence, it is making use of the expertise and knowledge of your suppliers rather than 'reinventing the wheel' each time a new product is developed. Those suppliers who have most to offer, and therefore deserve the business, should be used in the process.

The danger of the approach is that the product or service may become designed around the supplier, making it impossible to source elsewhere in the market. There may also be the potential for problems of ownership, particularly regarding intellectual property.

Early buyer involvement (EBI)

Generally, the approach is a cross-functional one whereby all of the parties with an interest take part in the design process. Also sometimes referred to as *early purchasing involvement* (EPI), this refers to the importance of involving the purchasing function at the outset of the product development process. This involvement ensures that costs are reduced and quality standards are achieved. Involvement in the specification stage ensures that:

- maximum use is made of standards
- tolerances are realistic
- materials are viable and obtainable at reasonable cost.

The contribution that purchasing can make at the development stage is considerable; possibly the most important result may be the avoidance of problems at a later stage, for example in production. The purchasing contribution may include many essential inputs before the design freeze is imposed. In addition to liaison with other internal departments and suppliers, purchasing can advise on issues such as standards, materials specifications and tolerances, materials availability and costs, value engineering suggestions and the setting of appropriate quality standards. The approach is generally one of consensus internally over design and a good communications bridge with the marketplace and suppliers.

Simultaneous engineering

This is a term originally coined by Tom Peters. The traditional approach to new product development was that it was seen as the domain of technicians only. As a result, a new design would be originated which would then be passed to production to assess the production viability; it would then go back to design for the incorporation of the production requirements. Next it would go to procurement who would assess it from their perspective where suggestions regarding issues such as standardisation, relaxation of tolerances, substitute materials and so on would be made.

The new project would then go to marketing where it would be assessed from the perspective of its marketability – going back to design for the incorporation of the marketing features. Finally, it would move to the marketplace.

The simultaneous engineering approach is that a new product design is not viewed as solely the domain of technicians; all of the interested parties form a cross-functional team consisting of design, production, engineering, purchasing and marketing: they consider all aspects of the design simultaneously. This approach has the advantage of incorporating all of the design, functional, commercial and marketing features at one time, producing goods that consumers want in a cost-effective manner. Estimates suggest that the approach can reduce the time to market for new products by up to two-thirds.

Plant visits

One of the most important aspects of the supplier selection process for important contracts is the **plant visit**, known variously as the *vendor audit* or *capability survey*. It is most important that such surveys for the determination of supplier capability are conducted objectively. To assist in this objective appraisal it is essential that standardised documentation is produced to form the basis of the survey – ensuring that the correct questions are asked and that the procedure uses the same criteria across all suppliers. Baily et al (2004) cover this aspect in some detail. Note in particular the example of the vendor evaluation form.

The following list represents some key factors you would include in a vendor audit for a large contract for an important assembly component that would run for several years.

- quality assurance and control procedures
- incoming and outgoing quality checks
- management capability
- plant capacity and vintage
- morale/employee attitudes
- housekeeping
- environmental procedures and conformance with environmental legislation
- planned maintenance
- tooling procedures/capability
- understanding of requirements
- samples
- order book
- corrective action procedures
- training and skill levels.

Selecting suppliers of capital items involves other considerations. The following list contains some examples from a DTI Committee on Technology:

- Check that the specification is clear and unambiguous.
- Check that it covers all aspects of the life cycle performance.
- Will it permit intending suppliers to prepare realistic estimates for costs and delivery?
- Check the process for dealing with proposed modifications by the intending supplier.
- Check the processes by which future costs and availability of components to be dealt with by the intending supplier.

Before placing any order:

- Is the information supplied by the intending suppliers sufficient to place an order?
- Conduct a contractual check on the supplier's terms and conditions if it is at variance with the buyers'.
- Has the specification been agreed by the parties?
- Have the quality aspects been checked with the relevant functions?
- Is there a vendor rating?
- Check the warranties that are in place.
- Check that the asset information supplied complies with the operation, repair and overhaul of the equipment during its lifetime.

Other general criteria:

- The supplier should be viable in the long term.
- The supplier would be able to participate in early design and development phases as discussed above.

- The supplier would openly share appropriate information.
- The supplier would be oriented to taking cost out of the product.
- The supplier would also be able to develop prototypes.
- The supplier would be prepared to agree cost-structure targets.
- The supplier would work with the buying company to achieve responsiveness and agility.

5

Self-assessment question 5.1

When sourcing internationally how will costs be influenced by the following considerations?

- Customs controls and tariffs.
- Intellectual property issues.
- Administration costs.
- Will payment terms be longer?
- Will currency fluctuations be a reality?
- Will agents have to be used at extra cost?
- Will insurance be higher?
- Will there be variations in the expectations of a profit margin?

Feedback on page 105

5.2 The contribution of vendor rating systems to supply chain management

Developing suppliers and improving supplier performance

Where there are few, if any, suitable suppliers, it may be necessary to add to the approved list of suppliers by the use of *supplier development*. The usual approach to this is to identify which suppliers have demonstrated the most potential and establish why they have failed to achieve approved status – and then to assist them to improve so that they can be reappraised and, hopefully, added to the approved list. This also has a beneficial effect of increasing the amount of competition among approved suppliers.

Supplier development can take several forms and consists of one or more of the following:

- financial assistance on favourable terms
- advice on production methods and technology
- advice on quality systems and assistance in developing such systems
- acquisition of equipment on favourable terms
- training in the required areas where expertise is deficient
- secondment of key staff to assist in raising standards of performance.

Once the supplier has reached the required standard and has been approved, it is very important that performance is monitored closely and feedback given on a continuous basis. One of the tools that can be helpful in this is some form of *vendor rating scheme*.

Supplier development can also be used where other suppliers have a dominant market position or monopoly. This power can be reduced by finding a supplier who is close to the area of production enjoyed by the monopolist; and then using the same techniques as outlined above to encourage and assist the firm to enter the particular market segment – effectively reducing the power of the monopolist.

Learning activity 5.2

Explain with reference to your own organisational experience whether vendor rating systems provide sufficient analytical information for effective supply chain management.

Feedback on page 106

Vendor rating

One particular technique which provides a useful framework for rating suppliers is based around vendor rating forms, which can help to construct an overall evaluation of a supplier. Typically a form will try to assess a supplier in terms of criteria relating to quality, costs and delivery, and the management and utilisation of resources.

The use of this type of rating mechanism can:

- create a system of rating suppliers, whether actual or potential
- enable a supplier-ranking system to be used for decision making
- promote self-evaluation by suppliers
- encourage partnership and a 'stakeholder' ethos, based around discussion and mutual advantage.

Vendor rating schemes attempt to rate the performance of a supplier in key areas in an objective manner. Generally, the two approaches are:

- *numerical (cardinal) methods* where a numerical assessment is made against predetermined criteria and the resulting figure is used to measure supplier performance over time
- *ordinal (categorical) rating* to compare supplier performance. Ordinal or categorical methods merely assess supplier performance against criteria such as good, medium, poor.

Vendor rating can also be used to improve supplier performance by regularly informing the supplier of current performance.

Numerical (cardinal) rating

The simple numerical vendor rating system outlined below is based on one originally produced in an early edition of Baily et al (2004). Although this is a simple example, it could easily be extended to include more variables. Such systems are easily computerised, which greatly simplifies their operation.

The first stage is to select the variables that are considered to be relevant to the organisation. For example:

- Quality : 40
- Delivery: 20
- Price: 20
- Cost reduction since contract start: 20

The sum of the weights equals 100, which is convenient for calculation.

- A numerical assessment is set against these standards, according to a formula which has been determined. The variables are as follows: *Quality* – number of rejects taken as a whole, deducted from 100; *Delivery* – 5 points deducted from 100 for each late delivery; *Price* – lowest price paid to the supplier divided into lowest price quoted; *Cost reduction* – current total acquisition must be divided by original total acquisition cost.
- Recorded actual performance is as follows: *Quality* 10% reject rate through quality failure; *Delivery* 5 late deliveries; *Price* 90% of that actually paid to the supplier; *Cost reduction* 90% of original cost.
- Calculated vendor performance rating:
  - Quality: $40 \times (1.00 - 0.10) = 36$
  - Delivery: $20 \times (1.00 - 0.25) = 15$
  - Price: $20 \times (90/100) = 18$
  - Cost reduction: $20 \times (90/100) = 18$
  - Supplier rating = 87%

This figure is recalculated each month; any decline in the figure indicates a decline in performance relative to these standards. Suppliers should be informed of the scheme and how it operates and their current rating communicated to them. This should act as a spur to improved performance.

Where there are two suppliers, the one with the higher rating is, of course, relatively better than the one with the lower rating.

One of the criticisms of this type of model is that it is still subjective: the choice of relative weightings is based on subjective opinion in the first instance. However, it is not unreasonable to expect that those choosing the weights understand the variables, and how important each variable is to the organisation. Provided that the rule of *consistency* is followed, once the variables and weight have been chosen, the result will be reliable.

Ordinal (categorical) rating

Here suppliers are rated against a series of headings. Providing knowledge, skill and consistency are applied, there is no reason why such a method should produce significantly worse results than cardinal (numerical) measurement.

Table 5.1 Category rating

	A	B	C	D
Price		✓		
Quality		✓		
Delivery			✓	
Supplier grade				C

Key:

A: Excellent

B: Very good

C: Acceptable with some improvements required

D: Unacceptable

In this example the supplier has performed well on the two variables of price and quality but delivery has not been as good. The overall grade is C and the assessment shows clearly where an improvement in performance is required.

It could be argued that this is highly subjective and favoured suppliers will benefit from the 'halo' and 'horn' effect – that is, some are felt to be good simply because we like them and others bad, because we for some reason dislike them or cannot relate to them in some personal way. If, however, we are acting in a competent and professional manner and only making assessments on the basis of recorded facts, this should not happen.

The benefit is that it is simple, easy to understand, and instantly meaningful. This, of course, is a highly simplistic example and more variables and sophistication can be introduced; however, over-sophistication may detract from the whole point of this method, which is ease of understanding.

No system of performance rating is without problems; the more objective methods can require the costly collection of data, across a wide range of performance delivery areas. However, this can be facilitated by the use of computers and the end result can assist decision making on whether to continue and develop business relationships or perhaps to look to alternative suppliers. The disadvantage of systems such as the above is that any quantitative system may incur costs in set-up and operation and there will be greater accuracy. The organisation has to decide whether to adopt the more costly option or use a less objective system based on experience and judgement. Feedback given to the supplier arising from the rating or assessment process is the vital component, and in this context it is worth noting how effective self-monitoring or assessment by suppliers has proved to be. Rating enables an organisation to judge a supplier and to decide whether or not to:

- grant preferred supplier status
- work with the supplier to develop and improve performance
- abandon the supplier.

Self-assessment question 5.2

List the key organisational KPIs that your organisation uses for effective supplier assessment.

Feedback on page 106

5.3 How vendor rating systems can contribute to overall value of the function

Introduction

Selecting the right suppliers is part of the risk of the operation. Risk management is based on being able to distinguish between an event that is truly random and an event that is the result of cause and effect.

Learning activity 5.3

With reference to your own vendor rating systems, produce a flow diagram which shows how problems are highlighted, recorded and dealt with in order of priority and risk.

Feedback on page 106

Risk reduction

Supplier selection and the resultant contracting is a risky business and there is no way of eliminating all the risk involved. Although it may be possible to eliminate the risk of quality failures by using Kaizen and lean supply methods, other risks such as lack of innovation may be introduced. This might be because suppliers become so lean that they have no spare resource for research and development.

Risk professionals know that they cannot eliminate risk, but by analysing costs, benefits and methods of risk reduction and mitigation, they can help enterprises and other bodies make informed decisions about risk. Increasingly, risk management rests upon the use of sophisticated analytical techniques for making sense of this information.

Ross (2003) writes: 'It's a revolution that affects each and every one of us. In essence, we as individuals can use these new intellectual tools and perspectives to become our own best risk analysts.'

The management of risk is a key challenge for supply management. Assessing risk accurately is a critical task for the purchasing and supply function. Systemising the risk elements is one way of minimising future problems. Approaches to risk can include:

- Assessment: to identify the nature of the risk within the supply base – is it a delivery risk, quality risk or a cost risk? Risk assessment requires that the supply chain be viewed as an end-to-end process and will often require extensive mapping exercises, as well as assessment. Vendor rating systems contribute to the management of suppliers and act as early warning systems for future problems.
- Reduction: where organisational spend is a high proportion of a supplier's total turnover. Some manufacturing groups in the Far East will not contract with a supplier unless their spend is over 80% of the supplier's total turnover, creating high levels of dependency. This tactic is clearly not available to many purchasers.
- Avoidance: one way of avoiding risk is to ensure that purchasing always works with the same suppliers that it has worked with in the past. A drawback here is the fact that existing suppliers may not let us down, but they may not give us the best possible performance either.
- Management: this is the use of contractual and relational tactics to ensure that risk is balanced with potential performance. The management of risk depends on the acquisition of good quality information which can be used to predict how often risks are likely to occur and what might cause them. This is how insurance companies operate, by collating risk data and using sophisticated analytical techniques to forecast, with degrees of confidence, the likelihood of those risks occurring in particular time periods and geographical location or within certain demographic groups. Purchasing can also collate data with regard to supplier performance and use similar techniques to forecast supplier failure.
- Allocation: much of the design and development of contracts is about the allocation of risk to different parties, but it can help to remember that sometimes risk needs to be allocated internally as well as across organisational boundaries.

Once sources and degrees of risk are known, it is possible to propose and implement strategies to reduce risk. It is generally true to say that preventing the occurrence of risk is more effective than dealing with risk once it has occurred. Therefore the vendor rating system if properly implemented will act as a management tool for minimising the risk of supply disruption and poor performance.

Managing risk

If risk analysis shows a high risk (valuable and vulnerable), then prevention activities are recommended. The vendor rating system should be sufficiently effective to give the management time to adjust the supplies, even in situations where the risk is high.

Risk management also includes balancing costs versus benefits for any reduction of risk. Simply put, the cost of risk management measures to reduce the threat should not exceed the value of what is being protected. Extensive assessment can be justified to protect a high value contract, but a more limited assessment may be required in a contract which had a lower impact on an enterprise's core activities, remembering the fact that it can be difficult to assess core and non-core activities. The resources put into managing each supplier should be balanced by the impact on the business.

The more serious the risk involved, the more the factors should be broken down and analysed into their individual sub-parts. By breaking down the risk factors into the smallest possible components, we are able to isolate key events and/or determinants and seek to determine how to best manage them. In order to do so, the purchaser must estimate the probability that one of these events that expose us to risk could occur. If the probability of incurring a loss is high, we may decide to avoid it altogether, avoid part of it, develop a contingency plan to deal with it and/or budget funds to deal with its occurrence. If a supplier's performance is particularly important at the moment, the rating system should enable preventative measures to be considered quickly. However, when the unforeseen occurs, it should be possible for contingency or crisis plans to be put into place to minimise the effect of the damage on the enterprise's key operations.

Self-assessment question 5.3

Undertake a review of the current vendor rating system within your organisation.

Construct a table outlining the problems encountered with supplier performance, and the outcomes of those problems, indicating what action was taken.

Feedback on page 107

5.4 Evaluating the circumstances when supplier switching will be considered

The switching of suppliers

If a supplier achieves an unsatisfactory performance rating, there will ultimately be consideration of the change of suppliers. Issues and problems surrounding the acquisition costs of supplies, the responsiveness and flexibility of a supply when faced with the challenges of changing supply levels will be a major consideration. Problems with the actual delivery of supplies and batches, the number of, and severity of, defects in the delivered goods, and the remedial action taken will all be a detailed focus of a good vendor rating system.

If the system delivers a rating that is substandard then, subject to feedback and corrective action, more radical action will be needed.

There will also be several other factors contributing to a decision to rethink the supplier's position, including wider but important issues relating to:

- the financial stability of the organisation and its changing viability
- the possibility of takeover or merger which might affect its ability to supply

- production capacity and capability as supplies levels alter
- changing environment within the production facilities
- quality standards and the relations to subcontractors, testing controls
- innovation and technology introduction
- the changing quality of the workforce
- environmental issues such as use of sustainable redundancies
- the use of information technology within the enterprise which leads to better lead times and shortened order cycles.

The drive for cost reduction and the increasing internalisation of the supply chain may be a constant pressure to examine the business case for switching to overseas suppliers to provide better placement of deliveries as organisations expand their geographical territories and of course the ability of suppliers in emerging nations to deliver components at reduced rates.

In addition, there is also the decline that occurs within supply relationships as products and services themselves are declining in the marketplace or being changed.

The contract between the purchaser and the supplier will also be instrumental in the relationship status.

Learning activity 5.4

Examine the commercial agreements that you have in place within your organisation. How effective are the agreements in controlling supplier performance?

Feedback on page 107

Nature of relationship life cycles

Because relationships are complex, interactive processes, it is difficult to describe a life cycle common to all commercial relationships. Parties to a relationship become acquainted, work more closely together, recede and approach in an ongoing fluctuation of states. During this time, they will consciously and unconsciously assess the state of the relationship. This means that any attempt to break relationships into stages in time is likely to be misleading. By and large all we can say is that some relationships go through a process of growth, maturity and decline in the same way that products do. However, it is important to recognise that not all relationships do, and that the rates at which they change vary widely from relationship to relationship.

One way in which relationships may change is in the degree of integration that takes place within them. Integration may include the integration of tools and systems such as information systems and ordering systems. It may also include the degree to which people within the respective organisations or enterprises 'think alike' as a result of shared experience and shared attitudes.

This change will be influenced by a range of factors including:

- Perceived needs: do both parties have a common understanding of the needs within the relationship and are these communicated effectively?
- Comparison processes: how the supplier compares to other suppliers.
- Conscious selection processes: around price, quality, innovation, for example.
- Unconscious selection processes: around personal liking, trust, for example.
- Interactional skills: such as communication or conflict management.
- Objectives: how much autonomy do the parties want to preserve? Is the goal a superordinate one?
- Cultural blueprints: what a relationship should be like.
- Public or private commitment: the degree to which the contract is known outside the relationship.
- The way in which the relationship is maintained: using bidirectional openness, communication, role and task clarity, for example.
- The way in which the relationship is ended: is any warning or feedback given?

Employing the relationship life cycle

Using the product life cycle approach, an enterprise launches a product priced at £200.00. Let's say that the technology of the product typically implies a product life cycle of five good years with little or no maintenance and then rapidly decreasing utility. After ten years it is assumed that the unit is useless. The seller optimises the deal around the individual transaction.

The customer life cycle approach extends this time line and, providing customer service is demonstrated throughout the life cycle of the product (free or discounted maintenance, for example), then the buyer might come back to the same seller to get a replacement. Therefore, the seller is not considering a single transaction, but a series of transactions, which might generate £1,000 over the duration of the buyer/seller relationship.

By looking at the relational life cycle, the skilled purchasing and supply professional can help the enterprise manage the flow of goods, services and information so as to optimise the resources within the relationship. This can result in effective communication, which can help the buyer and seller work jointly to better understand customer needs so that they can both serve them better than another competing value chain.

This can lead to both repeat business and new business. It can open new market segments, new locations or geographies and new industries. Such arrangements are rare, but can offer significant competitive advantage in value chain management.

Relationship violation and termination

It is important to remember that the environment in which contracts are used is changing. We can suggest that contracts rely on the perceptions of the parties involved. In a legal sense, companies, and some other organisational forms, are considered to be legal entities. In other words, companies can contract themselves, and the contract will be legally enforceable on the company as a whole. This means that regardless of the changes in personnel or management, the company still has to enforce the contract.

Of course, this is where many contract problems stem from. Although the contract is with the whole organisation, some parts of the organisation may not be 'involved' in the contract. This means that a tool operator who is not interested on a particular day could make a mistake and cause a problem for the customer, which costs millions in reputational and legal damages and equal amounts in legal fees.

The traditional answer to this problem was self-interest and self-protection, and a number of methods were deployed to ensure that this answer worked. These included supervisory management and payment by results at an individual worker level. Later, persistent problems led to the introduction of total quality management, which emphasised the involvement of the whole of the workforce in the task. How well this works over time is unclear.

In this sense, contracts can only ever be partial. One of the tasks of the purchasing professional is to embed the contract in the whole of the organisation. However, the problem still remains within a commercial relationship. How do we handle contract violation and termination?

There are a number of fundamental issues with regard to contract violation and termination including:

- In some senses, it is impossible to separate out the legal or transactional elements of the contract, and the relational element. Every contract has a relational element.
- Contract violation is commonplace. Individuals and groups break contracts all the time.
- Violated contracts will lead to some sort of adverse reaction by the injured party.
- Relationships can survive the breaking of a transactional contract.

Types of violation

Individuals and groups tend to consciously or unconsciously classify violations into types, depending on the capability and motivation of the party violating the contract. These are:

1   If the party is willing but incapable because of external factors such as a landslide destroying a supplier's plant.
2   If the party is capable but unwilling because circumstances have changed – another customer has ordered goods at a more advantageous price, for example.
3   If the party is capable and willing but violates the contract because of divergent interpretations. Both parties misunderstood the meaning of the contract.
4   If the party is incapable because they have perhaps lost key staff or because they were incorrectly selected. They may also be unwilling because the contractor has treated them poorly.

This classification will also tend to look at the reasons behind the motivation of the violating party. If they are motivated by opportunism, it can be considered a more serious breach than if they had been negligent. All of these classifications tend to take place in a framework of what is fair or just.

As well as classifying the type of violation, parties in a relationship tend to also classify the impact of the violation. Typically, classification tends to rest on:

- the size of the loss caused by the violation
- the type and nature of remedies offered
- the credibility of the explanations of the reasons for the violation
- the strength or value of the relationship.

In handling contract violations, it should be noted that individuals monitor each other's behaviour, and that the frequency of monitoring increases in relationships which are considered untrustworthy or untrusting. This will be the case when aspects of the vendor rating system are being discussed on a frequent basis because of poor supplier performance. The more monitoring goes on, the more likely we are to see problems and the worse the situation can become.

Just as in the transactional/legal contract, there also need to be procedures within the relational contract for managing violations, and these procedures need to be seen as fair by both parties.

Examples of such procedures might include:

- giving the violating party an opportunity to explain the violation
- being open to this explanation
- looking for evidence
- offering an opportunity to remedy the violation
- ensuring that the remedy is fair (supplier penalties for stopping production such as a £5,000 payment for every half-hour the line is stopped may not be seen as fair)
- building stages into the process to slow down escalation.

This type of informal procedure can help avoid termination of the contract. In some cases, however, the contract will require termination. This may be initiated for a number of reasons. These may be ongoing problems with the relationship, shifts in market conditions or technology or simply termination due to the end of a product life cycle.

Whatever the reason for termination, there are a number of considerations that can be taken into account where the aim is to preserve the relationship.

Successful terminations tend to:

- be well structured with proper procedures
- have valid, well-articulated reasons
- be clearly communicated
- involve accurate, balanced feedback

- be prepared for by both parties
- involve acknowledgement of the work within the existing contract
- frame the contract/relationship in terms of long-term objectives
- leave the door open for renewal or replacement of the old contract.

Self-assessment question 5.4

What steps do you take in your organisation with a failing supplier?

Feedback on page 107

5

5.5 The process by which a new supplier is adopted

Subject to the overall strategy of the purchasing function, the adoption of a new supplier will be based on a time-consuming and often costly appraisal.

Lysons suggests a number of reasons why before taking on a new supplier the buyer should be confident that a supplier reliably meets all the requirements of 'best fit' into the business. Initial desk research will assist any future visits to establish the reality of a potential relationship.

The key areas for assessment will be:

- finance
- production capacity and facilities
- human resources
- quality
- performance
- environmental and ethical conditions
- information technology.

The process

Factory visits or questionnaires sent to the suppliers will be the basis of the assessment. Arguably this more extensive review of supplier capability will not always take place but will be essential:

- where the supplier is required to have standards qualifications such as ISO 9000
- where there is to be the purchase of strategic, high-risk items
- purchase of non-standard items
- placing of construction and similar contracts
- expenditure on capital items
- when entering into JIT arrangements
- when contemplating a supplier association
- when engaged in global sourcing
- when entering into e-procurement arrangements with long-term strategic suppliers
- when negotiating TQM in respect of high-profit or high-risk items

5

- when negotiating outsourcing contracts
- when agreeing subcontracting by a main supplier in respect of important companies
- when negotiating service level agreements.

When assessing suppliers onsite, Lysons suggests that attention should be paid to the following:

- personal attitudes – including the general atmosphere of harmony of employees with their work, the degree of energy and the skilful use of manpower
- adequacy and care of production equipment – questions of modernity, maintenance, and capacity will be particularly important
- technological know-how
- means of controlling quality
- housekeeping
- competence of technical staff
- competence of management.

Final selection will take place after the appraisal process and confirmation of the information search that has been sent by questionnaire. In particular the purchaser will seek positive ways in which the supplier can contribute to the requirements of the visiting organisation.

The resolution of the potential conflicts and disputes will need to be discussed, including the implementation of any performance standards, rating systems, contractual criteria and adherence, plus a process by which personal relationships can be established between the key personnel of the two organisations.

Learning activity 5.5

Prepare a template for a visit to the premises of a potential new supplier which includes the criteria for assessing capability to be a key provider of goods to your organisation.

Feedback on page 108

Now move on to self-assessment question 5.5 below.

Self-assessment question 5.5

Following on from the need to replace a supplier, list the process by which you would undertake desk research of a new supplier and the sources of secondary information.

Feedback on page 108

Revision question

Now try the revision question for this session on page 341.

Summary

Supplier performance systems are at the heart of the purchasing function. Without some formal assessment and evaluation of supplier performance there is no structure for determining whether or not organisational objectives and targets are to be met. The risk of failure would increase with the consequent damage to the rest of the business. However, deciding upon and implementing an effective system requires skill and regular monitoring and evaluation.

Suggested further reading

Read the chapter on supply organisations and structures in Lysons and Farrington (2006).

Feedback on learning activities and self-assessment questions

Feedback on learning activity 5.1

The importance of obtaining supplies from different parts of the world is now established on grounds of cost, quality, expertise and volume. The logistics of bringing in supplies from overseas is now a major management aspect, and there should be some awareness of the costs of extending the supply chain as well as the benefits in terms of cost reduction and supply choice. Awareness of the growing expertise and quality of the world supply base should be in evidence and some thought given to emerging new areas of supply. There are a number of ways to identify a suitable buyer overseas:

*   trade exhibitions to gauge the level of competition, prices and technology
*   sales conferences where networking can take place
*   suppliers from trade directories and e-marketplaces
*   journals, newspapers and magazines
*   house magazines and bulletins from major suppliers
*   trade missions
*   contacts via trade ministers
*   business clubs and associations
*   internet searches.

Feedback on self-assessment question 5.1

A brief review of the cost and administrative impact of the lengthening supply chain is essential if margins are to be maintained. An understanding of the additional costs and logistical changes will need to be mentioned. Extending the supply chain brings further complications to organisational planning and requires specific expertise in logistical handling, either internally or as an outsourced facility. The additional costs may have an impact on the final margins.

- In particular there may be a licensing system in operation which restricts imports. A customs tariff may be imposed, which will increase the domestic price.
- The buyer will need to ensure that any components or finished parts are not infringing existing international trademarks or patent agreements.
- Administrative costs will increase because of the lengthening supply chain and for the need on occasions to have agents such as freight forwarders to ensure efficient shipment. Such agents will be paid a fee depending upon the complexity of the operation.
- Payment terms tend to lengthen as the supply chain and lead time lengthen.
- Most organisations entering into international sourcing will encounter exchange issues that need to be hedged or protected by forward exchange contracts.
- Use of Incoterms and the alignment with letters of credit usually require insurance protection.

Feedback on learning activity 5.2

Properly designed systems, which increasingly can be monitored using software, are an essential part of the process for ensuring compliance with organisational objectives. There needs to be some vigour in the assessment but should be administratively accessible so that the system can be used cost-effectively. Some understanding of the process, its measurement standards, and how feedback and evaluation are incorporated is required. How are vendor rating systems within the organisation implemented? How credible are they as a measure of supplier performance? How are they communicated and what impact do they have on supplier relationships and ultimate performance?

Feedback on self-assessment question 5.2

Typical KPIs will be based on price, cost reduction and quality standards. How are they set and implemented? What tolerances are allowed? What timescales are involved? Are costs of failure measured and the supplier informed?

Feedback on learning activity 5.3

This exercise will support learning by highlighting the process of assessing suppliers, with special emphasis on the risk elements. The flow diagram should indicate where the supplier problem might be picked up within the organisation and the purchasing functions. How is it actually recorded and who takes responsibility for dealing with the issue? Are the supplier problems broken down into major and minor issues so that they are dealt with at different hierarchical levels? What is the experience of failure by suppliers – this should be reflected in the process? Do the vendor rating systems in place help significantly in spotting and managing the risk of failure – does that mean that the point of contact will be the buyer responsible for the supplier? There should also be some indication as to when a problem is passed up the managerial chain and indication as to how it is managed.

Feedback on self-assessment question 5.3

A review of the major issues arising from suppliers is essential to understanding the buying process. The table should take the performance criteria from the existing vendor rating system – that is, KPIs on delivery, lean supply, quality and defects, cost reduction and pricing policy – and use these as heading for analysis. It may be possible to break these further into major or minor performance lapses. This is an opportunity to note the action taken from issues identified by the vendor rating systems, and a brief exploration as to how these issues were managed. There will be an indication of the complexity of the non-performance in that the recording of the problem and the assessment of the causes will vary from case to case. How often are issues recorded and responded to in reality or are the assessments periodic? This will be reflected in the table. A column will be needed to identify action points and who is targeted with dealing with the action and feeding back to the supplier.

Feedback on learning activity 5.4

It was seen previously that contractual agreements can provide a strong framework in which standards are set and action taken. However, it is important to understand the difference between the statements within an agreement and their use in dealing with poor performance. Legal action may be supported by the business but there are long-term relationship consequences to be considered. Is there any value in having detailed performance criteria within the contractual agreements? There should be some comment as to the circumstances as to when the contract terms are invoked. Would there be a formal response from the purchasing function? How and when does the legal team get involved? If the problem is resolved, how does this affect future relationships? When does the organisation actually sue?

Feedback on self-assessment question 5.4

An opportunity to review tactics in correcting poor supplier performance and the possibility of switching to more reliable suppliers. There should be some consideration of informal and formal approaches to issues and problems, and at what stages they are used. Steps will include discussions and negotiation, mediation, and use of contract clauses to enforce remedies. You will need to reflect on the skills needed to get the supplier up to speed wherever it is possible. This may involve a closer working relationship within the short term to help, assist and monitor remedial action. The strength of relationships in terms of importance to the buyer and length of the relationship between the two parties will inform the outcome of any buyer action. If the problem is serious and remedial action is not possible, then moves to redress the situation including switching suppliers will take place.

Feedback on learning activity 5.5

Lysons indicates that site visits should be based on the following:

- personal attitudes – including the general atmosphere of harmony of employees with their work, the degree of energy and the skilful use of manpower
- adequacy and care of production equipment – questions of modernity, maintenance, and capacity will be particularly important
- technological know-how
- means of controlling quality
- housekeeping
- competence of technical staff
- competence of management.

Feedback on self-assessment question 5.5

Good secondary background information on supplier performance is essential. Experienced buyers will through their networking have good knowledge of the industry supply base. There may an opportunity to consolidate the existing suppliers by increasing their supply commitment or perhaps seeing it as an opportunity for moving a supplier up from the second tier rank.

The usual secondary information on alternative suppliers gathered from trade directories, site visits of potential suppliers, trade fairs, internet searches and, of course, supplier enquiries will all provide new supplier possibilities. It is then a question of assessing their potential in terms of the usual criteria:

- financial stability
- production capacity and facilities
- human resources and skill base
- quality assurance and historical performance and means of controlling quality
- performance with test samples and trade references if appropriate
- environmental and ethical conditions
- information technology and capital resources
- personal attitudes – including the general atmosphere of harmony of employees with their work, the degree of energy and the skilful use of manpower
- adequacy and care of production equipment – questions of modernity, maintenance, and capacity will be particularly important
- technological know-how
- general competence of the organisation and its management.

Retrieving information from the supply chain

Introduction

Developing contacts and relationships with others in the supply chain is an important part of the purchasing function's quest to obtain the latest information and awareness of new developments and innovations. Market intelligence through contacts is important for keeping abreast and for devising strategies to move the organisation ahead of competitors. Systems need to be in place which systematically identify suitable secondary sources and track changes to the competitive environment. The value of more in-depth research is also considered, as is the need to have strong relationships with existing suppliers, as they will be an important source of new information.

'A corporate strategy will only succeed in a competitive market place if it is based on a thorough analysis of the organisation's competitors.'
Lynch (2000)

6

Session learning objectives

After completing this session you should be able to:

6.1 Describe the methods by which external contacts and relationships can be developed to gain market intelligence.
6.2 Evaluate the process for engaging external contacts within the supply market as a source of market intelligence.
6.3 Give examples of specific external information that could be valuable to the procurement business.
6.4 Describe the process of the adoption of a supplier innovation.

Unit content coverage

Learning objective

1.4 Develop and manage external contacts with the supply market to gain important information about new technologies, potential new materials and services, new sources of supply and/or changes in market conditions (specifically emerging risks and opportunities).

Prior knowledge

An understanding of the competitive environment.

Resources

Organisational resources on intelligence gathering.

Timing

You should set aside about 5 hours to read and complete this session, including learning activities, self-assessment questions, the suggested further reading (if any) and the revision question.

6.1 Gathering market intelligence

Information gathering

Achieving a competitive advantage and maintaining a competitive lead over others requires a sophisticated approach to the gathering of market intelligence. Information or market intelligence is required on potential new materials and services, new risks and opportunities within the market, new technologies and any other relevant change in market conditions.

Learning activity 6.1

Produce a source list that identifies the different types of market intelligence that will assist the purchasing function in supplier and component selection.

Feedback on page 120

The purchasing function can contribute (often in a collaborative sense) by establishing a market intelligence-gathering system that links the supply chain to world events.

The gathering of data from the myriad of sources will contribute to the basic understanding of what is happening in the external world. The gathering of market information from the supply chain will provide data that can be used in planning and forecasting after suitable analysis. Information-based decision making along the entire corporate value chain is the prerequisite for expansion of market share and an increase in cashflow and profits.

Basic information can be garnered or secondary research can be conducted on market changes from a regular review of:

- newspaper articles
- stockbroker analysis
- exhibitions and trade fairs
- company annual reports.

Government publications also provide a high-level statistical summary of many industries, and periodic research by agencies is often published. For example, National Statistics Online is a web gateway to UK government-maintained statistics about consumers and business markets (National Statistics Online: http://www.statistics.gov.uk). This will provide essential information on what is being manufactured, bought and sold.

Subjects such as purchasing policies, selection criteria, attitudes towards products, advertising and promotion, readiness to come to market with new technologies, brand loyalty and buyer preferences will appear as primary data through specialised published research.

Aspects of the broader changes in competitor activity or technological advances may also be picked up via the standard approach to gathering market intelligence from the strategic position. Most organisations will have some form of external analysis of the external environment through a number of models such as PESTEL or Porter's Five Forces.

The purchasing function in addition would wish to tap into this source of information, and generate its own intelligence through a number of particular and specific approaches.

The use of business networks will be part of that process. By developing sound businesses relationships with suppliers, the organisation begins to link to other relationships which the supplier has within its own supply chain and business experience. Not only does this mean that the buyer can receive examples of useful business data and solutions via the supplier, it is also possible for the supplier to provide tailored solutions, innovations or ideas based on its own experience within the network.

Buyers must work with suppliers in order to share experiences rather than just focusing on the immediate relationships. Within this definition of supply chain management, a collaborative approach would ensure that all those in the supply chain are effectively working towards common objectives characterised by sharing of information, knowledge, risk and profits. Sharing entails understanding how other companies operate and make decisions, which goes much deeper than cooperation. Collaboration is mutual goal setting that goes far beyond a written contract. Due to the level of commitment necessary, 'true collaborative relationships are anything but widespread' (Mentzer, 2001). Since it is not possible to collaborate with everyone, one of the challenges is deciding with whom to collaborate. The solution is to look for the key suppliers or customers and develop collaborative relationships with them alone. Just as determining the 'who' of the relationship is important, so is the 'what'. Not everything is of equal importance so research and information on key components, key commodities, key subsystems and key processes should be those that are prioritised.

The value of such relationships will be determined by a number of factors:

- The learning process will determine the strength of the developing relationship and network. There should be increasing subtlety and the ability to manage more complex situations.
- The investment of tangible and intangible resources from both sides, especially in this scenario of the investing in human resources into developing the relationship.
- Trust and commitment with the ability to adapt the relationship as short-term and long-term pressures emerge.
- Distance – both socially and culturally will have to be taken into account if useful contacts will be sustained.

6

Developing and maintaining a supply chain relationship, particularly under stress, requires considerable time and effort and certain enablers that can facilitate the task:

- *Common interest:* both parties have a stake in the outcome of the collaboration to ensure ongoing commitment.
- *Openness:* collaboration partners must openly discuss their practices and processes. Sometimes this means sharing information that is traditionally considered proprietary and confidential.
- *Mutual help:* when addressing supply chain problems or opportunities, look for cross-company solutions.
- *Clear expectations:* all parties need to understand what is expected of them and the others in the relationship.
- *Leadership:* without a champion, collaboration will never be accomplished.
- *Cooperation, not punishment:* focus on jointly solving problems, not looking for someone to blame.

Self-assessment question 6.1

Research the term 'reverse engineering' and how it may help the current business.

Feedback on page 120

6.2 Engaging external contacts within the supply market

Working successfully with suppliers

- *Trust:* this must be evident throughout both organisations – at every management level and functional area.
- *Benefit sharing:* in a truly collaborative relationship, partners share the pain, the risks and the losses.
- *Technology:* Advanced technology is essential to enabling a collaborative relationship across the supply chain. Without the other relational enablers in place, advanced technology means nothing; however, definite benefits can flow from the right technology, which:
    - allow a company to communicate with its suppliers at all levels
    - can help break down barriers between companies
    - speed up information flows
    - can turn data into useful collaborative information.

It should be emphasised that technology in and of itself is not enough – a human contribution is essential.

Impediments to collaboration

A number of factors can potentially cause supply chain collaboration to fail:

- *Doing things the old way:* There is a natural resistance to change that confronts any broad initiative such as supply chain collaboration.

- *Conventional accounting practices:* These focus on the traditional accounting role of determining the value for a single firm, rather than measuring cross-company values and providing the measurement tools necessary to guide collaborative efforts to share these gains.
- *Tax laws:* These dictate the need for a clear 'price paid' and 'price sold' to determine profitability – all of which obscures the synergistic, and often indirect, cost savings that are primary drivers of supply chain collaboration.
- *Antitrust or competition laws:* Information shared for the purpose of supply chain collaboration may be considered collusive activity.
- *Limited view of the supply chain:* This is a residual effect of the traditional silo organisational structure in which people think only about their own functional areas.
- *Annual negotiation process:* Annual negotiations consume time and energy, plus they are usually adversarial. There is no room for adversarial relationships in collaboration.
- *Time investment:* Collaboration takes time and a lot of hard work. To get people to make the necessary effort, they have to be clearly shown the potential benefits.
- *Inadequate communications:* When communication between supply chain partners is non-existent or inadequate, the potential for problems increases exponentially.
- *Inconsistency:* Behavioural attitudes and operational execution must be consistent at all interfaces in the supply chain relationship.
- *Betrayal:* Lying, misleading, misrepresenting – these may be the ultimate barriers to a successful collaborative relationship.

This all means that the culture within and between the partners must be established at the upper levels of the organisations and constantly reinforced. Without this positive attitude towards working together, collaboration is doomed to failure.

Benefits

If all the enablers can be put in place, and the impediments removed, the greatest benefit that can be expected is financial:

- reduced inventory
- improved customer service
- more efficient use of human resources
- better delivery through reduced cycle times.

In addition to these considerable financial benefits, certain non-financial benefits to flow from collaboration include the following:

- faster speed to market of new products
- stronger focus on core competencies
- enhanced public image
- greater trust and interdependence
- increased sharing of information, ideas and technology
- stronger emphasis on the supply chain as a whole
- improved shareholder value
- competitive advantage over other supply chains.

All of these benefits eventually affect the bottom line, whether directly or indirectly. Once companies understand this, they are ready to make the commitment to begin collaborating and sharing information with key supply chain members on key processes.

Using the internet

These efforts have been successful in driving substantial costs out of the overall supply chain and have contributed greatly to the growth of the electronics industry. However, improved internal planning and forecasting can only go so far in reducing supply chain costs. As supply chains rapidly become 'value chains', with increasingly complex relationships between product distribution channels, original equipment manufacturers, contract equipment manufacturers, component suppliers and others, an entirely new set of interactions will be required to sustain and accelerate the creation of new value.

The industry is looking increasingly to the internet as the source of these new models of interaction. Recently the emergence of the business-to-business (B2B) space has introduced a number of new business models that use the internet and powerful collaboration technologies to provide new ways for supply chain partners to interact.

These new models provide the innovative enterprise with an opportunity to leverage the power of market-based transactions, such as requests for quotes, auctions and structured negotiations, across homogeneous end-to-end systems. This ensures the efficient management of direct procurement functions, including the strategic sourcing of the goods and services that are most critical to business operations.

The new models address critical issues of transaction effectiveness in direct materials goods. These issues include concerns such as getting the best price, ensuring product availability, providing transparent visibility to inventories, managing component and product quality and making performance/price trade-offs.

To do this, internet sites in public marketplaces, as well as those focused within the enterprise or its direct value chain partners, provide a new form of market openness. In the electronics industry, public marketplaces mean leveraging the power of industry operating systems.

The sector trends and requirements are that:

- Companies must boost efficiency, lower costs and as a result change their corporate structures.
- Electronic cooperation is the highest and best form of business relationship between business partners.
- The end customer profits from cooperation in sourcing, production and selling, operating capital reduction, greater flexibility and visibility right across the end-to-end supply chain; and integrating the fields of advanced planning and scheduling, supply chain execution and enterprise resource management in line with corporate strategy,

rationalised business processes and appropriate corporate structures generates a decisive competitive advantage for companies.

Information-based decision making along the entire corporate value chain is the prerequisite for expansion of market share and an increase in cashflow and profits.

Competitive criteria

The competitive environment is constantly changing. Production quality alone is no longer a decisive competitive criterion. Success is based on the ability to meet customer requirements for time, delivery, volume, flexibility or responsiveness and service level. It is vital that efforts in the areas of sales and marketing be linked to supply chain planning and execution strategies to achieve and maintain competitive advantages. The integrated supply chains of different partners lead, in the end, to corporate networks that compete with other supply chain networks rather than company against company as it is today.

Customer requirements in the future will only be met by collaborative relationships among trading partners based on joint planning and execution. New developments in the area of information and communication technology, as well as software and support solutions such as e-business or e-commerce relationships, require end-to-end supply chain performance and develop over time from transaction-based exchange of data to real end-to-end cycles, ensuring assets do not sit idle in a production, source or delivery process.

Factors in the process are:

- Advanced information and communication technology; enabling strategic timing, availability and capability to promise, effective postponement; collaborative planning and execution processes leading to improved customer satisfaction, increased revenues and market share, and reduced cost.
- Economic value added focusing simultaneously on customer and shareholder value creation.
- E-business-enabled globalisation and strategic management driving responsive local operations, compressing overall cycle time and reducing the need for moving goods and materials around the globe; increasing operational excellence and customer intimacy.
- Partnership-based outsourcing concepts creating virtual supply chains or networks; enabling economies of scope and scale by replacing power-based, lowest-cost, winner-take-all contracts with long-lasting mutual partnership-based win-win relationships.
- Integrated SCM goes from vertical to internal and external integration, from the seamless to the extended enterprise.

The Net Initiative, founded by leading high-tech industries, is in the process of harnessing the global and pervasive reach of the internet by defining and leading the implementation of open and common processes of communication. These processes are designed to align the electronic business interfaces between IT supply chain partners, creating measurable benefits for the network.

During the past 10 to 20 years, business process redesign has created integrated processes within companies, made possible by database systems. During the next 10 to 20 years, the networking among companies (business networking) will link company boundaries: information technology, such as the internet, will provide the means. This inter-organisational coordination will change business more fundamentally than intra-organisational integration.

There will be a worldwide network of specialists, each of which will play its part in value creation with its core competence. The path will be led via the disassembly of existing enterprises into independent processes and via reassembly of enterprises and supply chains. Business is at the start of a dramatic transformation and business networking is a main driver.

Learning activity 6.2

Undertake a research activity into external sources of information linked to innovative development from among the supply base which has had a successful impact on the organisation.

Feedback on page 120

Now complete self-assessment question 6.2 below.

Self-assessment question 6.2

Explain what processes exist within your own job role which contribute to the use of market intelligence from the supply chain to improve functional performance.

Feedback on page 120

6.3 How external information can be valuable to the procurement business

Sources of information

The operating environment of the business is the one which can be controlled. However, it is the external environment which is of major interest to senior management because the changes in this environment will impact and inform the operating environment. It is the inability of the organisation to directly influence that environment that leads to market intelligence gathering in order to obtain quality data and information on trends and changes in that environment.

Depending on the structure of the business, information from the external environment will vary. Use of the strategic DEEPLIST will be a starting point for information gathering. This will no doubt be an organisational objective, but from a purchasing perspective it can be used to channel the information gathering.

- *Demographic:* Structural changes in society will be translated in variations in product range, style and choice.
- *Economic:* The purchasing function will be concerned about tax changes that can add to the cost of supplies, structural shifts in society away from traditional manufacturing 'smokestack industries', price movements, exchange rates and the shift in patterns of consumption. International agreements at Kyoto for example may increase fuel prices if governments seek to reduce dependence on fossil fuels. The costs of operating in other countries will be important is assessing sourcing globally.
- *Environmental:* Green issues such as global warming will eventually begin to impact on the wealth structure of society and buying patterns, as governments take steps to change the way business is organised.
- *Political:* The lowering of trade barriers around the world, the consolidation of the EU as a trading bloc, are important issues for the sourcing and trading of goods.
- *Legal:* The sourcing of goods around the world is made easier by the opening of borders as a result of EU membership and WTO agreements on tariff reductions. Increasing environmental legislation will have an influence on costs of supplies.
- *Informational:* The use of databases, the ability to store and transmit data, the ability to source online, the growing use of the internet to establish markets has begun to change the speed and scope of the buying function.
- *Social:* Changing buying patterns of consumers will need to be understood as these will translate into changes in consumer demand.
- *Technological:* Developments in IT such as digitalisation, electronic data interchange and software development generally has meant that e-business is transforming the face of industry.

Other sources of market intelligence will come from more specific primary and secondary research. These sources will be examined in study session 11.

Examples will include changes in market conditions.

Learning activity 6.3

Prepare a DEEPLIST template and include at least one example of external changes that could affect the purchasing function within your own organisation.

Feedback on page 121

Now complete self-assessment question 6.3 below.

Self-assessment question 6.3

List the key sources of information that are used to scan the external environment.

Feedback on page 121

6.4 The process for adopting a supplier innovation

Early supplier involvement in product innovation and development is beneficial to the organisation in terms of costs and quality, and will increasingly become an ingredient in the selection and management of suppliers.

The role of the purchasing function and its growing relationships with the supply chain has meant that its importance in strategic planning has also increased.

Learning activity 6.4

Describe the process of the adoption of a supplier innovation within your own organisation and how this is managed without loss of technical expertise in the industry.

Feedback on page 121

The drive for obtaining competitive advantage means that the extension of developmental aspects to the supply chain results in faster, more innovative products if the specialist skills of suppliers is fully utilised. Womack has documented the success of this approach with Japanese car manufacturers.

Organisations have to consider their own core competences and the level of detail required for developing specifications.

Supplier involvement will be considered if there are suppliers with the technical know-how and the potential to deliver innovation faster than the buying company.

Development risk

Calvi (Calvi et al, 2001) suggests consideration of the following risks before development is assigned:

- The link between the component and the final product.
- The level of differentiation brought by the new component.
- What is the reliability of the supplier?
- What is the newness of the production technologies involved?
- What are the weighted costs of the component to the final product?

- What is the technical complexity involved in the component?

The adoption process

The involvement of suppliers in the development process will depend upon the decision of the manufacturer (Wynstra et al, 1999):

- *Development management:* The extent to which the organisation wants to keep technologies in-house or outsourced and the overall policy on supplier involvement. This will involve the levels of management involvement in the various stages of development.
- *Supplier interface management:* Monitoring supplier markets for technological development, motivating suppliers to build up specific knowledge of products, exploiting the capabilities of suppliers and evaluating their development performance.
- *Project management:* Developing specific develop-or-buy solutions, selecting appropriate suppliers, managing the interface between the suppliers, the buyer and any other first tier or second tier suppliers. Ordering and chasing prototypes.
- *Product management:* Providing detailed specifications that give alternatives to products and suppliers and giving information about current developmental activities, evaluating product times under usual criteria such as quality, costs, lead times. Providing standardisation and simplifications assistance.

Self-assessment question 6.4

Outline an example of an improved supply component and its adoption with end users.

Feedback on page 121

Revision question

Now try the revision question for this session on page 341.

Summary

The purchasing function can assist the organisation to maintain competitive advantage by developing systems (in collaboration with the rest of the organisation) that systematically scan the environment looking for changes that affect the supply chain. The importance of close and strong relationships with suppliers is an essential feature of this gathering and assessing of market intelligence.

Such changes have to be responded to quickly and effectively if any advantage is to be gained or threats avoided.

Suggested further reading

Read the chapter on analysing resources in Lysons and Farrington (2006).

Feedback on learning activities and self-assessment questions

Feedback on learning activity 6.1

Information on market changes can be found in many secondary sources, and organisations should have some systems, both formal and informal, in place for data collection and analysis:

- newspaper articles
- stockbroker analysis
- exhibitions and trade fairs
- company annual reports
- internet sites.

In addition, information gathering through the supply chain should be examined. How is such information recorded and tracked? How is it updated?

Feedback on self-assessment question 6.1

An advanced form of intelligence gathering where insight is gained by deconstructing products and processes, **reverse engineering** (RE) is the process of discovering the technological principles of a mechanical application through analysis of its structure, function and operation. That involves sometimes taking something (a mechanical device, an electrical component, a software program, and so on) apart and analysing its workings in detail, usually with the intention to construct a new device or program that does the same thing without actually copying anything from the original.

Feedback on learning activity 6.2

Technical and innovative improvements will have aided supplier performance in the past. Their own need to change will ensure that suppliers will make a constant stream of improvements over a period of years which will enhance their standing and have a positive impact on the buyer. All suppliers will have capital improvement programmes, and will also adopt changes that come into the wider market that improve efficiency. Technological changes in the logistical operation are also streamlining and improving efficiency and should be noted.

How does the organisation track changes that improve supplier performance and how does it link into reduction in costs? Is this built into the contractual agreement?

Feedback on self-assessment question 6.2

Formal methods of gathering market intelligence might be included within the job role.

Is it part of the formal job description or a more informal aspect of the breadth of view required by the modern purchaser? Is this separately discussed at appraisals?

What is the organisational view on supplier knowledge development? Are supplier improvements systematically discussed at team meetings? What is the process for recording this improvement and using the information to change costs, prices and procedures? Do the purchasing function's procedures have a cross-functional role so that any technical improvements can be picked up and used elsewhere in the organisation with ultimate benefit for the end user?

Feedback on learning activity 6.3

This is an opportunity to examine the external environment, and to locate the most important sources for informing the organisation of external change. Examples of external factors impacting on the business will stem from competitor activity: How fast is the market changing? How quickly do new entrants appear? Consider economic changes – including costs of fuel and packaging, government investment, and changes in customer confidence. How is the UK economy doing? There may be a new form of breakthrough technology – are there any new significant technological introductions?

Feedback on self-assessment question 6.3

Current secondary sources that are used by the organisation should be listed. Sources are varied and numerous and indeed some organisations may subscribe to specific agencies that provide summaries of their interests which may be in macro-economic information, regulatory and legislative changes, or perhaps consumer attitudes, health, lifestyle, technical and product liability issues. Whatever the industry, failure to identify and anticipate any crucial factors can mean the difference between success and failure.

Scanning of general news, specialist journals, government statistics, website intermediaries all provide invaluable information.

Feedback on learning activity 6.4

This involves the building of trust and confidentiality between the parties so that as much of the innovation can be made specific and protected so that some technological lead can provide a competitive advantage. It is difficult to prevent the supplier from using their technical know-how on other projects but a close relationship and a fast-paced development in conjunction with supplier assistance will give a temporary lead over competitors. If technological innovations can be incorporated into more sophisticated organisational processes, then it is possible for the competitive edge to be sustained over the longer term if imitation is more difficult.

Feedback on self-assessment question 6.4

This is a requirement to scan the supply base for examples of component improvement, and how they have been adopted, and how quickly. How

6

frequently do they occur? Who has responsibility for engaging with the suppliers on these matters? What is the review process? How is feedback undertaken?

- Hewlett-Packard, for example, is working closely with suppliers to eliminate lead, mercury, cadmium and hexavalent chromium in 100% of electronic products sold worldwide, as defined by the EU's Directive.
- BAe Systems has developed a supply chain excellence (SCE) process to involve key suppliers in improving delivery, quality, cost and management systems and reduce waste.

Identifying supplier capability

Introduction

Effective supply chain management makes a significant contribution to the ultimate performance of an organisation, the ultimate margin, and creates a competitive advantage. Systems that monitor and evaluate supplier performance are essential for maintaining standards, and for identifying those supplier characteristics that drive success.

'Many companies are discovering that effective supply chain management is the next step they need to take to increase profit and market share'
Simchi-Levi et al (2003)

Session learning objectives

After completing this session you should be able to:

7.1 Evaluate the effectiveness of supplier performance systems that segment the supply base.
7.2 Demonstrate how competent and valued suppliers contribute to competitive advantage.
7.3 Explain the key characteristics of enhanced supplier performance.

Unit content coverage

Learning objective

2.1 Propose and manage systematic organisational efforts to create and maintain networks of competent suppliers, and to improve various supplier capabilities necessary for an organisation to meet increasingly competitive challenges.

Prior knowledge

Understanding of the procurement process and the competitive stance of modern business.

Resources

Access to supply base performance criteria.

Timing

You should set aside about 5 hours to read and complete this session, including learning activities, self-assessment questions, the suggested further reading (if any) and the revision question.

7.1 Segmenting the supplier base

Tiering the supply base

Organisations have for many years sought to reduce their supplier base as they seek to implement a lean supply regime. Segmenting the chosen supply base into tiers gives a measure of prioritisation in the management of the supply chain. The first tier is reserved for the immediate and direct suppliers of assemblies and other final stage components, whereas second and third tier suppliers are reserved for component suppliers who supply the first tier suppliers, thus removing them from direct involvement with the manufacturer.

Tiering enables the manufacturer to develop a closer relationship with fewer suppliers and to delegate to the responsibility for second tier suppliers where, for example, components are an integral part of the assembly.

A further third level tier can be introduced for low-value-added items required by first and second tier suppliers.

First tier suppliers become more integrated in the direction and management of the supply chain as they are responsible for ensuring the buyer's specification with all its complexity is adhered to.

Further responsibilities identified by Lamming (1998) include:

- the management of subcontractors
- adopting a JIT philosophy
- customer-dedicated staff who work in conjunction with the design and production team of the supplier
- responsibility for warranty and end-user customer claims
- research and development into technologies that are being applied to the supplier's product.

Tiering is important in building a very strong relationship of trust and commitment between the buyer and the first tier supplier.

Supplier associations

Supplier associations or Kyoryoku Kai are a major feature of Japanese manufacturing, and also reflect the cultural aspects of Japanese business life, in that integration between businesses within an industry is normal practice. Supplier associations help develop a climate of trust between the parties involved.

In the UK there has been some interest shown and some coordination of efforts between suppliers and manufacturers by means of seminars and workshops.

Aims of supplier associations

- To improve the abilities of the suppliers especially in techniques such as JIT, TQM, SPC and so on.
- To produce uniformity in the supply system.
- To facilitate the flow of information and strategy formulation between the parties.

- To increase trust between the parties.
- To keep suppliers and customers in touch with market developments and therefore aid the translation of the voice of the customer.
- To enhance the reputation of the customer as someone the suppliers should do business with.
- To increase the length of relations.
- To allow the sharing of development benefits.
- To provide an example to subcontractors of how to coordinate and develop their own suppliers.

The success of such associations in different cultures such as the UK requires strong leadership from the customers in putting techniques into action and disclosing how they are used on site. The selection of members must be from those who favour collaboration so that the use of members over time is productive and expertise is imparted. There must be some tangible results to prevent it from becoming a mere talking shop.

7

Learning activity 7.1

Outline in a report how suppliers within your own organisation are tiered.

Feedback on page 133

Now try self-assessment question 7.1 below.

Self-assessment question 7.1

Identify the current electronic software systems that contribute to measuring and evaluating supplier performance.

Feedback on page 133

7.2 How competent and valued suppliers contribute to competitive advantage

Obtaining a competitive advantage

Porter (1998b) argues that an organisation's performance is driven by the need to respond to its marketplace by modifying its internal and external competences so as to best position itself in relation to its competitors.

This is done by using distinctive competence to create and exploit linkages in what he calls the internal value chain so as to create value for the customer. Further value can be created by encouraging the organisation's network of suppliers to do the same, thus delivering superior value to the final customer in the chain. This is the basis for sustainable competitive advantage – the 'holy grail' of business.

It requires an effective strategy and focus – organisations that become 'stuck in the middle' because they have multiple strategies will be less successful. It requires an organisation to have a differentiation strategy that either concentrates on low-cost production or one where quality-oriented aspects are the focus.

Learning activity 7.2

Research a significant example of the impact to the business of a supplier failing to perform.

Feedback on page 134

A competitive advantage through world-class status

Schonberger in 1986 popularised the word 'world-class' in relation the manufacturing effort. Organisations that achieve 'world-class' recognition in full or in part inevitably have a strong competitive advantage. The characteristics of such organisations are as follows:

- commitment to total quality management
- commitment to just-in-time
- commitment to total cycle time reduction
- multidimensional and integrative strategic plans
- supplier relationships
- strategic cost management
- performance measurements
- training and professional development
- service excellence
- corporate social responsibility
- learning
- management and leadership
- a push for world-class status requires suppliers of a similar stature.

Organisations must therefore search for suppliers that not only deliver on the key KPIs, competitive price, quality and lead times; they must in addition have the following characteristics:

- a commitment to continuous improvement
- a commitment to being leaders in their industry in terms of technology and innovation
- adaptability and the ability to invest in new areas and technologies.

The management of these suppliers will involve collaborative, long-term working arrangements and specifications that deal with the purchaser's expectations and the performance standards to be measured.

Self-assessment question 7.2

From the list of world-class descriptors, comment on your own organisation's performance against each one.

Feedback on page 134

7.3 The key characteristics of enhanced supplier performance

Competitive advantage

Supply chains are being managed to obtain competitive advantage. Suppliers that perform well and to the objectives of the organisation will contribute significantly to that organisational success. Supply chains built around design concepts and manufacturing principles, such as build-to-order (BTO), continuous replenishment or integrated make-to-stock, can offer enterprises a significant source of competitive advantage. Other labels for different types of supply chain and the relationships that underpin them include:

- agile: focused on fulfilling a wide range of fast-changing customer product needs
- lean: focused on the elimination of waste (which equates to cost) and inventory
- leagile: focused on both customer needs and waste
- design: focused on innovation
- clockspeed: focused on time-based competition
- full service: focused on an extended range of customer product and service needs.

Learning activity 7.3

Prepare a report on a specific improvement from a supplier: how is this managed and sustained?

Feedback on page 134

The type of supply chain and the relationship that underpins it will depend on the basis upon which the enterprise chooses to compete. Thus, if the enterprise chooses to compete on cost, it may adopt a lean supply model. If it chooses to compete on customer retention and customisation, it may adopt an agile model. If it chooses to compete on time it might adopt a clockspeed model.

Of course, this is not to say that enterprises will employ one type of supply chain. Different product lines may require different types of supply chain and different types of relationship and some product lines may be based around more than one performance driver.

Increasingly, we can see that certain performance dimensions are 'order winners' and others are 'order qualifiers'. Order winners are dimensions of product and process performance which will lead to customer orders and reorders. In the 1980s quality was seen as an order winner. Order qualifiers are the minimum requirement for an organisation to gain a foothold in the market. The performance characteristics that allow organisations to offer order-winning or order-qualifying products change over time. Some commentators now say that quality is no longer an order winner. Customers now expect quality as a right, rather than as a need, and consequently it is now only an order qualifier.

Developing relationships for agility

Agile supply chain management grew out of the quick response and effective consumer response of supply chain management. It focuses on the customer. An important difference is that lean supply is associated with level scheduling, whereas agile supply means reserving capacity to cope with volatile demand. Whereas information transparency is desirable in a lean regime, it is obligatory for agility. Lean forecasting is algorithmic, but agile forecasting requires shared information on current demand captured as close to the marketplace as possible. Real-world supply chains are cyclical in character.

Within the agile supply chain, demand is managed using inventory strategies. The aim of the agile supply chain should be to carry inventory in as generic a form as possible, that is, standard semi-finished products awaiting final assembly or localisation. This is the concept of 'postponement', a vital element in any agile strategy. Postponement, or delayed configuration, is based on the principle of seeking to design products using common platforms, components or modules but where the final assembly or customisation does not take place until the final market destination and/or customer requirement is known.

The advantages of the strategy of postponement are several. First, inventory can be held at a generic level so that there will be fewer stock-keeping variants and hence less inventory in total. Second, because the inventory is generic, its flexibility is greater, meaning that the same components, modules or platforms can be embodied in a variety of end products. Third, forecasting is easier at the generic level than at the level of the finished item. This latter point is particularly relevant in global markets where local forecasts will be less accurate than a forecast for worldwide volume. Furthermore, the ability to customise products locally means that a higher level of variety may be offered at lower total cost, enabling strategies of mass customisation.

Supplier characteristics for agile supply

Obviously, in all cases, supplier selection will depend on a range of factors and it is impossible to identify supplier characteristics that may be appropriate for a particular contract. However, some general characteristics of an agile supplier in a manufacturing supply chain may include:

- flexible or cell-based manufacturing capacity
- flexible training programmes in place
- JIT system in place
- supplier understanding of trade-offs between set-ups and inventory
- EPL methods of inventory planning
- total productive maintenance programmes in place
- multiple constraint synchronisation modelling in place
- 'single minute exchange of die' (SMED) training and tooling

- collaborative scheduling capacity
- purchasing has a role in capacity allocation
- marketability cost tracking.

Developing relationships for lean supply

Lean supply chain management focuses on the elimination of waste. For example:

- Overproduction waste: Make only what is needed now.
- Waiting waste: Eliminate bottlenecks and streamline processes.
- Transportation waste: There is a demonstrable relationship between damage/deterioration and the number of materials handling operations. Can these be eliminated or reduced?
- Processing waste: Does this product or part need to be made?
- Inventory waste: Inventory hides problems. Can it be eliminated?
- Movement waste: First improve, then mechanise or automate.
- Defect waste: Accept no defects and make no defects.

Lean supply rests on the concept of supplier networks, where suppliers are part of a stable consortium. These networks are based on long-term relationships rather than competitive tendering (although the original sourcing is tender-based).

Open book costing is an important element of these relationships. There is expectation that once the learning curve has been mounted and continuous improvement has taken hold, costs and prices will reduce in subsequent years and that these savings will be shared. This is not necessarily a 'cosy' or a 'soft' relationship. Target costing creates tensions which, in some situations, has led to suppliers walking away from some major customers. Asset linkages are made where tooling is partly or fully funded by the OEM or first tier supplier. Asset linkages can lead to problems because the supplier can face difficulties in persuading the customer to fund major overhauls which may be needed despite total productive maintenance programmes.

Demand is managed with the aim of smoothing production. Examples are quoted of production personnel being moved to sales in times of low demand. This is one of the major differences between 'lean' and 'agile' manufacturing.

Supplier characteristics for lean supply

Some years ago, the difference between 'pragmatic just-in-time' and 'romantic just-in-time' inventory management and manufacturing systems were made. Romantic JIT aims for zero inventory and therefore zero waste. Pragmatic JIT will work with minimum realistic inventory (MRI). In many ways suppliers for lean supply chains are romantic JIT suppliers and characteristics may include:

- strong team emphasis
- JIT system in place
- total quality management systems in place

- waste reduction teams
- electronic data interchange (EDI)
- extensive forecasting and modelling capacity
- order status tracking capability
- vendor-managed inventory
- product development cost tracking.

Developing relationships for design

The management of early supplier involvement has been shown to offer significant cost, time and quality advantages in the new product design process. Effective integration, once an organisation has decided to use suppliers in new product or process development, includes a number of issues:

- careful supplier selection
- co-location (physical or virtual) of supplier and buyer personnel
- shared physical assets (information systems and manufacturing equipment)
- formalised risk/reward sharing agreements
- shared education and training programmes
- direct cross-functional, inter-enterprise communication, project management and collaborative working systems
- formal procedures for inducting suppliers
- information partnerships – sharing of technical information and customer requirements on a continuing, as-needed basis
- intellectual property agreements
- supplier role definition – where are the cut-off points for supplier involvement?

Supplier characteristics for design supply

Choosing suppliers for early involvement in the design process or to act as elements of an integrated product design (IPD) team will clearly depend on expertise in the requisite design area. Specific issues may include:

- shared CAD/CAM/VRML software
- rapid product deployment experience
- rapid prototyping capability
- co-location of buyer and supplier personnel
- creativity training
- FMEA capacity – the ability to test and analyse the likelihood of failure in a part or component, under given conditions
- nature of R&D portfolio
- R&D strategy
- integration between own production systems and R&D
- modular planning and assembly cost tracking
- team building across functional and organisational boundaries
- clear design briefings
- effective project management
- joint end user/consumer research teams
- gain-sharing agreements
- technology licensing agreements.

Developing clockspeed relationships

Competitive advantage is a constantly moving target. In order to compete effectively, many businesses are choosing to compete on the basis of time. As a strategic weapon, many authors see time as the equivalent of money, productivity and quality. Managing time has enabled some enterprises to reduce their costs and also to offer broad product lines, cover more market segments and upgrade the technological sophistication of their products. These companies are time-based competitors.

Time-based competition (TBC) is defined as a strategy for the development of a sustainable competitive advantage, characterised by three major traits:

- First, it deals with only those lead time areas that are most important to the customer.
- Second, these reductions in lead time derive from the removal of waste from the processes involved.
- Third, these lead time reductions must be achieved through system analysis and attack of the underlying processes; they must not be product-driven.

In such environments, TBC must be a strategy which achieves reductions in lead time through changes in the processes and structures used to design, manufacture and deliver products for a firm's customers.

It should be remembered, however, that time-based competition will vary depending on the clockspeed within an industry sector. Clockspeed is the rate at which products and systems evolve within the value chain. One hypothesis suggests that a common characteristic of supply chains is the fact that the industry clockspeed a company faces increases the farther downstream it is located in the supply chain. Thus, in computer hardware industries, personal computer manufacturers experience faster clockspeeds (for example, shorter product life cycles) than semiconductor manufacturers, who, in turn, experience faster clockspeeds than the semiconductor equipment suppliers. Managing these differences means developing the right type of relationships.

Supplier characteristics for clockspeed supply

Again, clockspeed suppliers will share some of the same characteristics of lean and agile suppliers. In addition, there may be an increased emphasis on inventory issues. Characteristics may include:

- geographic location or distribution hub location
- line-side inventory holding
- cross docking
- EDI/e-markets
- radio frequency identification (RFID) tracking systems
- automated picking and kitting
- process redesign and re-engineering
- lead time reduction programmes in place or completed
- commitment to continuous improvement

- product cycle time tracking
- order configuration checking.

Developing full service relationships

Full service supply has been described in some quarters as 'a myth'. Others believe that achieving full service supply is a realistic aim. A full service supplier would be an integrator or a provider of a complete range of services in all possible performance dimensions. These may include:

- cost
- delivery accuracy and lead time reduction
- quality as in reliability and consistency
- customer service in all dimensions
- flexibility and agility in terms of product line changes and mix
- innovation as a cost reduction method and a customer order.

In addition, the full service supplier would be positioned and skilled so as to be able to manage large elements of the overall supply chain. Full service suppliers would have in place technological, management and enterprise-wide systems and philosophies that would integrate processes throughout the supply chain.

At the time of writing, a number of enterprises had made claims to represent full service suppliers, but whether the actual management of all these supply performance drivers throughout the whole of the supply chain is achievable is open to question. Like lean supply, full service supply may be a target that is never realised, although aiming for such targets is often beneficial and sometimes necessary.

An enterprise's requirement for appropriate commercial relationships arises from massive changes in the trading environment. Shifts in the way in which purchasing and supply contributes to the organisation mean that the management of the purchasing function is now much more complex. This complexity is reflected in the type of relational strategies that are employed. Relationships reflect the objectives of the enterprise, and these depend on the performance dimensions in which the enterprise chooses to compete. Some enterprises choose to compete on cost and quality, others choose to compete on mass customisation and still others on innovation or first-mover advantage. In some industries there has been an attempt to compete on combinations of different performance dimensions to meet differing customer needs.

Self-assessment question 7.3

A full service supplier would be an integrator or a provider of a complete range of services in all possible performance dimensions. These may include:

- cost
- delivery accuracy and lead-time reduction
- quality as in reliability and consistency
- customer service in all dimensions
- flexibility and agility in terms of product line changes and mix

(continued on next page)

Self-assessment question 7.3 *(continued)*

• innovation as a cost reduction method and a customer order.

List examples of these factors being achieved from your own supply base.

Feedback on page 134

Revision question

Now try the revision question for this session on page 341.

Summary

Suppliers that can achieve reliability, consistency and accuracy as well as a spirited response to buyer demands will assist organisations in achieving their pressing and demanding schedules. If at the same time they have some of the attributes of world-class organisations, then a real competitive advantage is achieved.

Suggested further reading

Read the chapter on specifying and managing quality in Lysons and Farrington (2006).

Feedback on learning activities and self-assessment questions

Feedback on learning activity 7.1

The tiering of suppliers is an aspect of lean supply. The tiering of suppliers will be determined by their importance to the organisation in terms of the influence that the supplier exerts within the supply chain.

The tiering of suppliers can be based on:

• First tier suppliers of high level assemblies (or those that supply indirectly but have significant technical influence).
• Second tier suppliers who are approved by the assembler and managed by the first tier.

There may also be a tier of tertiary subcontractors.

The second tier suppliers tend to supply to the first tier supplier, who is responsible for the management of that second tier.

Feedback on self-assessment question 7.1

Examples include:

• commercial systems that manage the supply chain in terms of performance and relationships in ways that are similar to marketing-led CRM systems
• systems that integrate sales, production and product availability within the supply chain

- systems that trace the movement of products through product coding, for example fresh food
- specialist systems that concentrate on a particular industry such as retail or wholesale
- systems that help manage KPIs and related supplier performance issues
- systems that help gather and manage business intelligence
- systems that manage distribution.

Feedback on learning activity 7.2

Suppliers that fail to perform in terms of the essential KPIs such as quality, delivery of time, cost reduction, lean supply and so forth will impact on an organisation's ability to differentiate itself from competitors. An organisation that is unable to deliver high-level performance to the end user will ultimately find it difficult to compete.

Feedback on self-assessment question 7.2

Becoming a world-class organisation requires compliance with a number of high performance standards. Schonberger's descriptors are not easy for an organisation, but many will have systems in place that address total quality management, attempt to reduce lead times, have strategic plans that focus on the development of the business and will seek to select high quality suppliers.

Feedback on learning activity 7.3

Examples of supplier improvement will identify cost savings from the supplier as a result of innovation within their production process, savings gleaned from their suppliers or perhaps improved systems that cut out waste. Alternative examples will report the speed at which the supplier is able to adjust supplies as products are customised for end users. Or perhaps there is faster response in terms of delivery times as customer demands have changed. The improvements have to be sustainable so there needs to be evidence that systems are in place to monitor compliance and the new performance standards become embedded in the vendor rating system.

Feedback on self-assessment question 7.3

Quality in terms of reliability or consistency is an important attribute of any supplier; examples will include the reduction in quality errors, defects and rejects over a period of time. This should be matched by delivery accuracy, with reasons given – is it because the logistics is outsourced? Or perhaps regular liaison with the supplier detects possible production delays? Some examples from the response by suppliers to changes to the supply order and the way and spirit in which changes are implemented should be included. The standard of performance from the supplier will be driven by the management systems in place by:

- the buyer who sets KPIs and monitors and evaluates, and
- by the suppliers themselves, because of their own internal systems that drive cost-effective change.

Communicating effectively

Introduction

Clarity in buyer communications is essential. This covers the formal transmission of dealings with the supply chain, as well as the need to ensure that the communication of the objectives of the purchasing function is undertaken successfully. In addition there will also be informal interpersonal aspects within the communication process that ensures the maintenance and sustainability of essential relationships.

'Without adequate or successful communication, any hope of achieving results would be confounded'
Armstrong, Gallagher and Watson (2005)

Session learning objectives

After completing this session you should be able to:

8.1 Describe the importance of effective communications with suppliers.
8.2 Assess how specification issues are effectively communicated.
8.3 Explain the techniques for ensuring compliance with the buyer's specification.

Unit content coverage

Learning objective

2.2 Develop, manage and maintain effective communications between an organisation and its suppliers to ensure that correct quality specifications are given to suppliers and subsequently delivered back to the business in measurable terms. To include early supplier involvement and risk transfer techniques.

Prior knowledge

Understanding of some of the skills required for effective communication including an introduction to negotiation.

Resources

Access to buyer specifications.

Timing

You should set aside about 5 hours to read and complete this session, including learning activities, self-assessment questions, the suggested further reading (if any) and the revision question.

8.1 The importance of effective communications with suppliers

Communication and relationships

Several of the units have discussed the importance of commercial relationships in establishing trust and mutual respect which can then lead to a more embedded and long-term relationship between the buyer and supplier. Good communications between the two parties is important in maintaining that relationship. Organisations have tended to shift from the 'bow-tie' structure evident in early key account management (McDonald, 2000), to one in which effective relationships must be maintained throughout the organisation as contacts can come in at several levels, for instance board, administration and operations. However, in relationships between buyers and first tier suppliers there will inevitably be a key account manager responsible for the buyer's account.

Defining communication

In order to improve communication effectiveness, it is necessary to agree a number of issues. These are:

1 Communication uses symbols: Symbols are things that are used to represent something else, and are open to misinterpretations because they may be understood differently by different users – the word (symbol) quality might mean very different things to different suppliers.
2 Communication is about creating a meaning: We are often involved in meaningless conversations.
3 Communication involves the transmission and interpreting of messages.
4 Communication takes place at different levels of awareness: Much communication is routine and we rely on existing patterns of behaviour when communicating in a routine way.
5 Prediction of communication: People who communicate predict the outcomes of their communication. In the same way that we like consistency, we also like our predictions to be accurate. People we know well are generally more predictable than strangers.
6 Unintentional communication: Although we may intend to communicate in a particular way, we can communicate without intending to. Non-verbal behaviour, relative positions, clothing or gender can all be unintentional communication.
7 Every message has a content dimension (what is said) and a relationship dimension (how it is said).
8 Structured communications: Communicators structure their communications in order to explain them. Sometimes people have differing explanations of the communication (a supplier may say that a delivery failed because of poorly organised cross-docking arrangements at your warehouse; your warehouse manager may say that cross-docking didn't work because of delivery failures).
9 Communication involves uncertainty: Every time we make a communication effort, we experience some uncertainty and therefore some anxiety. This may not be noticeable, but when it reaches high levels it interferes with communication effectiveness.

When people are really serious about improving their communication effectiveness, there are a number of areas of knowledge that they need to acquire and skills that they need to develop.

Communication knowledge

1   In terms of the knowledge people require to communicate effectively, perhaps the first item is knowledge of their own motivation. Without understanding their needs in communicating, it is unlikely that communication will be successful.
2   The second item is knowledge of how to gather information. Good quality communication rests upon good quality information, and competent communicators use active and passive strategies to acquire information that will help them tailor their communication to the situation in which they find themselves. This involves gathering information through questioning, active listening and research.
3   The third item is that communicators need to understand that groups are different, and that these differences will impact on communication.
4   The fourth item is knowledge of likely alternative interpretations. Once the communicator understands how the communication could be interpreted, he or she is more attuned to the likelihood of misunderstandings which can be costly in a commercial relationship.

8

Learning activity 8.1

Using organisational examples describe how specification standards are effectively and accurately communicated to suppliers.

Feedback on page 142

Communication skills

Skills for communication include the ability to think systematically. Skills also include the ability to tolerate ambiguity and uncertainty. Where there is a lot of uncertainty, and people do not tolerate this well, they tend to make judgements on first impressions. An ability to perceive how a message may be received is an important skill, as is precision. A professional buyer learns to be succinct in their communications, gaining credibility for that precision and relevance. Indeed, it is a good tactic to minimise the number of messages sent, so that information overload is avoided. Although human information gathering about people tends to be quite accurate within their own groups, it may be inaccurate elsewhere, and this can also lead to costly mistakes. A third skill is the ability to empathise, or see the other person's point of view. This is a critical skill because it allows the communicator to understand the effects of his or her messages but it also improves predictive accuracy about what the person will do. This feeds into the fourth skill, which is the ability to make accurate predictions and explanations. If the communicator can be accurate in this area, he or she can reduce uncertainty and therefore anxiety, reducing the possibility of misunderstandings.

A good communicator will always allow for feedback from the other party so that there is an opportunity for correcting misunderstandings and avoiding conflict.

Finally, the ability of the communicator to remain congenial is important if the other party is to continue to be willing to continue relationships despite differences that may arise.

Self-assessment question 8.1

List the issues that create the most problems for tying down specifications with suppliers.

Feedback on page 142

Feedback on page 142

8

8.2 The effective communication of specification issues

Introduction

The primary purpose of the purchasing function is to obtain the best possible products and services at the most efficient cost.

Buyers contribute to this aim by being aware at the design and development stage of factors that could contribute to cost reduction without impairing performance. They will also be in a position to advise if the planned production is likely to infringe any commercial, legal or environmental codes. They then select the right supplier and ensure that the requirements of the specification are correctly communicated to the selected supplier.

The purpose of specifications

Specifications can be of several types, dealing with anything from raw materials to final products, and including systems and complex structures. They will also have an element of process in that they will describe what is expected in terms of action. The preparation of a specification is a normal part of the buying process and will be used for all new buying situations, unless a branded good has to be incorporated into the process, or if the quantities purchased are so small as to make it impracticable to prepare a specification.

Lysons and Farrington outline the key functions of a specification:

- It should indicate the fitness for purpose and use.
- It should clearly communicate the requirements of the user or purchaser to the supplier.
- It should provide the basis of what is actually supplied with the purpose, quality and performance stated in the specification.
- It should provide evidence in case of dispute as to what the performance standard should have been.

The specification is usually an integral part of the contract between the two parties so that the agreement can be used as leverage if performance standards slip. Irrespective of the specific clauses, implied statutory protection such as the Sale of Goods Act 1979 imposes particularly high compliance standards on the supplier.

The British Standards 7373 gives a good order for the presentation of a specification:

- identification – title etc
- issue number
- contents list
- forward
- introduction
- scope
- definitions
- requirements/guidance/methods/statements – the main body of the specification
- index – cross references
- references to organisational, national, international standards.

8

Learning activity 8.2

A good specification can ensure the right performance standards are incorporated into the sourcing of supplies. Construct a process chart that would be used in your organisation to show sequencing of specification approval internally and with the supplier.

Feedback on page 142

The specification will obviously be fleshed out with considerable detail as appropriate. The tactics used in compiling a specification require the buyer to be aware of several variables in its preparation. The tendency to construct an overlong specification will increase input costs. Every requirement will lead to a price increase, but if there are omissions this will mean that it is unlikely to be supplied. Performance standards are to be preferred rather than a detailed design. Finally they must be open enough for other suppliers to be able to adhere to the specification if required. Compliance with legal standards is also essential. Some of the key areas included will be whole sections on:

- performance – including testing of the product, acceptance conditions, certification
- the life of the product
- its reliability
- the control of quality and the checking for compliance
- storage conditions
- characteristics, evidenced by drawings, design samples, models, materials to be used, appearance and finish, marking, preparation for manufacturing, interchangeability of parts and so forth

- packing
- information on installation and maintenance from the supplier.

Self-assessment question 8.2

Identify how you as a buyer respond to supplier queries over complex specifications, ensuring that the substance of the specification is not corrupted.

Feedback on page 143

8.3 The techniques for ensuring compliance with the buyer's specification

Contractual determination

The successful execution of a contract to specification and to time depends upon the cooperation of both parties. The contract with the attached specification is a means of communication, defining the obligations of the parties in as precise a manner as possible, taking account of the realities under which the contract is performed.

As we have already discussed, the construction of the contract is important as it is the description of the performance expected. If there is any aspect that is unclear or uncertain then the buyer runs the risk of non-performance. Too detailed a specification can lead to confusion and an increase in cost as suppliers seek exact compliance.

A team approach to the development of products in which suppliers are involved will overcome problems caused at the design stage.

Assistance from the supplier in the drawing up of the specification is increasingly common. Traditionally the contract specification was based on conformance standards. Using the expertise of the supplier and a measure of trust, a contract with performance criteria is perhaps a better approach for compliance as the supplier's expertise will be capable in constructing a satisfactory specification.

Some agreements will be based on model contracts if the contract involves civil engineering, construction work or the supply of mechanical or electrical works, whose terms will be known to the industry and obligations and responsibilities clearly understood. In other areas standard contract terms used repeatedly will become established performance practice.

Contractual clauses will inevitably deal with potential breaches of the performance criteria and will cover areas such as description of the product or service, quality and delivery standards. Breach of contract will be met with a clause giving the buyer the option to terminate the contract, reject the goods and claim damages for compensatory loss and possibly consequential damages which covers any economic loss. Such potential claims could be encapsulated into a liquidated damages clause.

Irrespective of the construction of the contract specification, the supplier must still conform to the quality standards and deliver on time. Buyers need to manage the contract by first identifying and ascertaining the possible risks and then assessing the impact on the organisation. Service level agreements linked to the specification could be used to agree parameters for performance which will guarantee the success of the contracts. Examples of SLAs include:

- delivery to due date and time
- adherence to agreed cost
- adherence to agreed reliability standards
- adherence to agreed standards of consistency
- ability to change in response to changing conditions or requirements
- ability to innovate and improve in design or production
- quality of service in delivery.

Learning activity 8.3

Analyse the contractual terms used by your own organisation relating to supplier performance criteria, indicating the potential pitfalls for compliance.

Feedback on page 143

Standardisation

Specification performance can be improved with the application of performance standards.

These can be compiled by the organisation to enable consistent functional processes, or they can be borrowed from associations to which the parties belong. Commonly used are national or international standards such as ISO 9000:2000 which is a useful benchmark for quality systems. Standards will improve performance through the reduction of waste, reduction in error, less reliance on specialist suppliers, less need to buy expensive brands, reduction in costs for material handling and the reduced investment in spares. International standards have contributed to the successful growth in international sourcing.

Self-assessment question 8.3

Draft a contractual term that seeks compliance with standards of quality expected by your organisation.

Feedback on page 143

Revision question

Now try the revision question for this session on page 342.

Summary

Effective relationships must be maintained throughout the supply chain if organisational performance is to be maintained over a long period of time. This requires specific skills of those communicating to ensure clarity of purpose and ensures compliance with the organisation's objectives, but also in a style which ensures consideration of supplier needs. Support systems in the form of clear contractual agreements and accurate and precise specifications provide the formal structure to the buyer-supplier relationship.

Suggested further reading

Read the chapter on matching supply with demand in Lysons and Farrington (2006).

Feedback on learning activities and self-assessment questions

Feedback on learning activity 8.1

We have seen from the text that effective communication involves a clear message and transparent meaning. Communications can easily be distorted through the injection of 'noise' so it is essential that the communicator has the appropriate skills (drafting expertise?) and knowledge, especially in technical areas such as specifications. Some clarity can be obtained by the use of templates and other supportive systems. Specifications require precision and accuracy of language. Ambiguity will lead to possible confusion or non-compliance, and potential complications in the relationship with the supplier.

Feedback on self-assessment question 8.1

Much depends upon the scope and demands made upon the supplier, who will respond according to their capability. With first tier suppliers, who may have been involved in the initial stages of product design, the problems will mainly be to do with any subsequent changes. Where involvement has not been a major factor then the supplier will naturally have some concerns about standards imposed in the specification if they are non-routine. Issues about cost and price will arise, which must be resolved if production is to be of a satisfactory level. Other issues may surround the capability of untried suppliers and their capability in complying with tight buyer specifications. Materials used, production processes and achievement of performance standards will all be potential issues.

Feedback on learning activity 8.2

It is essential that the process of agreeing the specification is sound. An organisation will usually base the specification around some template structure to ensure consistency, such as the British Standards 7373. Because of its importance in establishing clear supplier standards, the process of agreeing the specification will require a layered process of involvement of other cross-functional personnel, for example engineers and designers and possibly the legal team, plus approval of a senior company official, depending upon the importance of the specification.

Feedback on self-assessment question 8.2

There can be no deviation from the specification otherwise there will be an unacceptable corruption of the internally agreed performance standards, and also the contract of purchase may itself be varied. However, there must be a procedure for dealing with points of clarification, and if this does lead to changes to the specification, a process of formal approval must take place.

Feedback on learning activity 8.3

Key terms within buyer's contracts will include conditions relating to quality, delivery, risk, pricing, the detailed specification, and so on. The involvement of lawyers will ensure that all foreseeable events are covered by a contractual stipulation. However, it is still a good exercise to consider and examine the detail surrounding the quality issues, for example, the extent to which the supplier must comply with performance standards post delivery. Is there a warranty in place and how long does it last? Another area of occasional ambiguity surrounds the precise moment when delivery and risk passes to the buyer. Who, for example, is responsible for the goods during transit? Is there a force majeure clause in place and how is it actioned?

Feedback on self-assessment question 8.3

A quality clause should be clear and unambiguous. The standard of quality should be referenced to any specification in place and perhaps indicate the consequences of non-compliance, a reference to an inspection process, the right to reject and any potential claim for damages. Buyers might also include a clause stating the warranty that would be required post delivery.

8

8

Managing costs and improving value

Introduction

Cost reduction is an essential aspect of modern life as organisations seek to maintain a competitive position within the market. Only by working closely with supplies will systems become embedded that ensure the achievement of minimal stock levels, and prices and costs controlled and reduced over a period of time as improvements enter the supply chain.

A lean supply organisation is one in which 'there is dynamic competition and collaboration of equals in the supply chain, aimed at adding value at minimum total cost'
Lysons and Farrington (2006)

Session learning objectives

After completing this session you should be able to:

9.1 Explain how cost reduction programmes are a normal part of business strategy.
9.2 Evaluate the techniques for delivery of acceptable price changes.
9.3 Describe how contracts are used to produce price decreases.
9.4 Give examples of how the customer can contribute to cost reductions.
9.5 Assess the importance of introducing tighter stock control systems.
9.6 Describe and evaluate JIT and stockless purchasing models.

Unit content coverage

Learning objective

2.3 Manage cost reduction for organisational efficiency and provide added value to customers.

Prior knowledge

Familiarity with issues of cost as part of the whole procurement process.

Resources

Access to organisational strategies and procedures on cost and price.

Timing

You should set aside about 5 hours to read and complete this session, including learning activities, self-assessment questions, the suggested further reading (if any) and the revision question.

9.1 Cost reduction programmes

The strategic direction

The strategic direction of the business will be based on the three broad approaches:

- Stability: in which the organisation continues with the same line of products and makes steady improvement.
- Growth: a more aggressive look for new products, markets and processes.
- Retrenchment: where any improvement is at the expense of cutting back.

Learning activity 9.1

Review of the Supermarkets code of practice by the Office of Fair Trading

The OFT's review of the Supermarkets Code of Practice, in early 2004, found widespread belief among suppliers that the Code is not working effectively. There is no hard evidence to support this, however. The OFT therefore proposed to commission further work to establish how supermarkets deal with suppliers under the Code.

Following a consultation with suppliers, their trade associations and Asda, Sainsbury's, Safeway and Tesco, 80 to 85 per cent of respondents claimed the Code has failed to bring about any change in the supermarkets' behaviour.

Despite anecdotal evidence that the Code is not working, no cases have gone to mediation under the Code. Nor has the OFT received any detailed information from suppliers or trade associations about alleged breaches of the Code. This has made it impossible to draw any firm conclusions as to how individual supermarkets are operating under the Code, though it is clear that widespread dissatisfaction amongst suppliers continues.

Fear of complaining was the main reason identified for the Code's perceived lack of effectiveness. Seventy-three per cent of respondents reported a fear of complaining amongst suppliers.

The concept of 'reasonableness' used in many of the Code's terms was also seen by suppliers to allow the supermarkets to interpret the Code to the detriment of suppliers, leading to uncertainty about some of Code's key provisions and increasing reluctance to complain.

The four supermarkets themselves each express a commitment to the Code and believe that relations with suppliers are generally good. However, the OFT has no evidence from the supermarkets that their relationships with suppliers had changed significantly since the introduction of the Code.

Given the reluctance of suppliers to provide specific evidence of alleged breaches of the Code, the OFT intends to obtain information from the

(continued on next page)

Learning activity 9.1 *(continued)*

supermarkets by conducting a focused compliance audit of each of the four supermarkets' dealings with suppliers.

The audit will involve a sample examination of the supermarkets' records of dealings with their grocery suppliers, focusing particularly on the clauses of the Code where claims of breaches were more frequently identified by suppliers.

Question

The above extract from the website of the OFT indicates the success of the major supermarkets in driving down costs in order to secure a competitive position in the market. To what extent do you feel that this is a successful strategy and a template for future procurement strategies from powerful buyers?

Feedback on page 157

A competitive position

Irrespective of the strategy, the business needs to compete in its marketplace. In competitive markets the organisation must take decisions on how to combat the strategies of rivals. If a business fails to grow at the rate of its competitors it faces the possibility that the competitors gain a cost advantage through economies of scale and experience as they tackle larger and more complex markets with the accompanying logistics.

Porter (1998a) proposed three generic strategies for organisations:

* Differentiation: where the quality, service, speed of response or brand distinguishes it from other competitive products. Small improvements may not be enough.
* Cost leadership: in which customers are attracted because the business operates more efficiently than others. Low costs that can be transformed into something that customers see as value is a major competitive advantage.
* Focus: a differentiation or cost leadership strategy aimed at niche segments of the market.

Whatever path is adopted, it can be seen that cost is at the centre of many strategies, and even those organisations that differentiate themselves at the higher end of the market will still need to keep an eye on costs so that profits generated satisfy key stakeholders. It is just as important that Fortnum & Mason makes a good profit as it is for a mainstream supermarket.

At certain times organisations will be pursuing a position in a growing market as for example when implementing new technology. Using the terminology of the Boston Consultancy Group's matrix, new products need to appear as 'stars' rather than 'question marks' with low market share. Building a position in any market requires substantial investment, which in itself can only come initially from cash reserves or borrowing. The more profitable companies are in a stronger position to adapt to the fast pace of growing markets and make the necessary investment.

The 'lean' production model is only successful if supported by a 'lean' supplier base, which has at its heart a concentration on both cost and value for the ultimate customer. While the price on a contract is important, an attempt to share costs and to examine the total costs of the supply is a more effective measure.

Supply costs are clearly an influence on the organisation's overall costs and can be particularly important in supply chains where competitive pressure means margins are low. Managing input costs becomes critical if any value added is to be achieved.

Lamming argues that target costing is a successful partnership arrangement within the Japanese manufacturing industry, and by working closely to seek out ways in which cost reduction can be made, costs and prices can be driven downwards.

It is recognised that organisations should expect their unit costs to decline over a period of time or face the consequences of competitive pressure.

9

Self-assessment question 9.1

Examine your own organisation and outline the steps taken to achieve cost reductions through logistical adjustments from order through to delivery.

Feedback on page 157

9.2 The techniques for delivery of acceptable price changes

Obtaining the best price

Buyers obtain prices from the suppliers in several ways:

- price lists
- quoted prices from an internal price list or estimated on request
- bids or tenders.

In addition, negotiation will take place to seek the best available price in line with business needs.

Obtaining competitive prices in new and existing supplier agreements is a fundamental task of the buyer. There are several techniques for delivering the best price including *competitive bidding or tendering*.

A standard approach to obtaining bids for supplies streamlines the process and makes comparisons easier. Bids should only be requested from suitable suppliers otherwise time and money is wasted on making comparative assessments.

Learning activity 9.2

Review the events within your own organisation that contribute to price changes and show how procedures ensure that the best price is incorporated into the contract.

Feedback on page 157

The impact of the product life cycle

As a product moves through the cycle of introduction, growth, maturity and decline, the price will vary dramatically during these stages. For example, at the earlier stage of the product cycle it may be possible for the supplier to implement a differential price because of the scarcity of the products – a pricing strategy known as 'skimming'. As other competitors enter the market, lower prices will be offered to obtain market share.

Costs and prices

Whether the goods supplied are priced on a cost-price, cost-plus or target pricing basis, buyers will be able to look for justification of the costings and will have scope for negotiation over time in competitive situations.

Discounts

There are a number of ways in which a discount can be negotiated by the buyer including:

- Recognition of prompt payment.
- Quantity discounts, although there is some risk in taking additional quantities if they are to be stored, and this has to be compared with the benefits of possible additional production at marginal costs. If a contract is extended beyond the typical twelve months (subject to acceptable termination or option clauses), it may be possible to secure an additional discount for the longevity of the contract.
- Discounts for technical breakthrough by the supplier. It would be expected that some of the benefits will be passed down the supply chain.
- Discounts can be given to intermediaries, where stockists or agents take responsibility for the distribution down the supply chain.
- Special discounts are possible for seasonal variations in demand, and promotional offers.

Irrespective of the price discounting offered by the supplier, buyers will often undertake a price analysis of the offered price to ensure that by breaking the price down into constituent elements the reasonableness of the price or price change is determined. This analysis will be based upon previous experience of price increases, information supplied by the vendor and other comparative market factors.

9

149

Traditionally the buyer has concentrated on price but by working closely with the supplier it is possible to drive out unnecessary costs in the supply chain.

9.3   The use of contracts to produce price decreases

The negotiation of contracts with suppliers

Effective negotiation ensures that prices are reduced wherever possible and price rises are contained within agreed limits or formulae. By incorporating a bidding process for the larger contracts, the buyer can achieve greater savings. The increasing use of e-procurement where it is linked to e-auctions has seen buyers obtain keener prices in competitive supply situations.

The negotiation of contracts centrally will enable the consolidation of demand and the aggregation of all orders into one contract, therefore benefiting from the maximum quantity discounts. Establishing master contracts for all of the major suppliers will also eliminate any potential disputes in the future if standard contracts are used by both parties, and in doing so precipitating a potential 'battle of the forms'. Such negotiations will be preceded with a detailed value analysis to eliminate unnecessary features.

Proactive sourcing rather than reliance on repeat ordering will generate a competitive spirit amongst the supplier base. The specification should also include as much standardised components as is possible, and also should look to source complete sub-assemblies rather than individual components.

Incentives

As contracts become more complex and the need for superior performance greater, then the buyer may consider incentivising the contract to achieve increased performance including cost reductions. These contracts will work if they align closely with the corporate strategy and direction of the organisation, and have mechanisms that deliver mutual gain (win-win) from the achievement.

There is a variety of incentive types but they could include:

- Extending the contract if performance criteria are met.
- Achievement of a project ahead of time.
- Target cost achieved or reduced.
- A discretionary award if ultimate customer satisfaction is achieved.

Learning curves

In complex work it has been proven that organisations learn to shorten the manufacturing times per unit, and as a result bring about a reduction in the unit cost. This learning rate can be expressed quantitatively and be built into the purchase agreement.

Self-assessment question 9.3

In what circumstances would a supplier wish to increase prices during the lifetime of the contract? What mechanism is used to ensure that any price increase is acceptable?

Feedback on page 158

9

9.4 The buyer's contribution to cost reductions

End-use customers are becoming more demanding so it is important for organisations to continue to innovate by making continuous changes to their products. Every aspect of the customer offering must be reviewed if customer loyalty and interest is to be maintained.

In addition, 'breakthrough' innovations will secure a more substantial competitive advantage for the innovator and the potential for enhanced profits, until competitors respond with similar products. Sometimes it is macro forces that give the incentive to take on new markets, a technological breakthrough, a shift in the economic fortunes of a country or region, changes in government policy or legislation, new material inventions, shifts in customer expectations or new distribution channels.

Opportunities for innovation arise from many sources. Doole and Lowe (2005) identify a number of sources:

- scientific invention
- adjusting products to anticipated customer needs
- redefining the product so that further market segments are reached
- applying existing techniques and technologies in new sectors

- eliminating a link in the supply chain
- revamping products in mature markets.

Technology is a factor behind many breakthrough strategies, and R&D investment can create much change in the marketplace, and set new standards for the rest of the market to catch up with. However, all technology has in itself a life cycle and eventually improvements to the existing technology slow and the search is on for something more innovative.

Learning activity 9.4

The performance of computers has improved considerably in recent years with the development of faster and smaller microprocessors. Research the background to the development of the microprocessor. What are the trends in increased performance? To what extent do you think the technology is reaching the end of its life cycle? What would be the best methods for selecting an appropriate source? You might want to track the rivalry between the major players, Intel and AMD, to explore the extent of choice in the market.

Feedback on page 158

Also, the extent of the organisation's fortunes with any new product will depend upon its acceptance in the marketplace. The speed at which it is 'diffused' into the marketplace and taken up by competitors will determine the eventual profitability of this particular product. The rate of diffusion will depend on whether the new innovation within a product or service is continuous, whereby the behaviour of the buying end user does not have to change, or discontinuous, whereby the end user will have to adapt to new processes and technology.

Any new product launch will have a degree of risk attached to it, especially proactive new product innovations which may require considerable sums of money to establish in the market. This reinforces the idea behind early supplier involvement in the design and development of the product so that the product development has a greater chance of success.

As new products are developed, the buyer will be contributing to the effective procurement of materials and components through its specification in a number of ways:

- quality assurance or defect prevention
- value engineering and value analysis
- discussion with the design department about the availability and cost of materials
- evaluation of cheaper alternative methods
- agreement of alternatives when specified materials are not available
- importance of buying complete systems rather than individual components

- discussions about buying rather than making
- building co-makership/designership relationships
- creation of an information centre surrounding the design and development.

In addition, the buyer will contribute a different approach to the purchasing process which may be different from the design orientation. In particular the focus on costs and waste, the importance of just-in-time delivery, the emphasis on the lowest ultimate costs and elimination of unnecessary costs will bring a commercial edge to the development process. The buyer will also be able to advise on acceptable levels of quality and tolerance, and the suitability of materials, rather than pursuing standards that are not appropriate for the design build.

Self-assessment question 9.4

Research three examples of a specific technological breakthrough that has reduced costs within your own organisation.

Feedback on page 158

9

9.5 The importance of introducing tighter stock control systems

Introduction

The management of inventory fulfils many objectives including:

- The provision of a quality service to customers.
- The avoidance of overstocking and bottlenecks.
- Keeping costs to a minimum by variety reduction, economical lot sizes and cost analysis of carrying inventories. Variety reduction can make substantial cost savings on the inventory if there is both rationalising and standardisation of components and parts kept in stock.

Learning activity 9.5

Provide an overview of your organisational approaches to stock levels and the impact of excessive stocks to the cost and efficiency base of the business.

Feedback on page 159

Baily et al (2004) refer to a number of policies used by purchasing in selecting stocks including:

- Blanket orders so that inefficiently small quantities are not ordered.

- Capacity booking orders in which reserve supplier capacity is made.
- Period contracts whereby an estimated total quantity for the agreed period is made, and an agreed price.
- Period contracts with specified delivery dates and quantities.
- Spot and futures contracts, especially for commodities.
- 'Order-up-to' systems – often used in the retail sector.
- Part-period balancing and other systems used by manufacturers operating MRP or Kanban systems.

Whatever system is operated by the organisation and the purchasing function, control of stock levels is important so that there is an efficient balance in providing a service to the organisation, including situations when mistakes are made in the planning process, against control of costs and waste. Some organisations adopt an ABC or Pareto analysis in which more attention to order quantities, price comparisons and stock levels is paid to those stocks that have the greatest impact on the business.

A good, efficient stock ordering system reduces the ordering and set-up costs and lead times so that ordered quantities are smaller. Lead times involve the whole process from the time a need is ascertained to the delivery of the goods and components. A substantial part of this process involves administration by the buyer, and is therefore within their control and can be improved with more efficient systems. This will be complemented with accurate forecasts of future demand.

For greater efficiency, models are used to assist the ordering process. Algebraic formulae can be used to establish an economic order quantity (EOQ) quantity discount model (see Lysons and Farrington (2006) for an account of the mathematical approach).

Self-assessment question 9.5

Undertake primary research into the costs and potential savings from using intermediary sourcing organisations.

Feedback on page 159

9.6 JIT and stockless purchasing models

The impact of JIT

Tight control leads naturally on to just-in-time (JIT). Originally developed in the Toyota Motor Company in the 1960s, this is a 'philosophy of manufacturing based on planned elimination of all waste and continuous improvement of productivity'. It is about the meeting of customer needs when required but by using the minimum resources of people, machinery and material. 'Big JIT' or lean production concentrates on eliminating waste from all sources of the organisational processes, whereas 'Little JIT' concentrates on material scheduling and inventory levels.

Learning activity 9.6

What are the benefits of your own organisation implementing JIT techniques?

Outline the disadvantages of moving towards stockless systems.

Feedback on page 159

The objectives of JIT:

- zero defects so that the quality expectations of the customer are exceeded
- zero set-up time
- zero inventories
- zero handling – wherever possible eliminate all non-value added handling
- zero lead time – impossible in some industries but the aim is to use small batches of components or assemblies
- lot size of one, which enables speedy adaptation if the market changes.

To be successful, JIT requires:

- uniform master production schedules
- 'pull' production systems, with a close linkage with the design function
- good relationships with suppliers over a longer period of time
- short distances between customer and supplier
- reliable delivery, all parts must arrive on time
- consistent quality with zero defects
- standardisation of components and methods
- material flow system
- a reliable supplier certification programme
- effective evaluation of supplier performance.

The JIT purchasing system works classically with production and links to a Kanban system (meaning a ticket or signal) and refers to an information system in which instructions relating to the type and quantity of items to be withdrawn from the preceding manufacturing process are conveyed by a card that is attached to a storage and transport container.

The advantages of JIT include:

- reduced stock levels of purchased supplies
- enhanced product quality and reduction of scrap and waste
- greater productivity and less rework
- shorter manufacturing lead times
- greater flexibility in changing the production mix
- faster design response
- smoother production flow and fewer disruptions through late deliveries

9

* greater workplace participation
* higher productivity
* reduced space relationships
* improved relationships with suppliers.

There are, however, organisational problems:

* Adequate systems must be in place to allow effective communication down the supply chain.
* Forecasting must not be faulty.
* Suppliers do not always perform to specification.
* Failure to hold any buffer stocks can be a considerable risk, and this includes the class C goods which can on occasions cause major disruption if not available.
* Short life-cycle goods do not fit well with JIT systems because of the pace of change.
* JIT is more suitable with flow production lines rather than batch production.
* It may not always be possible to negotiate the necessary savings with JIT contracts.
* Transportation disruptions are a feature of congested economies.

Any JIT system needs careful appraisal before implementation, including transportation and environmental costs.

9

Self-assessment question 9.6

Explain what technology is needed to ensure tight stock control and its effectiveness in complex logistical chains.

Feedback on page 159

Revision question

Now try the revision question for this session on page 342.

Summary

Costs and prices can be reduced over time as a result of buying and stockholding strategies, that incorporate price reduction programmes with an expectation that suppliers will seek to reduce the costs in their own operations, plus a willingness to cooperate with the buyer for the benefit of both organisations.

Suggested further reading

Read the chapter on sourcing and supplier information in Lysons and Farrington (2006).

Feedback on learning activities and self-assessment questions

Feedback on learning activity 9.1

Price reduction is a key strategy for buyers because of the need to remain competitive. Use of bargaining power is a legitimate tactic in all negotiating situations. However, it is a strategy not without some risk if it alienates suppliers, or attracts attention from the regulatory powers. It must also be noted that a competitive market for the suppliers will ensure that they in turn remain competitive and look to improve their performance and reduce waste. In addition there will often be a response to a buyer's perceived power within the supply chain as suppliers seek alliances and mergers to build their own negotiating position.

Feedback on self-assessment question 9.1

Cost is at the centre of most businesses and is often the key focus as indicated in the Porter model. The rate of cost change by suppliers will depend upon many factors. Profitability is an issue as this will enable investment in greater step changes if appropriate. In all cases a business which is to survive must be looking for some changes throughout these processes from inputs to outputs. Organisations will usually scan the environment to establish what incremental and breakthrough technologies are available which might create a more efficient workplace.

Feedback on learning activity 9.2

Many buyers will have a strategy of constant price reduction from suppliers as a result of competitive activity or the need to establish market share within an industry. In addition there should be examples of price changes as a result of improvements in technology, systems and administration, supplier initiatives and, of course, the extension of the supply chain sources to cheaper markets.

Buyers will also be looking for price improvements from existing and new suppliers as a result of the normal activities of offering discounts, seeking tenders for more important supplies, and regular negotiations.

It is essential, for example, that a discounting strategy bears fruit with savings for bulk supply.

Feedback on self-assessment question 9.2

1   Discounts: There are a number of ways in which a discount can be negotiated by the buyer including:
    - Recognition of prompt payment.
    - Quantity discounts: some discounts can be given to intermediaries, where stockists or agents take responsibility for the distribution down the supply chain.
    - Special discounts are possible for seasonal variations in demand, and promotional offers.

9

- In addition, negotiation with the supplier as a result of regular pricing reviews and analysis will secure additional reductions.
2 The contract can provide for greater discounts if the length of supply is extended beyond the traditional one year, subject to contractual clauses that allow for some variation of the length of contract.

Feedback on learning activity 9.3

- The use of tenders or a bidding process will often be successful in obtaining discounts on larger orders. The increasing use of e-auctions often leads to keener prices.
- Positive sourcing will ensure a constant competitive edge amongst the supply base.
- Value analysis of all products purchased will eliminate any unnecessary waste.
- The use of supplier incentives if price reductions are achieved.
- An expectation, which will be established during the negotiation process, that suppliers' costs will fall as they become more experienced in the production process.
- There will be some supplier resistance to changes in the negotiation process and the expectation of price reduction. Some resistance will be overcome because the business approach is one that becomes sound practice. Other specific resistance will be discussed as part of the negotiation process and where possible help and support given to overcome barriers.

Feedback on self-assessment question 9.3

Supply costs will increase as they face increases in the cost base over a period of time. Negotiations and contract clauses will ensure that the cost is only passed on if it is appropriate, and after some of the cost increases are absorbed by the supplier. Benchmarks against price indices and other competitors will ensure that the increases are not ahead of the competition in the market.

Feedback on learning activity 9.4

The microprocessor revolution is a demonstration of how some technology increases at a pace faster than first expected, with huge gains in speed being achieved in a relatively short period of time. Buyers have to keep abreast of such breakthrough technology as it will have a significant impact on their product development and cost base. However, not all technology moves at the same speed. In addition, there has to be some understanding as to when the technology reaches the end of its own life cycle and therefore future investment will diminish.

Feedback on self-assessment question 9.4

Answers no doubt will include the microprocessor and related computer technology, software programs, robotics and enhanced material development.

Feedback on learning activity 9.5

Most organisations have adopted some form of lean supply to reduce the cost of stockholding and the possibility of unsold or obsolescent stock. Examples should be given from JIT techniques to reserve supplies held by suppliers. Commodity buying may be mentioned, in which the future contracts are made to ensure regular supplies as required.

Feedback on self-assessment question 9.5

Where supplies are difficult to achieve through the usual channels, the use of intermediaries such as for the commodity markets, export houses and e-markets will ensure regular supplies at a competitive price.

Feedback on learning activity 9.6

The use of zero stock levels, lead time and handling can create a strong competitive edge through cost reduction and the expensive management of the stockholding. The improvements in manufacturing and design response times will be significant, smoother manufacturing operations and potentially higher productivity.

This is an objective of many organisations, although it does require good logistical systems that ensure an efficient materials flow system, good tracking, monitoring and control systems, sound inspection and quality systems and of course reliable delivery.

Feedback on self-assessment question 9.6

There is a requirement for administrative and software systems that are good at forecasting, a system that accurately and speedily communicates all aspects of the JIT system including the tracking of supplies, their quality and potential disruptions.

9

9

Involving the suppliers

Introduction

The supply chain must be protected from risks to the business and risk of supplier underperforming. The effective management of supplier development, the building of long-term and sustainable relationships will help manage that risk, as will a careful assessment and management plan to protect the business from any major supplier problems.

On Tuesday morning, September 11, 2001, the US is attacked by terrorists in New York City and Washington, and the world changes forever.

Worldnews.com

Session learning objectives

After completing this session you should be able to:

10.1 Compare joint performance systems with standard vendor assessments.
10.2 Explain how more complex feedback systems can improve performance of suppliers.
10.3 Evaluate the effectiveness of supplier risk management.

10

Unit content coverage

Learning objective

2.4 Plan and develop a well-structured approach to measuring the performance of suppliers.

Prior knowledge

Awareness of the concept of risk.

Resources

Access to the organisation's disaster recovery plan.

Timing

You should set aside about 5 hours to read and complete this session, including learning activities, self-assessment questions, the suggested further reading (if any) and the revision question.

10.1 Joint performance systems

Partnerships and cross-functional relationships

Partnering relationships

Increasingly, in many sectors enterprises are considering, or have ventured into, a partnership agreement with suppliers. In the face of rapid changes occurring in drivers, such as cost management and increasing competition, suppliers have made drastic changes in the way they conduct business. Changing regulations, a consolidation of the supply base and changing consumer demands are some of the market forces that have played a role in the growing number of partnerships between an enterprise and its trading partners. Partnerships or alliances make sense when there is:

* synergy, where customers and suppliers seek to identify opportunities that arise from joint activities
* collaborative strategy development
* risk and gain sharing
* joint problem-solving activity
* mutual incentive to improve products and processes
* creation of common goals
* trust
* a long-term commitment
* increased information sharing
* increased communication.

It has been suggested that collaborative alliances are suitable for organisations where:

* there is a possibility of adding value to a product
* strengthening operations by lowering systems costs
* adding technological strength
* enhancing strategic growth
* enhancing organisational skills
* building financial strength.

Cross-functional relationships

Cross-functional collaboration, when individuals attempt to integrate their diverse knowledge and experiences into solutions that provide synergy more than the sum of the parts, or add value, is often difficult. Such relationships involve moving towards a partnership style agreement, which becomes essentially long-term and emphasises cooperation and community of interest between the purchaser and supplier.

Concepts such as team, group, cohesiveness, group maturity, creativity or decision making cross these boundaries and influence each other in complex ways. Different individuals and groups have diverse, often conflicting, perspectives and insights on the process.

One of the common approaches to organisational design is the bureaucratic organisation in which managers coordinate the work of multiple functional specialists on various tasks which are then integrated into a common whole.

However, this situation is changing in response to a variety of driving forces. These include the need to control costs in the face of higher levels of

10

competition and increasingly demanding customers. The introduction of new technology which has allowed for speedy communications throughout the supply chain has increased the possibility of easier collaboration.

The increasing complexity and specialisation of business has meant that in order to survive and thrive, a company has to use other organisations, including suppliers who have specialist knowledge and technical expertise to perform some of the functions. The traditional view of such a relationship is conducted at arm's length. This view is changing with first tier suppliers, and a move to more integrated strategic alliances is occurring more frequently.

The implementation and success of cross-functional working depends on a range of factors and decisions. The first of these decisions relates to the way in which relationships are supported.

Policy deployment

If the purchasing and supply function chooses to use a purchasing policy, there are a number of challenges. Effort is often spent in introducing and agreeing purchasing policies. This is time-consuming as well as costly, and when introduced they are very difficult to regulate. The purchasing department may find that much of its time is spent dealing with disparate staff groups who feel that purchasing and supply is trying to erode both their authority and autonomy, and are resisting attempts to ensure that they optimise spend, or even adhere to purchasing policies. In addition, these policies can often become outdated very quickly, which makes the work of the purchasing and supply function even harder.

Of course, this situation is changing as more and more enterprises install electronic procurement systems where spend limits can be preset and all procurement takes place through a desktop buy-side system, but principles still apply.

Cross-functional teams

Here the purchasing and supply department might wish to consider the operational stimulus for cross-functional working. Is the process going to be based around and focused on:

- Quality?
- Customer service?
- Innovation in product or service design or delivery?
- Cost reduction?
- Delivery improvement?
- Improvements in product or service flexibility?

Learning activity 10.1

Develop and present a model for collaborative teams, indicating the areas where collaborative work is possible within your own organisational supply base.

Feedback on page 174

10

Collaborative working in practice

Where intra-functional relationships are supported by information technology, there are still issues that relate to both structure and information. There is often no proven basis for the modelling and sharing of information to support decision making by cross-functional and multiorganisational teams.

It is a challenge to combine different disciplines and cultures and to integrate sets of information and representations to support cross-functional access, interaction and decision making.

However, essentially all decision making by cross-functional teams needs to consider large, disparate data sets. They need, though, at least some access to each other's information, which is typically embedded in discipline-specific legacy applications or paper-based systems which may be robust, but are frequently time-consuming and inflexible.

Organisations also have to consider the downsides, not least the fact that their core competences might be weakened by an alliance or partnership. For example, the entry into the PC market during the 1980s by IBM was facilitated by an alliance with Intel, who designed the microprocessor. Although IBM quickly captured market share over Apple Computers, it later suffered damaging competition from Compaq who entered the market with the microprocessor that was developed through the alliance. This loss of control has to be balanced against logistical strengths. Many large organisations have divested aspects of their logistics to other suppliers so that they can concentrate on their core competences.

The success of the retail industry in meeting customer expectations has been attributed in part to the closer relationships that have developed within the supply chain, which have enabled point-of-sale data from retailers to be transmitted to the suppliers, who can synchronise their production efforts to match sales within the retail establishments. This can either be done through a system that continuously replenishes the retailers' stock or is based on the vendor managing the stock levels in response to trends in demand and responding rapidly to retailer demands.

The closer relationship will also need to be supported by contractual agreement that deals with confidentiality as well as the usual measures dealing with performance, ownership, and ordering responsibilities.

However, a major strength of collaborative working comes through quality of performance. Negotiations that concentrate merely on price may lead to quality suffering. In addition, concepts such as JIT, communication and replenishment are difficult to manage with multiple suppliers, so the reduction of the supply base brings greater efficiency but also greater interdependence.

Establishing closer relationships or 'partnerships' with first tier suppliers will be a dynamic relationship, with change a constant process. Improvement in performance will stem not just from the standard vendor rating and assessment system, which is a traditional buyer-supplier assessment, but from a constant dialogue and the seamless integration of a number of activities.

Self-assessment question 10.1

Explain how your collaborative partnerships with first tier suppliers might lead to improved and consistent high quality service.

Feedback on page 174

10.2 Developing the performance of suppliers

Supplier development?

As with so much else in the field of supply chain management, supplier development means different things to different people. Some people refer to competitive tendering as 'supplier development' as it helps the supplier develop tendering skills. For other buyers, supplier development may consist of statistical process control workshops.

For the purposes of this section we can suggest that supplier development consists of a range of activities integrated into a relatively seamless whole to ensure effective supply chain management. These activities may include:

- sourcing strategy
- vendor assessment (surveys, site visits)
- supplier rating and qualification
- supplier award programmes
- use of new technology (for example, computer-supported collaborative working, advanced planning and scheduling)
- cross- or multidisciplinary teamworking
- supply base reduction
- joint supplier problem-solving team
- supplier development 1 (Kaizen teams)
- supplier development 2 (redesign of internal processes)
- electronic data interchange
- supplier associations (Kyoryoku Kai)
- longer-term contracts
- partnership (win-win negotiation, partnering agreements)
- lean supply (JIT, for example)
- standards development
- supplier tiering
- cost analysis methods (VA, ABC, WLC, TCO)
- cost management.

As can be seen, many of these processes refer to the manufacturing sector. This is because much supplier development work grew from quality control and assurance problems experienced in that sector. This is not to say that the principles of supplier development cannot also be applied in service industries. The use of process redesign across organisational boundaries can also be useful to service enterprises, as can the use of contracting strategies.

10

Sourcing strategy for supplier development

The objectives of a sourcing strategy should be in keeping with the philosophy of the extended enterprise, which is to ensure that suppliers have the capacity and capability to match systems and policies with the enterprise's current and changing needs. Communications and feedback to the supply base are essential if these needs are to remain aligned to the organisational strategy.

Many organisations that are global in scope base sourcing policy upon raw materials and labour costs. This can be mitigated by the need for technical innovation. Enterprises that work in technically sophisticated markets may need to consider a range of issues when sourcing. Environmental pressure groups, ethical issues, plant and distribution hub locations all contribute to make sourcing decisions politically sensitive as well as price sensitive.

In addition, an emphasis on early supplier involvement in the design process and supplier innovation will impact on sourcing decisions, as will the need to ensure continuity of supply. This can also have an effect on sourcing policies, as an enterprise may prefer, in some cases, supply assurance over part price. In some industries, the majority of an enterprise's suppliers will be situated in areas contiguous with their plants.

Supply base reduction or rationalisation also has an impact on sourcing. Suppliers may be brought into an extended enterprise to act as first tier supply team leaders. An enterprise may assign a particular supplier to act as team leader for particular platform groups.

10

Learning activity 10.2

Examine the methods by which your own organisation contributes to supplier development.

Feedback on page 174

Analysis strategy for supplier development

Objectives

Supplier development is expensive. This means that it is important to target efforts carefully. There is little point in carrying out supplier development with a first tier supplier if the problems lie in the second or even third tier. This means using an analysis strategy to identify the capabilities and competences of different suppliers within different supply categories or platform groupings. These capacity profiles can be used to match suppliers to particular projects and issues within the product development and manufacturing process.

Processes

It can require considerable effort to identify suppliers in both first and lower tiers. This, in the case of manufacturing enterprises, may be carried out on a platform-specific basis. 'Platform' in this case refers to a specific group of manufacturing processes carried out to produce a particular product.

One way of analysing data is to develop supplier capability profiles. These profiles can be used to identify suppliers with complementary skills and capacity to carry out specific projects.

As well as looking at individual suppliers, analysis also needs to look at the relationships between suppliers. In this way an understanding of the complexity of the supply chain becomes clear and the supplier development task can be broken down into manageable chunks.

Analysis enables purchasing and supply to identify opportunities for cost savings and innovation by eliminating gaps and overlaps within the extended enterprise and enabling better distribution of work tasks across business processes.

Carrying out an analysis might involve a range of actions including supply chain mapping and business process analysis workshops.

Communication strategy for supplier development

Objectives

Communication is perhaps perceived as the major tool in supplier development. Communication is the way in which trust can be developed, information acquired and shared and business opportunities identified. The objectives of a communication strategy may be to create seamless relationships across an extended enterprise, which will involve and motivate suppliers to identify opportunities for improvement.

Processes

There are a number of elements within any communication strategy which contribute to its overall effectiveness. Perhaps the most important of these is to introduce and maintain a strong, unambiguous message that both staff and suppliers within an extended enterprise can understand and then subscribe to. In many organisations this message has been about price or total quality. Increasingly, we can see organisations turning to the fulfilment of customer needs as a message. Some enterprises in technically complex sectors, such as aircraft assembly or semiconductor manufacture, may flag innovation as a way of avoiding future costs. The quality and credibility of the message is a key factor in supplier development.

Once the key message has been designed, it needs to be supported by an internal programme of education and training. Effective internal communication is supported by extensive use of cross-functional teams (CFTs). These may, in turn, be supported by trained facilitators to help avoid some of the problems CFTs face in their initial stages. This is also assisted by the use of a range of information and communication technologies.

Communication for the purposes of supplier development means that everyone needs to hear the same message and buy in to the same key objectives. Everyone needs to work to manage costs, improve quality, ensure delivery, improve customer satisfaction or capitalise on existing technological advances. One critical element of communication is also about the future. This may involve committing to existing suppliers when developing a new technology or process.

Message effectiveness can be improved by ensuring that it is repeated by the buying enterprise, and also by other enterprises and trade associations. In this sense, communication is marketing. Multiple communication channels increase message credibility and effectiveness where messages from one customer may be ignored. One way in which external communication infrastructure can be developed is through supplier conferences. Conference areas may be dedicated to specific issues: cross-platform issues or strategic issues.

The purpose of these conferences is to improve the business relationship with the suppliers through a bi-directional communication channel and provide recognition for their efforts and work in achieving preferred supplier status (if supplier awards and tiering are used). Strategic conferences may address the accomplishments of suppliers as a group and recognise their achievements through a supplier certification process. Platform-specific conferences may look at suppliers for a given programme and discuss current platform plans and future marketing strategies with the specific suppliers.

In addition to the conferences, transactional and relational communication can take place using a variety of EDI and intranet/extranet functions. Communication also takes place through supplier development programmes and supplier award programmes. These are explained in more detail on the following pages.

Infrastructure strategy for supplier development

Objectives

In order to communicate effectively, there is a need for a simple, powerful and consistent message that can be easily communicated, and also for a range of tools that will support that message. Two types of communication can be identified, which rely on different tools. These are:

- relational communication: which may require frequent face-to-face communication supported by phone/email, for example
- transactional communication: which may involve EDI, electronic procurement systems, for example.

This involves developing a broad-based information and communication technology (ICT) infrastructure that will enable the message to be transmitted both internally and externally. This can involve heavy expenditure on both EDI technologies and communication technologies, such as dedicated extranets and e-marketplaces.

Processes

Communication tools need to extend along the chain, but also through the enterprise itself. Where enterprise resource planning (ERP) systems are employed, these may assist in lateral intra-enterprise communication, but within large enterprises this still requires a great deal of investment.

This is not, however, to suggest that even with ERP implementation there is always a total enterprise-wide information infrastructure in place. Again, a lack of strategic planning can mean that more than one corporate intranet exists and that ERP fails to include some functions.

Although comprehensive information infrastructure may be in place, this does not necessarily mean that information is used to its fullest extent. Information can still too often be filed rather than being used, and the very complexity of the information systems used means that there is little cross-referencing between different information systems. In addition, information is not introduced systematically into an overall risk management framework.

Self-assessment question 10.2

Measuring tangible performance from suppliers is relatively straightforward. List some examples of intangible supplier performance that benefits the organisation.

Feedback on page 174

10

10.3 Management of supplier risk

Introduction

Risk management is based on being able to distinguish between an event that is truly random and an event that is the result of cause and effect. Certainly the closer relationships that are being developed with first tier suppliers and their relationships with suppliers further down the supply chain will enable collaborative systems to be in place that detect many risks.

Learning activity 10.3

Identify how your organisation manages supply risk under the following headings:

- Assessment of the risks to the business
- Avoidance of the risks to the business
- Management of the risks to the business.

Feedback on page 174

Risk reduction

Contracting is a risky business and there is no way of eliminating all the risk involved. Although it may be possible to eliminate the risk of quality failures by using Kaizen and lean supply methods, other risks such as lack of innovation may be introduced. This might be because suppliers become so lean that they have no spare resource for research and development.

Risk professionals know that they cannot eliminate risk, but by analysing costs, benefits and methods of risk reduction and mitigation, they can help enterprises and other bodies make informed decisions about risk. Increasingly, risk management rests upon the use of sophisticated analytical techniques for making sense of this information.

The management of risk is a key challenge for supply management. Assessing risk accurately is a critical task for the purchasing and supply function. Approaches to risk can include:

- *Assessment:* To identify the nature of the risk within the supply base – is it a delivery risk, quality risk, a cost risk, a business failure risk? Risk assessment requires that the supply chain be viewed as an end-to-end process and will often require extensive mapping exercises, as well as assessment.
- *Reduction:* Where organisational spend is a high proportion of a supplier's total turnover. Some manufacturing groups in the Far East will not contract with a supplier unless their spend is over 80% of the supplier's total turnover, creating high levels of dependency. This tactic is clearly not available to many purchasers.
- *Avoidance:* One way of avoiding risk is to ensure that purchasing always works with the same suppliers that it has worked with in the past. A drawback here is the fact that existing suppliers may not let us down, but they may not give us the best possible performance either.
- *Management:* This is the use of contractual and relational tactics to ensure that risk is balanced with potential performance. The management of risk depends on the acquisition of good quality information which can be used to predict how often risks are likely to occur and what might cause them. Purchasing can collate data with regard to supplier performance and use similar techniques to forecast supplier failure. The relationship approach that has been discussed in this and other units which forges closer partnership working, its sharing of information, working on product solutions, appraisals, including supplier involvement in the purchasing function's appraisal, and vendor ratings systems, will mitigate against most of the controllable risks.
- *Allocation:* Much of the design and development of contracts is about the allocation of risk to different parties, but it can help to remember that sometimes risk needs to be allocated internally as well as across organisational boundaries.

Once sources and degrees of risk are known, it is possible to propose and implement strategies to reduce risk. It is generally true to say that preventing the occurrence of risk is more effective than dealing with risk once it has occurred.

Managing risk

If risk analysis shows a high risk (valuable and vulnerable), then prevention activities are recommended. For example, a hacker attack on a company's website is easy to attempt and can have a considerable negative impact on the company's reputation and ability to do business. So risk management strategies would put prevention strategies in place such as upgraded firewalls and other security features which would make it harder for the attackers.

On the other hand, if value is high but vulnerability is low, then insurance and back-up activities are recommended. For example, the loss of a key supplier would have a high impact but low probability of occurrence so back-up procedures such as contingency contracts for secondary suppliers are required. In addition, trade disruption insurance might be obtained which, although time limited, would give the enterprise sufficient time to reconfigure the supply chain.

Risk management also includes balancing costs versus benefits for any reduction of risk. Simply put, the cost of risk management measures to reduce the threat should not exceed the value of what is being protected. For example, purchasing managers must be able to justify the cost of security measures, both financial costs and user inconvenience, in light of the expected frequency of risks and the anticipated loss resulting from a risk occurring. So, extensive assessment can be justified to protect a high value contract, but a more limited assessment may be required in a contract which had a lower impact on an enterprise's core activities, remembering the fact that it can be difficult to assess core and non-core activities.

The more serious the risk involved, the more the factors should be broken down and analysed into their individual sub-parts. By breaking down the risk factors into the smallest possible components, we are able to isolate key events and/or determinants and seek to determine how to best manage them. In order to do so, the purchaser must estimate the probability that one of these events that expose us to risk could occur. If the probability of incurring a loss is high, we may decide to avoid it altogether, avoid part of it, develop a contingency plan to deal with it and/or budget funds to deal with its occurrence.

However, when the unforeseen occurs, contingency or crisis plans must be put in place to minimise the effect of the damage on the enterprise's key operations.

Crisis management

The impact of disasters

The 11 September attack on the World Trade Center affected supply chains in a number of ways. Manufacturers that used the web to regulate incoming parts and keep inventories to a minimum were thrust into chaos that day when parts didn't come and assembly lines were brought to a halt. Lean inventories, which had been a source of competitive advantage, quickly became a handicap following the terrorist attacks in New York and Washington, which grounded air traffic and slowed or stopped cross-border commerce. These delivery failures shut down many assembly lines and cost some large original equipment manufacturers £8,000 per minute. This was a risk that enterprises had never had to factor into their supply chain planning before.

In an increasingly global economy, purchasers face trade-offs between cost and risk. Suppliers' factories may be damaged by earthquakes, their logistic channels may be destroyed by mudslides and their credit be attacked by financial terrorism.

In the event of such risks, it is vital that the enterprise develops and maintains a disaster recovery or business continuity plan.

According to one model of dealing with crisis there are three levels of activity. These are:

- Primary prevention: activities designed to prevent a crisis from occurring.
- Secondary prevention: steps taken in the immediate aftermath of the crisis to minimise the effects (financial, reputational or other) which occurs.
- Tertiary prevention: provides long-term follow-up to those most affected.

A contingency plan needs to be developed by a team representing all functional areas of the enterprise, and this team should include suppliers wherever feasible. If the enterprise is a large, complex business, this may involve the establishment of a formal project team, which should have senior management approval and support.

Perhaps the first contingency planning task is to prepare a comprehensive list of the potentially serious incidents that could affect the normal operations of the business. This risk register should include as many incidents as possible, no matter how remote the likelihood of their occurrence. Generating such a list requires cross-functional teams, and a series of brainstorming sessions, which may be iterative in the same way as scenario planning workshops, are used in developing strategy.

Again, each occurrence should be assigned a probability rating. Each occurrence should also be rated for potential impact severity level. From this information, it will become much easier to frame the plan in the context of the real needs of the enterprise. Once the assessment stage has been completed, the structure of the plan can be established. The plan will contain a range of processes designed to move the organisation from its disrupted status to normal operations.

The first important process would deal with the immediate aftermath of the disaster. This might involve emergency services or other specialists who are trained to deal with extreme situations. It might also involve communication strategies for reassuring staff, shareholders and family members. The next process would be to identify which operations should be resumed and in what order. Such a plan will hold detailed task sets, and should identify key individuals and their key responsibilities in the event of an occurrence.

Once a plan has been developed it should be tested rigorously. The testing process itself must be properly planned and carried out. It should be remembered that individuals often find crisis difficult to deal with, and the way to overcome the problems that stem from this is to make sure that testing is rigorous, regular and carried out by the individuals responsible in the event of an occurrence. Test procedures should be documented and the results recorded. This also gives feedback, which can be used for fine tuning.

It is necessary for contingency arrangements to be communicated effectively to all staff and that that they are aware of their own duties and responsibilities. Equally, it is important to audit both the plan itself, and the contingency and back-up arrangements supporting it.

Contingency planning must always be kept up to date and applicable to current business circumstances. This means that changes to key business processes should be reflected within the plan. A risk manager can be assigned responsibility for ensuring that the plan is maintained and updated regularly. This individual can also, therefore, ensure that information concerning changes to the business process is properly communicated.

Longer-term effects of crisis management can range from personal trauma experienced by staff through to the need to recalibrate forecasting models. Plans may need to allow for counselling of staff or families, and this may include financial, location and other assistance to help individuals come to terms with crisis.

In other cases, many industries' supply chain applications rely on demand forecasts developed over time by collating data from ERP, sales and historical reporting tools. In the face of disruptions, companies may have to discard old forecasts and recalibrate their applications without knowing when demand will rebound.

10

Self-assessment question 10.3

Outline the contingency plans in place for your organisation and any key suppliers.

Feedback on page 174

Revision question

Now try the revision question for this session on page 342.

Summary

Ensuring that the business maintains a profitable profile requires constant development of suppliers to assist them in maximising their contribution to the buyer's operations. Involving key suppliers in the decision-making process will also develop long and trusting relationships. Finally, all businesses must be aware of crises that can severely disrupt their operations. Only if a clear contingency plan is in place will the business be able to cope with such disruptions with the impact minimised.

Suggested further reading

Read the chapter on specifying and managing quality in Lysons and Farrington (2006).

Feedback on learning activities and self-assessment questions

Feedback on learning activity 10.1

A simple model or diagram should show the importance of members from different departments working in cross-functional teams in order to have more meaningful discussion on changes to design, production issues, and customer perspectives. The involvement where possible of suppliers if the organisation wishes to have improvements in: quality, customer service, innovation in product or service design or delivery, cost reduction, delivery, product or service flexibility.

Feedback on self-assessment question 10.1

A close relationship with first tier suppliers will develop greater interdependence and the ability to respond more quickly to customer demands, will develop tighter stock control systems, the mutual sharing of risk and gains and a longer, more trusting relationship.

Feedback on learning activity 10.2

The increasing involvement of the supply base in fulfilling organisational objectives requires a number of communications and development activities. The implementation of JIT systems is a good example, as is formal vendor assessment, longer supply contracts and the reduction of the supply base which creates greater interdependence.

Feedback on self-assessment question 10.2

Examples might include the responsiveness to changes to supplies, the willingness to discuss and share improvements and seek solutions to supply problems through their own experience and networks.

Feedback on learning activity 10.3

Risk reduction within the organisation will only occur if the organisation takes steps to assess the potential risks. Examples would be an impact assessment of the consequences of a supplier failing to deliver to the right specification. Avoidance of the risk might be possible if the buyer works with trusted and long-term suppliers. Relationships and the discretionary use of the contract will help manage the supplier risk.

Feedback on self-assessment question 10.3

Such a plan would be based on measurement of the impact of a variety of events, and then a planned response – alternative supplies, alternative

10

operational location and so forth. An example of the need to have a plan occurred with the UK oil depot fire at Buncefield, Hertfordshire, that destroyed a number of business premises in the vicinity.

10

10

Study session 11
Doing research

Introduction

Research on purchasing and supply chain management issues can contribute significantly to the stock of knowledge of an organisation and contribute to future decision making. It provides stimulus to original thought as well as providing valuable information to the organisation. In addition it can be seen as a developmental activity for members of staff.

'But he never could think which he ought to do first and so in the end he did nothing at all.'
AA Milne

Session learning objectives

After completing this session you should be able to:

11.1 Assess the contribution that research can make to the organisation.
11.2 Give examples of the potential for research into supply markets.
11.3 Demonstrate the link to ongoing research and improvements in logistics.

Unit content coverage

Learning objective

2.5 Compare and contrast – through purchasing research – different supply markets and conditions, and liaise closely with logistics/suppliers to co-ordinate inbound logistics and associated materials flows.

Prior knowledge

An understanding of the purpose of research and the basic information-gathering processes.

Timing

You should set aside about 5 hours to read and complete this session, including learning activities, self-assessment questions, the suggested further reading (if any) and the revision question.

11.1 The contribution that research can make to the organisation

Introduction

Purchasing research involves the application of research methods to the specific field of procurement. It is 'the systematic gathering, recording and

11

analysing of data about problems relating to the purchasing of goods and services'.

Research generally involves investigating some issue in greater depth even though it can be for a straightforward purpose such as assisting in the determination of pricing strategy. Research is about obtaining information that will provide a competitive advantage for the business. In addition it can contribute to the reduction in costs of purchased components and materials. It can also be used to look for sources of greatest value within the supply chain.

The increasing development of the purchasing function into strategic elements such as the management of the supply chain, world-class status, lean supply, cost of ownership, and so forth, requires market intelligence to achieve best results.

JIT, for example, is one of the world-class strategies that have improved the efficiency and performance of an organisation. The speeding up of lead times, greater quality focus and the reduction of stock costs are possible outcomes if cooperation from the supplier is achieved. It is often difficult to make such concepts work in practice. Research provides information about the market, other industries and supply chain problems that can be used to improve the techniques and systems.

Research is about gathering intelligence concerning competitors and suppliers, 'the creation of an intelligence system that helps managers assess their competition and their suppliers in order to become a more efficient and effective competitor' (McDaniel and Gates, 1999).

Although competitor intelligence will be driven by organisational needs, the purchasing function will be involved in those aspects of competitor activity which have a bearing on their activity, such as production resources and locations, product lines and their specifications, distribution channels used, contracts won and lost, prices and pricing policy. The way a company distributes its products is a way in which competitive advantage can be gained, and also efficient delivery systems, warehousing and stock levels through JIT management. Financial performance of suppliers is important because of the risk impact to the business and also a business opportunity for the purchaser or competitor with the potential to extend the supply chain by buying out the supplier.

Learning activity 11.1

Produce a report to identify what research information relating to the purchasing or logistical function would contribute most to your organisational success.

Feedback on page 183

Research can be primary or secondary

Primary research involves the obtaining of new data and information, data that does not already exist. It can be collected in several ways including

11

qualitative and quantitative research. If an organisation wishes to look at whole systems and economies, then macroeconomic research can be undertaken. Microeconomic research involves research into individual producers, suppliers, markets and industries.

Secondary research discovers information and data which already exists. Such data is usually readily available, and is, therefore, generally cheaper than conducting primary research.

Sources are numerous and include:

* catalogues
* trade directories
* databases
* the internet
* trade journals
* chambers of commerce
* government sources such as the Department of Trade and Industry, the Office for National Statistics
* banks
* importers
* *The Journal of the European Union*
* competitors' annual reports
* news items
* competitors' promotional material
* research centres, for example, universities, professional institutions such as the CIPS, consultants.

11

Self-assessment question 11.1

Prepare an outline research proposal for the purchasing function with a clear objective and a list of potential sources of information.

Feedback on page 183

11.2 How research benefits the business

The impact of research

Purchasing research should be designed to contribute to savings and efficiency. Therefore it makes sense for the organisation to look at the areas of greatest expenditure.

It is suggested that purchasing research can be broken down into four major research areas:

* purchased materials, products or services
* major purchased commodities
* vendors
* the purchasing system.

Another approach is to look at aspects that deal with the organisation itself and its relationship with suppliers, prices, JIT, and so on or to research external markets and the whole macroeconomic environment relating to the supply of materials and components from around the world.

Learning activity 11.2

Design a potential research project for a member of staff that would contribute significantly to current organisational knowledge.

Feedback on page 183

Major areas of potential research include:

Materials, commodities and services:

- substitute materials or items
- alternative production methods
- life cycles and the purchase of capital items
- variety reduction
- standardisation and specifications.

Purchasing policies and procedures:

- Research topics within this area would include global sourcing, make-or-buy decisions, comparative studies of purchasing policies and studies relating to the growing environmental issues.

Economic aspects:

- economic trends affecting material purchasing; currencies, interest rates, inflation
- price analysis
- supply and demand analysis
- market trends
- purchasing and its impact on competitive advantage.

Purchasing organisation:

- The management of the supply chain would be a key research topic, possibly linked to logistics as well.
- Benchmarking research of other organisational approaches to purchasing is always useful for market intelligence, as is the interface between the different internal functions.

Human resource aspects of purchasing:

- Training and development of purchasing personnel.

Suppliers:

- performance rating systems
- supplier appraisal and feedback

- quality assurance and control
- buying centres and sourcing decisions.

Inventory:

- The whole topic of inventory management is relevant including stock management systems, just-in-time and variety reduction.

Negotiation:

- strategies for negotiation
- different negotiation styles in other cultures.

Support tools:

- Information technology, accounting approaches and costing.

Purchasing performance:

- Benchmarking research, audits, management by objectives.

Self-assessment question 11.2

List the skills that are required to conduct research effectively.

Feedback on page 183

11

11.3 The link to ongoing research and improvements in logistics

Research over the last few years has contributed to many areas of operational development that are directly or indirectly linked to the purchasing function. Matters relating to quality, business process engineering, lean operations and world-class performance, benchmarking and process technologies have all become recognised and accepted techniques within the business world.

For example, the writings of management gurus in the 1950s such as Deming, Juran, Feigenbaum, Ishikawa, Taguchi and Shingo pioneered the development of total quality management as a transformational process. Research continues in this area as shown in the writings of Peters, Crosby and Moller, which demonstrates that, as with all suggested management techniques, further research is essential for continuing validation and to suggest refinements or other approaches as business situations shift and change.

Learning activity 11.3

The concept of lean operations and just-in-time (JIT) production was introduced to the automotive industry through the Toyota Production

(continued on next page)

Learning activity 11.3 *(continued)*

System. These interconnected concepts describe a process in which waste is eliminated by reducing inventory holding costs and continuously improving to maintain production quality. Integrating and synchronising the entire supply chain and manufacturing process is a key goal of lean manufacturing. This requires a more efficient use of logistics, increased flexibility and reduced variability.

Identify potential areas of waste in your own organisation from:

- overproduction
- waiting
- transportation
- processing
- inventory
- unnecessary motion
- defects.

Explain how your organisation is attempting to eliminate or reduce waste in each of these areas.

Feedback on page 183

Now try self-assessment question 11.3 below.

Self-assessment question 11.3

Research the potential delays in your own organisation in the following operations:

- preparation of requisitions
- forwarding of requisition to purchasing
- processing by purchasing from enquiry to preparation of order
- transmission of order to supplier
- execution of order by supplier
- transportation of order
- receipt, inspection and storage
- issue to production or sales.

Feedback on page 184

Revision question

Now try the revision question for this session on page 342.

Summary

Although academic research drives much of the in-depth debate about business life, organisations need either to support such research or initiate their own research into aspects that affect their micro performance, as well as the impact of the macro environment. Without comprehensive market intelligence an organisation is in danger of only reacting to change rather than being proactive in new initiatives.

Suggested further reading

Read the chapter on purchasing research, performance and ethics in Lysons and Farrington (2006).

Feedback on learning activities and self-assessment questions

Feedback on learning activity 11.1

Any research which is about gathering intelligence concerning competitors and suppliers would be of value. Research, which can use secondary sources, could, for example, identify key competitor activity within the supply chain with a view to identifying the buying techniques, systems and processes as well as their supply source. Research into new potential sources in different geographical areas would also be beneficial.

Feedback on self-assessment question 11.1

A clear title and objectives needs to be identified; objectives or an hypothesis, plus some indications as to the sources of information. If primary research is to be undertaken then the methodology needs to be outlined.

Feedback on learning activity 11.2

Examples would include modelling the supply chain to examine the extent and range of the supplier source, the importance of some suppliers, the potential for bottlenecks and the impact of a supplier failing to perform, benchmarking internally and other competitor organisations, business process engineering and the scope for structural changes within the purchasing function. Global sourcing opportunities would also be a valuable research activity, as would any broad examination into market trends.

Feedback on self-assessment question 11.2

- task definition
- information-seeking strategies
- location and access
- use of information
- synthesis
- evaluation.

Feedback on learning activity 11.3

Research into lean operational tools will enable an organisation to assess the extent of change that is needed in its continuing search to become efficient.

11

Few organisations will not be familiar with the concept of 'leanness' and have used that knowledge to look for savings within the operational and support services. Examples from dealing with bottlenecks and planning operations will highlight areas of waste caused by overproduction, waiting and inventory. An analysis of the extent to which just-in-time techniques are used will raise issues of inventory and transportation. A review of production techniques will address issues of waste in the process itself and any resultant defects. Suppliers too will be part of the waste cycle if goods are not delivered according to schedule and on occasions are not of the require standard.

Feedback on self-assessment question 11.3

Administrative systems should be striving for real-time delivery. By examining the speed, response and flexibility of current systems, areas of potential improvement will be identified.

Using technology

Introduction

Most organisations now have increasingly sophisticated data management and procurement systems that have streamlined and increased the capacity and efficiency of the purchasing function. Increasingly the integration of these systems towards virtual management of the supply chain will create a significant competitive advantage.

'Aware that we are living in the midst of a technological revolution, we are becoming increasingly concerned with its meaning for the individual and its impact on freedom, on society, and on our political institutions.'
Drucker (1985)

Session learning objectives

After completing this session you should be able to:

12.1 Explain how a technological approach to information flows can improve organisational efficiency.
12.2 Show diagrammatically the impact of technology on information gathering and flows.

Unit content coverage

Learning objective

2.6 Appraise the benefits of automated processes and information flows and their impact on the supply chain in terms of efficiency, productivity, quality improvement, cost reduction, payments and materials flow management.

Prior knowledge

Awareness of electronic data interchange systems.

Resources

Access to organisational software systems.

Timing

You should set aside about 5 hours to read and complete this session, including learning activities, self-assessment questions, the suggested further reading (if any) and the revision question.

12

12.1 Technological approaches to information flows that improve organisational efficiency

E-business

Information technology is seen by many organisations as an important factor in providing a competitive advantage. The increasing standardisation of the technology has given the opportunity for many large organisations to introduce automated technology which allows for fast flows of information, for example Wal-Mart's satellite connected information systems and the Federal Express tracking system.

E-business is increasingly being applied to the process of automating various aspects of the supply chain to simplify and speed up those processes. The benefits include:

- The potential to be available on a 24-hour basis – the timeless availability of information may be critical to business operations.
- Allows for the aggregation of information from several sources and permits access from a single point of contact.
- Collects information on all products throughout the supply chain process.
- Allows for managers to track transactions through audit trails and seek areas of greatest efficiency and cost savings.
- Enables the business to customise its information flows.
- Allows collaboration with supply chain partners and helps to manage risk and uncertainty.

Examples of automated systems include:

- Production focused processes which include electronic links with suppliers includes Manufacturing Resource Planning (MRP II).
- Enterprise resource planning (ERP): The growth of collaborative relationships has transformed ERP into ERPII as the whole supply chain becomes involved and the system has moved from an internal system to an open web-based system.
- Advanced planning and scheduling (APS).
- Customer-focused process including customer relationship management (CRM).
- The provision of internal employee services through the intranet.

Advanced computer-driven communication capabilities enable many applications including:

- intranet portals which allow employees to access all the information they need to do their job via a desktop application
- email
- data exchange including EDI
- transportation product tracking
- supply chain management
- exchange platforms to share information and trade with supply chain partners
- databases.

12

Learning activity 12.1

Prepare a report on processes within the organisation that have improved as a result of the technological impact on information flows, and suggest future improvements that technological innovation can bring.

Feedback on page 191

Software systems and the supply chain

Supply chain software has made a significant impact on the ability of buyers and sellers to collaboratively plan, forecast and replenish inventory, enabling organisations to determine whether or not customer orders can be fulfilled.

E-procurement software systems allow buyers to streamline and automate their procurement processes.

A number of benefits should ensue:

- *Cost reduction* as a result of operational efficiencies through the reduction of search and process management. Integrated systems such as those used by major retailers enable goods to be reordered from the cash till of the retailer.
- *Speed and efficiency* in terms of ordering, delivery, reductions in inventory levels, improvements in warehousing and distribution logistics and information flow that assists demand forecasting.
- *Quality improvements* because of the greater access to suppliers through the automated systems.

It has been recognised that the key to success in supply chain management is the information system. The internet has transformed the ways in which the supply chain can connect with each other and provides a vehicle for the establishment of a virtual supply chain. Global markets can be accessed at minimal cost and information can be shared with suppliers in a cost-effective way via extranets.

IT capabilities

- Advanced solutions enable organisations to develop a strategic network design which allows planners to pick the optimum sourcing arrangement in terms of who should produce which product, what are the best distribution channels, which warehouses should service which customer, and so on.
- The ability to plan ahead to take into account seasonal variations, promotions and related capacity issues.
- Inventory planning and the amount of safety stock that would be needed.
- Transportation planning.
- Production scheduling.
- Supplier relationship management.

12

E-commerce

E-commerce allows for a much more efficient interaction between companies as physical processes are replaced with electronic ones.

Using extranets

The building of intranets that reduce or eliminate problems with internal communications can be applied by using the same technologies that work for intra-organisational communications. CAD files, purchase orders, design specifications, payment instructions, or any other information can be processed by extranets effectively and efficiently. They can be used to electronically route product shipment schedules, order information, CAD files for product designs, purchase orders and other financial information. The improved exchange of information should result in new business practices between vendors and manufacturers throughout the supply chain.

Self-assessment question 12.1

How does your organisation deal with the security issues on increasing data interchange and the consequences of breaches of that security?

Feedback on page 191

12.2 An integrated IT system?

Information and the virtual supply chain

The internet has transformed the ways in which supply chain members can connect with each other and provides a model for the development of a virtual supply chain.

It enables global markets to be connected and accessed at minimal cost, allows customers to shorten search time and reduces transactional costs. Furthermore it enables the buyers and suppliers to share information with each other through cost-effective extranets. The emergence of integrated logistics systems can link the operations of a business such as production and distribution with the supplier's operations and ultimately the customer. Companies can link the replenishment of products in the marketplace with their upstream activities.

Learning activity 12.2

Construct a diagram to show how your own organisation has embraced integrated IT solutions to move towards a virtual supply chain.

Feedback on page 191

In addition, integrated software solutions can provide opportunities to virtually manage most of the procurement functions such as:

- collaborative e-design and R&D: including planning of new products, digital modelling and the management of the projects
- e-sourcing: including market analysis, auctions, negotiations, and cost reduction management
- e-category management: including purchasing analysis, contracts, compliance and scorecards
- e-ordering and ERP systems
- e-logistics management: including demand and capacity planning.

Self-assessment question 12.2

Research into available supply chain IT solutions and identify the potential costs for the system against the costs of implementation and maintenance.

Feedback on page 191

Improving the supply chain interaction

Most organisations will now engage in several levels or layers of electronic commerce. Simchi-Levi et al (2003) identify a number of levels.

Level one: one-way communication

This is perhaps the oldest and simplest of communications using email, file transfers and browsing.

Learning activity 12.3

In relation to system development, produce a table which compares past and present practices within the organisation with examples of real gains.

Feedback on page 191

Level two: database access

Accessing the database for personal or tailored information by entering data through data entry forms. Status enquiries and purchases can be made via the internet through customised supply websites. Company knowledge bases can be accessed for data on suppliers and problem reports. Increasingly internet sites are being created that match buyers and sellers. The progress has been quite slow in terms of e-procurement systems because of the difficulty of implementing and integrating the software into existing legacy systems. The existing software does not always live up to expectations and there has been difficulty in managing cross-functional processes. The costs of running e-catalogues have at times proven to be more than first thought.

12

As with many new approaches to business, evolution, although striving for standardisation, has been through different IT solutions creating an 'e-patchwork' which has slowed commonality of systems.

There has been some development of commercial e-marketplaces:

- vertical e-marketplaces which provide goods or services to a specific industry
- horizontal marketplaces which provide goods or services to a range of organisations in different market segments
- supplier marketplaces which are controlled by a particular supplier.

Level three: data exchange

The prime example is electronic data exchange (EDI) between buyers and suppliers.

Level four: sharing processes

The development systems for supplier relationship management (SRM) and customer relationship management (CRM) are examples of the sharing of more than data. SRM systems provide for a number of capabilities:

- *Strategic supply management*, which focuses on obtaining and managing the right set of suppliers linked to price paid and quality delivered.
- *Supply chain collaboration*, which allows for the sharing of information with suppliers in an attempt to cut material costs, minimising inventory and expediting deliveries.
- *Direct materials procurement execution* uses the internet to automate the purchasing of supplies, which can cut cycle times and reduce inventory levels.
- *Collaborative planning, forecasting and replenishment systems.*

12

Self-assessment question 12.3

Outline how information technology systems have permitted an increase in the number of suppliers that can be handled by one employee.

Feedback on page 192

Revision question

Now try the revision question for this session on page 342.

Summary

The future management of purchasing will centre on the use of e-systems as organisations seek to efficiently manage supply chains, build in flexibility and responsiveness and, of course, minimise costs.

Suggested further reading

Read the chapter on purchasing procedures in Lysons and Farrington (2006).

Feedback on learning activities and self-assessment questions

Feedback on learning activity 12.1

The report should contain a range of examples of increased use of software to assist in the gathering and dissemination of logistical information within the business, data exchange, the tracking of goods and the more effective management of the supply chain. There should also be some mention of the sourcing potential that is now available as a result of internet capabilities.

Feedback on self-assessment question 12.1

The increasing involvement of suppliers in the business planning cycle does raise considerable concerns about confidential information. A standard response would be to tie this up with a confidentiality agreement within the contract that establishes the relationship with the supplier.

Feedback on learning activity 12.2

The diagram should show how the internet and the intranet are used to manage the purchasing transactions more efficiently. Many organisations will have systems that order electronically, but increasingly the use of sourcing software has enabled more competitive prices to be obtained. More sophisticated systems also look to manage the supply chain performance in an integrated way. There will also be some need to show how the data on the supply chain is managed and stored.

Feedback on self-assessment question 12.2

This is essentially an exercise in drawing up a shortlist of different commercial integrated IT systems for procurement and examining the cost of the software and its implementation, plus costs for licensing and any maintenance update agreements, compared with the suggested improvements in speed, responsiveness and indirect cost savings.

Feedback on learning activity 12.3

A table would, for example, show how a largely paper-based system has improved as a result of the use of email, and file sharing systems.

The use of databases to manage the supply chain will have made significant manpower savings, as will the ability to source electronically through the use of EDI systems.

12

Feedback on self-assessment question 12.3

An analysis of file sharing systems and the use of databases should reveal that the number of suppliers that can be managed by the procurement team is increased per capita.

Negotiation strategies and styles

'The ability to negotiate successfully is crucial for survival in today's changing business world.'
Ed Brodow

Introduction

Successful negotiation requires the development of a 'negotiation consciousness'; assertive behaviour which challenges everything, but is based on aiming high for the organisation. It is a professional process which requires the development of advanced skills and tactics to succeed.

Session learning objectives

After completing this session you should be able to:

13.1 Describe the negotiation process in commercial situations.
13.2 Compare and contrast different approaches to negotiation.
13.3 Identify cultural issues that would have to be taken into account in international transactions.
13.4 Assess examples of approaches that maximise the reward in negotiation.
13.5 Assess the risk in negotiations.

Unit content coverage

Learning objective

3.1 Compare, contrast and evaluate different negotiation strategies, styles and levels in different supply chain contexts (e.g. open and closed-book negotiation). Formulate appropriate strategies for negotiation within and across the supply chain and to manage risk and reward in the negotiation process.

Prior knowledge

Background knowledge on negotiation skills.

Resources

Examples of organisational negotiations, the processes and outcomes.

Timing

You should set aside about 5 hours to read and complete this session, including learning activities, self-assessment questions, the suggested further reading (if any) and the revision question.

13

13.1 The negotiation process in commercial situations

Introduction

Negotiation is important. It is through negotiation that buyers achieve their objectives. The more effective buyers are in negotiation, the better their performance will be in obtaining the best possible outcome for their organisation.

Negotiation is defined in the *Oxford English Dictionary* as 'discussion with another with a view to compromise'. This suggests obtaining a mutually acceptable outcome, and is therefore different from 'haggling' as it involves a more orderly and logically developed pattern of discussion.

Negotiation should not be confused with *bargaining*, which is part of negotiation but a narrower term implying only giving and taking; negotiating involves a wider range of activities and attitudes such as persuasion, posturing, warnings, threats, flattery.

Most definitions of negotiation stress a number of elements in the process:

- communication and information exchange
- the relative strengths of the participants
- implicit and explicit objectives.

It should be recognised that most negotiations are rarely win-win (where both parties meet their objectives) or win-lose (where one party meets their objectives and the other doesn't) situations. Instead, negotiations are mixtures of common and conflicting interests and objectives and call for a mixture of negotiating strategies.

Uncertainty is unavoidable in negotiation. The very substance of negotiation is to manage communication in such a way as to manage the way the other party looks at the situation. Negotiations can be 'poisoned' by existing sources of potential conflict such as the historical relationship between the parties. Managing these elements in the course of a negotiation can be very difficult.

As a negotiator the buyer is a representative of an organisation. This places them in a leadership position. Negotiators often have to 'sell' or 'force' agreements both on the party they are negotiating with and on their own organisation – while maintaining credibility with both.

The organisation might be represented by a number of different negotiators over time – or even at one point in time. A critical role for the effective negotiator is to manage and conserve accurate knowledge about the management of previous and concurrent negotiations.

Although negotiations can seem difficult, there are a number of approaches that can make them easier. This includes:

- paying attention to preparation
- structuring the negotiation

- managing the timeline
- managing the information exchange
- understanding the process taking place and the way that process links to other processes.

Whereas the structure of a negotiation will shape the negotiation strategy used, the skilled negotiator will shape the underlying structure.

Learning activity 13.1

Outline your experience of the reality of negotiation in relation to the theoretical approach, especially in markets where the buyer is not the dominant party.

Feedback on page 217

Planning the negotiation

Planning the negotiation is absolutely essential if objectives are to be met with some success. Buyers often underestimate the time required for successful planning of the more complex scenarios in which they will be involved. Failure to plan properly often leads to poorly formulated objectives for the negotiation, and the use of inappropriate negotiating styles or tactics. The negotiation will centre on a number of specific questions concerning the context, what the parties expect to achieve from the negotiations, and any anticipated problems.

Negotiation always takes place within a context. Some of the important issues to consider in understanding the context of a negotiation include:

- The **supply market** in terms of:
  (a) competition: Is the market fully competitive, dominated by a few larger suppliers, filled with unsophisticated suppliers?
  (b) growth: Is this a new market, a growing market, a mature market, a retracting market? What is the impact of new technology on this market?
  (c) geography: Is this a global market, a distributed market, a rural market? Is distance an issue?
  (d) power: Who owns the suppliers? What level of turnover do the suppliers have? What is their financial status? What proportion of their turnover does this contract represent?
- The procurement decision in terms of:
  (a) purchasing risk: What is the nature of the purchase that is being made in terms of its level of risk, and level of expenditure?
  (b) complexity: How complex is the good or service that is being purchased? The buyer will also want to consider whether this is a negotiation with a new supplier, and whether there are any sensitivities attached to the negotiations. An assessment of the current relationship would be important and whether this is to be a relationship that is to be maintained.

13

- The *relationship* between the parties in terms of:
  (a) history and timeline: how much time is available for the negotiation?
  (b) The skill base of the negotiating parties.
  (c) how skilled and experienced is *your* negotiating team?
  (d) how skilled and experienced is *their* negotiating team?

Objectives

Once the context for the purchasing negotiation is understood, the next step is to plan the negotiation. Controlling the negotiation is vital, and the first step in controlling the negotiation is to set clear, realistic and achievable objectives.

Knowing the overall objectives of the negotiation is essential, because this helps the buyer decide the most appropriate strategy or approach to be used for the negotiation. Without broad goals or clarity of desired outcomes of the purchase, it is very difficult to control the negotiation. Once a strategy is clearly defined, it is possible to decide on consistent objectives for the negotiation and to develop a negotiation plan.

This plan should include, for example, details of negotiating team composition, time frames for the negotiation, negotiation styles to be adopted, strategies and tactics to be applied, limits on the negotiators' authority and process requirements. Obviously some consultation with other stakeholders in the business will ensure support for the end result of the negotiations.

Team negotiation

Negotiation doesn't always take place between individuals. For significant purchases, such as complex and expensive capital equipment, buyers may decide that a team of negotiators would be appropriate. Consideration should be given to the make-up of the team (for example, whether technical and financial experts or end users should be involved). A leader needs to be selected, and roles of members need to be established and clarified. These negotiators need to be appropriately trained and supported. Negotiators may wish to spend time rehearsing and role-playing the options that are likely to arise. If negotiations with suppliers are an ongoing activity in the organisation, then a pool of skilled negotiators within each function who can participate in a team are developed.

Negotiation variables

Three critical variables have a major impact on the nature of negotiation: power, time and information. Let's look at these in some more detail.

Power

It is important to make a realistic assessment of the power relationship in any purchasing negotiation. Power involves being able to control or manage the decisions of the other party. There are many ways in which this can be done, which range from managing their perceptions of potential loss through to reducing their alternative networks.

Sometimes the balance of power will sit with the organisation, simply because of the size of the contract and buying power. Sometimes the balance of power is in the supplier's favour, where the organisation is a small customer or a supplier has an actual monopoly, a geographical monopoly or a virtual monopoly position in the market.

Being the powerful party in a negotiation is, in itself, neutral. It is neither good nor bad, neither ethical nor unethical. However, market power should not be misused to damage, eliminate or exclude competitors from the market. Misuse of power will often incur costs later in the relationship.

Organisations can increase their negotiating power by identifying a number of alternative products/services that could meet their requirements and by having a range of possible suppliers, thus reducing their dependence on buying a particular item from a particular seller.

Time

Most people describe negotiation as if it were an event. This implies that it has a definite start and finish within a fixed time frame. In fact, negotiation is a process rather than an event; the actual starting point of a negotiation is always long before the start of the formal face-to-face negotiating phase. In the preparation phase it is wise to gather as much information as possible both about the organisation's interests and alternatives and the interests and alternatives of the supplier. After the formal negotiating phase has finished and an agreement has been reached, it must be documented, formally agreed, implemented and monitored.

The management of time within the negotiation, slowing the process down and speeding it up according to the needs of the organisation, is a common tactic. It also helps one party when situations change in an unexpected direction. Taking control of time is often a way of taking control of the rest of the negotiation.

However, it should be noted that, generally, good outcomes in purchasing negotiations cannot be achieved in tight time frames. It is worth investing the time that is necessary to explore issues, identify the needs and interests behind expressed positions and develop creative and innovative solutions of mutual benefit to the negotiation.

Time is a valuable commodity in a purchasing negotiation. The organisation can often make best use of available time to improve its negotiating position substantially by gathering useful information – which allows the development of alternatives to the solution being proposed by the supplier.

Information

Information is at the heart of any negotiation. Adequate attention to gathering information during the preparation phase of a negotiation can significantly enhance the likelihood of a mutually satisfactory agreement being reached during the formal phase of the negotiation. During the formal phase, it can be a common strategy for parties to try to conceal their true interests and priorities. The chance of obtaining accurate information from an experienced negotiator during an adversarial negotiation is quite low. Information is normally easiest to gather during the preparation phase before the formal negotiation begins.

The more information about the other party's financial situation, real priorities, needs, deadlines, costs and organisational pressures, the easier it will be to develop negotiating proposals which address these issues, and the stronger the negotiating position will be.

There are many sources of information on suppliers and markets. Sources include the media, libraries, government publications and statistics, product and consumer reports, online services and professional bodies – and the supplier themselves, through their literature, their websites and through their sales force at any exhibitions at which they are displaying their goods or services. Other interesting sources of information include contact with third parties who are familiar with the other party, including current and previous customers or even competitors of the other party, who may be able to give you an insight into industry issues and prevailing conditions, cost and/or price structures, product availability and design features.

Developing a 'BATNA'

Negotiators should consider a contingency plan, should the negotiation not prove successful. 'BATNA' stands for the **best alternative to a negotiated agreement**. Researchers developed the idea of a BATNA as part of the Harvard Negotiating Project in the 1970s.

Having a well-developed and attractive BATNA is a source of great power in any negotiation. The BATNA can be identified in any negotiation situation by asking the question, 'What will we do if this negotiation is not successful?' Vigorous exploration of the options that might exist outside the current negotiation can tip the balance of power in a negotiation.

However, attractive alternatives may not always be immediately obvious. Sometimes it will take time to identify what these alternatives are, and more time again to make them attractive. This is almost always time well invested as having a strong alternative improves the ability to negotiate a good deal in the current negotiation.

One of the main reasons for entering into a negotiation is to achieve better results than would be possible without negotiating. The stronger a negotiator's BATNA is, the greater the range of alternative courses of action. This means that the stronger the BATNA, the greater the ability to walk away from an unsatisfactory negotiation.

Preparing for negotiation

The checklist below covers the activities required in completing a thorough preparation and planning process for your negotiation.

Prepare for negotiation by:

- forming a team (if appropriate), specifying roles, rehearsal

- reviewing your own position and underlying interests
- obtaining input and advice from key stakeholders
- reviewing the possible positions and underlying interests of the supplier
- developing some possible outline proposals which consider the needs and interests of both parties to use to start the negotiation rolling
- developing a bottom line, and some desirable targets for the negotiation (these may shift during the course of the negotiation)
- identifying your BATNA
- determining any deadline when a decision must be reached
- considering location – office, conference room, your facility, the supplier's premises, or on neutral ground
- considering seating arrangements and the impression that you may create by your choice of seating layout
- developing a plan for dealing with interruptions
- providing facilities for the other party's use (telephone, fax and photocopier access, refreshments)
- setting an agenda for the first meeting after consultation with the supplier
- being prepared personally. being well rested and alert, well briefed, confident and informed on the issues, and dressed appropriately.

A version of the BATNA approach, taken by Dobler, Lee and Burt in *Purchasing and Materials Management* (1990) is the MIL approach. Here, categorisation of objectives is those that:

- *Must* achieve
- *Intend* to achieve
- *Like* to achieve.

Competition

A competitive style is characterised by the desire to 'win at all costs'. It is often described as a win-lose approach, or playing hardball. In this approach, one party seeks to have all of their requirements recognised, without giving any reciprocal recognition to the (valid) needs of the other party. Competition can be an appropriate approach when:

- quick, decisive action is necessary
- parties have predominantly conflicting goals
- a belief in being right
- you are dealing with someone who will take advantage of non-competitive behaviour (but beware of escalation)
- other options are not possible.

Using a competitive negotiation style may, however, create problems which include:

- reduced communication and possibly a lost opportunity to generate and explore alternative approaches
- reducing diversity of opinion on your own team, because it is easier to agree than to get into an argument
- damage to relationships with your own team and with the supplier

13

- no real commitment from the other party, which incurs more costs due to the need to keep 'selling' or policing the agreement during implementation.

Accommodation

An accommodative negotiating style is characterised by the *desire to please others at the expense of your own interests*. This approach is often called 'lose-win negotiation' or 'soft negotiation'. Accommodation is very appropriate when the issues are more important to the other party and there is an opportunity to build 'credits' for later use on more important issues. This is the principle of making concessions in negotiation. Other uses for an accommodating approach include times when:

- goals are potentially shareable or unimportant
- you find out that you are in the wrong
- you want to seem reasonable
- continued competition would only damage the situation or the relationship
- preserving the relationship is especially important
- you want to minimise losses by making early concessions.

Potential negative consequences of accommodating include:

- frustration as own needs are not met
- relinquishing the optimum or best solution
- self-esteem being undermined.

Avoidance

Avoidance is where the real *issues at the heart of the negotiation are ignored* completely. Avoidance can be an appropriate style when:

- the issues are trivial, and more important issues are pressing
- there is no chance of getting what you want
- there is a need for both parties to take time to cool down and regain perspective
- you need more time to gather information
- someone else can handle the issue more effectively than you
- the issue is a symptom of another, bigger issue.

Potential negative consequences of using an avoiding style are:

- decisions may be made by default
- unresolved issues are never addressed, and may surface later in the relationship
- creative solutions and improvement opportunities are prevented
- exclusive use leads to damage to personal credibility, and it may be difficult to recover when a different style is required.

Compromise

Compromise is a negotiation approach where the *parties meet at midpoint*. Both parties achieve a moderate, but incomplete, satisfaction with their

13

agreement – a type of sub-optimal win-win. It is typified by the 'split the difference' tactic in negotiation. Compromise is an appropriate style when:

- goals can be accommodated
- issues are not worth the effort of being negotiated in full
- a temporary settlement to a complex issue is needed
- an expedient solution under time pressure is needed
- back-up is needed because collaboration or competition is not working.

Potential negative consequences of compromising include:

- no one is fully satisfied with the agreement and this leads to short-lived agreements, which require a lot of selling or policing
- perception of a sell-out on important issues
- principles and long-term objectives may be lost, by focusing exclusively on the practicalities.

Collaboration

Collaboration is characterised by a *desire to satisfy all interests in a win-win solution*. Collaboration is appropriate when:

- joint goals can be agreed
- finding a long-lasting or creative solution is required
- both sets of interests are too important to be compromised
- reaching a consensus is required
- developing and maintaining a relationship with the supplier is wanted
- there is a need to learn – to test assumptions or better understand the views of others.

Potential negative consequences of collaborating are:

- it is very time-consuming to reach agreement
- too much time can be spent on insignificant issues
- unfounded assumptions about trust can lead to the other party taking advantage of your position
- ineffective decisions result because too many people input into the process.

Phases of a negotiation

Negotiations tend to be complex, and move forward in surges of activity. This means that there may be many stages. Before we consider these in some detail, you should review the case study below which indicates some of the many facets of a protracted and highly technical negotiation.

A staged approach to negotiation can help in managing structure.

During the closing stages of a negotiation, it should never be forgotten that reaching agreement is in fact only the beginning of the relationship with the supplier. It will be necessary to work together productively to implement the agreement. The working relationship must be sustainable.

13

Documentation

There are essentially two types of documents involved in negotiation:

- Contracts: Many negotiations will be embodied in a contract. However, a written contract is not essential for the agreement to be legally enforceable.
- Minutes and records: It is good practice to keep written records of all negotiation meetings. Negotiations can move along at a very fast pace and it is easy to lose track of what concessions were offered by whom, and what follow-up actions need to be taken. Proper record-keeping is also an important part of ensuring proper accountability for the negotiation process. Negotiation records may be needed if the deal is subject to external scrutiny.

When it goes wrong

Sometimes the purchasing negotiation simply does not run according to plan. This might be due to both parties failing to understand the structure, 'poisonous' elements in the negotiation, or a whole range of other causes. There are a number of situations that might arise when things do not go according to plan, and a number of things that can be done.

Deadlocks

A deadlock exists when negotiations reach an impasse or stalemate. Both sides appear to have exhausted all possible concessions that might get the negotiation moving again. Deadlocks can be recognised because there is no progress, frustration levels rise, emotions become more heated and there is a sense of going over old ground again and again. Deadlocks can be broken in two main ways:

- changing something: making the situation different
- explaining something: making the situation seem different.

Some options that might assist in achieving breakthroughs include:

- lead negotiators for both sides meeting informally in a neutral environment
- team leaders meeting informally, as above
- forming sub-groups to thrash out issues from various areas of the negotiation such as technical, financial, or product testing
- redefining the problem and then both parties working together to brainstorm possible solutions
- bringing in an outside 'expert' to give a different perspective on the problem
- repeating the organisation's position and adding new support or a new angle
- changing the subject to more easily resolved issues, and then returning to the deadlock issue
- suggesting an adjournment for both parties to consider more fully the other party's position

13

- offering a minor (pre-planned) concession as a gesture
- offering to trade concessions.

In the case of a deadlock, it is often useful to summarise the negotiations to date, to identify issues agreed and those outstanding and endeavour to identify some issue which could be conceded to bring the other party back to the negotiation table.

Deciding to walk away

When a party breaks off negotiation, this has the potential of ending the negotiations completely. It is a sensitive situation that raises questions about how to get negotiations moving again. If it is the supplier who is walking away, it may be worth making the effort to persuade them to return to the negotiation.

If the supplier walks away from the negotiation this is an opportunity to review and rethink the process. If the supplier eventually returns to the negotiation, then this is always recognised as a positive point, and negotiations can be resumed without acrimony.

The purchaser may also make the decision to walk away from a negotiation if it seems impossible to satisfy important objectives by dealing with this supplier.

In walking away, it is important to consider the BATNA again. Before walking away, buyers should compare the present situation with the BATNA. If the present situation is *better* than the BATNA, then there is no realistic alternative but to stay with this negotiation and try to improve the outcomes. If the BATNA is more attractive than the set of conditions that can be agreed, then it makes sense to walk away from the negotiation and pursue the more attractive option presented by the BATNA. This approach allows the decision to walk away from a negotiation to be made on rational grounds, rather than in the heat of the moment.

It is vitally important to walk away from a negotiation in a manner that leaves open the option for the purchaser to continue to do business with this supplier at some point in the future. Be cautious not to overestimate the attractiveness of your BATNA if you intend to follow this approach. Some form of correspondence should be sent to the supplier to cover the following key issues:

- Summarise the final position, using hedging language which allows the supplier room to change position without losing face.
- Summarise the position, using hedging language to let the supplier resume the negotiation gracefully.
- State that the negotiation simply could not proceed because of the differences in these interests.
- Avoid blaming the supplier.
- Thank the supplier for their investment of time and effort.
- Give the other party an idea of your BATNA so they know what time frame is appropriate if they do wish to resume negotiations.

13

Unreasonable behaviour

When confronted with a difficult situation or an unreasonable person, it is natural to rely on emotions such as anger or frustration. Often this causes us to act without thinking of the consequences. This can lead to a loss of focus on the negotiating objective or goal. Responding calmly to provocation allows time for the parties to distance themselves from emotional responses and to act in more constructive ways.

When faced with unreasonable behaviour, there are a number of issues to keep in mind.

- Focus on the goal: The goal of a negotiation should not be to force the other party to give in to your demands, but rather to satisfy your interests and as many of the other party's interests as possible. When confronted by a difficult situation or unreasonable person, it is useful to remind yourself of your negotiating interests. Then resume the negotiation, calmly pursuing your interests.
- Empathise: Listen to what the supplier is saying, acknowledge their point of view and, if possible, agree with them. Acknowledgement does not mean agreement, but rather that their point of view is accepted as one of many potentially valid points of view on the matter. By acknowledging the point the emotional content may be defused.
- Make it easy for them to agree: It makes no sense to force the other party into an agreement if it is expected to be a lasting one. Instead, it is better to make it easy for the other party to reach their own conclusion that the agreement is desirable.
- Use the BATNA to your advantage: As you yourself would, the other party will refuse to reach agreement if they believe *their* BATNA is better than the negotiated terms. You need to convince the other party that this belief is incorrect. A useful approach is to point out factors to the other party that would convince them that they have simply miscalculated the strength or attractiveness of their BATNA; or that they have underestimated the negative consequences of not reaching an agreement with you. Let the other party know what these consequences are. This can be achieved by asking leading questions until the other party has had the opportunity to think through the impact of not reaching an agreement. Some useful questions to encourage this are:
  - (a) 'What do you think will happen if we don't agree?' Perhaps the other party simply hasn't thought about this issue.
  - (b) 'What do you think I will do?' Perhaps the other party might be underestimating the strength of your BATNA.
  - (c) 'What will you do?' Perhaps the other party is overestimating the attractiveness of their BATNA.

Tactics

The first step in successfully negotiating with a party who is using tactics is to *identify the tactic*. Most tactics depend on the fact that you will not recognise that you are being manipulated, and that you will react in a predictable way. If you are able to identify the tactic, you are less likely to respond to it in the way the other party hoped, and you thus gain a degree of control over the negotiation situation.

There is a vast range of possible negotiating tactics which you might employ in your negotiations, or which you might encounter from the other party. Many of these tactics are quite obvious and you will easily recognise when they are being used against you. Others are more difficult to identify.

Some tactics or ploys that are used to pressure parties to do things they would not otherwise do include:

- 'good guy/bad guy'
- highball and lowball
- bogey
- the nibble
- chicken
- intimidation
- aggressive behaviour.

There are a number of counter tactics that can be used in these situations which include:

- Ignore the tactics: Ignoring might appear to be a weak response, but in fact it can be a very powerful way to deal with hard negotiation tactics. It takes a lot of energy to use intransigent tactics; while the other party is wasting their energy, you can be working to achieve your goals.
- Discuss the tactics: Negotiate the negotiation process. Offer to change to less aggressive methods.
- Respond in kind: Although this response can result in chaos and hard feelings, it is not an option that should be dismissed. Once the smoke clears, both parties will realise that they are skilled in the use of hardball tactics and may recognise that it is time to try something different!
- Co-opt the other party: Try to befriend negotiators who might use hard practices. It is more difficult to attack a friend than an enemy.

As noted above, these are only some of the tactics that might be used. Others include appealing to external allies, pretending incompetence in negotiation or shifting the make-up of the negotiating team. The key issue to keep in mind is that the use of such tactics often signals fear or need on the part of the other party. This shifts the balance of power in the negotiation.

A standard negotiation approach might consist of the following:

- opening
- exploring issues and inventing options
- making offers
- offering concessions
- reaching closure
- documentation.

Opening

It is important to establish control and set the right tone from the opening moment of the negotiation. It is essential to enter the room confidently and to exchange pleasantries in a relaxed and confident manner. Interruptions

13

such as mobile phones should be taken care of. Some care should be taken in arranging the accommodation to maximise the potential for getting the negotiations off to a good start.

Exploring issues and inventing options

It is at this stage that the parties begin to form an understanding of each other's positions and the interests behind those positions. This stage allows identification of areas where mutually compatible interests exist. Identifying areas with the potential for mutual benefit is an essential skill in this stage of negotiation. There are several techniques for attempting to identify the other party's negotiating interests and the potential for mutual benefit from satisfying these interests. These techniques include:

* empathising with the other party: trying to put yourself in their place and imagine the issues from their perspective
* asking questions that demonstrate your interest in understanding the other party's position
* considering possible reasons why the other party has not made a decision along the lines that you would like
* analysing the short- and long-term consequences for the other party agreeing to the type of decision to which you are asking them to agree. Areas of potential mutual interest should then be explored together, with both parties generating options that might work and putting these on the table for discussion.

The choice and sequence of issues for discussion is an important element of the negotiation. It is usually wise to start with an issue that is not too important, so that you can afford to make a concession and thereby show readiness to compromise. The next issue should also not be too important. This gives the opportunity to see whether the other party will offer a reciprocal concession or is interested in playing a competitive style.

Next, it is suggested that the buyer should deal with the major issues on which serious concessions from the other party are looked for. By this stage, both parties have made an investment of time, effort and money in the negotiation and will feel some commitment to discussing the issues until an agreement is reached. Major issues should be followed with minor ones, finishing with a minor issue on which the buyer can afford to give a concession as a final gesture towards closing the deal.

Making offers

At some point, clarifying interests and inventing options for mutual benefit must develop into the making of an offer. Once an issue has been thoroughly explored, the buyer should be prepared to make an offer, but should be aware that doing this too soon can make the other side feel that they are being pressured.

Suppliers will typically start with the highest defensible offer on each item and purchasers would normally respond with the lowest defensible offer.

Offers should be put clearly and firmly and without any hint of apology. Initial offers are very important because they create an impression of the sincerity and the realism of each party's position. Often, the initial demand will become the anchor for the negotiation – the central point around which the negotiation proceeds. This can be a disadvantage if the opening offer is pitched too low or too high. When deciding what to offer, keep in mind the following points.

- The buyer has other alternatives – there is recourse to the BATNA
- Clarity about other alternatives (including your BATNA). Develop not only your BATNA, but also your second-best alternative, third-best and so on. The more options, the easier it is to negotiate a good agreement
- Stick to the agreed limits. Developing limits is not much use if they are constantly broken. At the resistance point, the other party know that they are getting close to the limit and that soon the best option will be to walk away and follow the BATNA.

Offering concessions

A concession is a revision of a previous position that has been held and justified. Making concessions is essential in reaching a negotiated agreement. The challenge when making a concession is to make a concession on a particular point without creating the perception of weakness, and without developing the expectation that other points will be readily conceded. Making a concession brings a number of issues into consideration, including:

- When should the concession be offered? Make the other party work for the concession, and encourage the other party to offer the first concession. Do not offer a concession without specific pressure from the other party. If a concession is offered without pressure being applied, it is probably not worth much to the party offering the concession.
- What should be offered in return? Concessions should be traded and not be made without a return. Concessions are important, so do not give them lightly. Always pair concessions: 'If we can agree to extend the deadline for delivery, would you be able to offer better payment terms?'
- How much should be offered? The concession you make need not match the one offered to the buyer, but it must not be disproportionate in a marked way. Try to value the concession from the other party's point of view. Identify items that are cheap for your organisation to give up but are of real value to the other party, such as access to key decision makers, access to information or minor process streamlining for example.

Reaching closure

Practically, a negotiation closes when the parties agree on enough of the terms and details and are ready to formulate the agreement. In a legal sense, a negotiation closes when the parties have reached agreement on all the points under negotiation and have entered into a legally enforceable agreement with each other. This agreement is usually evidenced in writing.

The most effective way to close the negotiation is to simply ask the supplier whether they will agree to the current terms. The initial response will often be 'No' but, by asking, the need for closure has been signalled.

13

A negotiation cannot be effectively closed while the supplier still holds objections to some of the current terms. These objections must be identified and legitimate objections dealt with. This is easier in a climate of trust where there is willingness to work through the legitimate objections until both parties are satisfied. Failure to address and resolve objections will lead to deadlock, not closure.

Addressing objections involves:

- Avoiding arguments over the objection: Treating all objections as reasonable and logical, even if they seem superficial or irrelevant. This places the supplier under an obligation to accord the same respect to your objections.
- Rephrasing and repeating the objection: This is an opportunity to check that you have understood the objection, and shows that you were paying attention to what they said. A useful phrase here can be, 'You seem to be saying that…' It also provides an opportunity for the supplier to tell you how they would like to see the objection resolved.
- Identifying hidden objections: Sometimes the expressed objection is not the real one. You can use questions such as, 'There seem to be other concerns that are bothering you at this stage. Do you want to talk about these concerns?'

When it seems that closure is drawing near, it may be useful to consider offering the other party something small but of value to them as a sweetener to reach closure. It is crucial to be clear that this is a final gesture and that there will be no further concessions. Such a gesture can often break through any last-minute hesitation about reaching closure. The supplier will leave the negotiation feeling satisfied and fairly treated, a situation that can pay high dividends during the implementation phase of your arrangement.

Measuring the effectiveness of negotiating performance and outcomes

It is very important that after a major negotiation the team hold a debriefing session in order to evaluate their performance during the negotiation and the extent to which the negotiation could be considered to have been successful. In terms of outcomes the measure should be against the extent to which the targets set for the negotiation were achieved or not, and the easiest way to do this is a comparison against the original MILs (must, intend, like to achieve) set at the planning stage of the negotiation.

The debriefing sessions should be used as an opportunity for learning and improvement in future negotiations. The team should identify what was done well and what was done badly so that good practice can be reinforced and mistakes learned from and not repeated. Note that this is an opportunity for learning, not for blaming; the discussion should be open and not specifically critical of individuals, by referring to the team at all times as 'we'. The analysis should cover:

- How good was our preparation?
- Were our entry and exit points realistic?

- Did we follow and achieve our MILs?
- Did we make too may concessions?
- Did we maintain relationships?
- Did we close correctly and at the right time?
- Are all parties happy with the deal?
- Did the team perform well – if not, what did we do wrong?
- How did we perform in the face-to-face sense; did we handle the situation well?

The results should form learning points for the team so that good performance can be maintained and hopefully built upon in the future.

Self-assessment question 13.1

List the negotiation objectives that would be typical in your own negotiations with a supplier.

Feedback on page 217

13.2 Negotiating styles

Adversarial or partnership?

Negotiators have to decide whether their approach is to be adversarial or partnership, or a mixture of both.

An adversarial approach is referred to as a win-win or distributive style. Such a style will have a number of characteristics, and might be used in a one-off situation, or when a quick simple solution to an agreement is required.

Adversarial negotiations will emphasise competing goals at the adversary's expense and negotiation will be conducted in an air of secrecy, with outcomes often misrepresented so that the opponent is unclear as to the direction of the negotiations. Strategies are often unpredictable, and tactics are threats, bluffs and estimations, infused with hostility and aggression. Negotiations will be broken off if the goals are not achieved.

Partnership negotiation is known as a win-win or integrative style and develops around openness and high trust with a belief in shared goals. The atmosphere is one of solution-seeking, not threats, which are seen as counterproductive, and infused with clear predictable strategies discussed in an imaginative and friendly way.

A negotiating style will be influenced by many factors. All negotiations will be a reflection of the personality and interpersonal skills of the negotiators. Styles will vary according to the situation; therefore training should be given in behavioural analysis and tactics so that the most effective style is determined. Lack of understanding of behaviour will potentially damage relationships and the negotiations.

13

Learning activity 13.2

With regard to the objectives outlined in the self-assessment question 13.1 above, how do your negotiations obtain a balance between immediate reward and long-term supplier relationships?

Feedback on page 217

Personality and behaviour

An individual's personality is a relatively enduring pattern of behaviour, thinking and attitudes. Their personality will have an impact on negotiations in obvious ways; if it is friendly or courteous or aggressive, vulgar or rude. Evidence also suggests that the mix of personality variables will affect the outcome of negotiations, through personality traits such as authoritarianism, dogmatism, self-esteem, anxiousness or suspicion.

Behavioural styles in negotiations have been categorised by Lee and Lawrence (1991):

- *Proposing behaviour* is used to elicit development behaviour and support for solving complexity.
- *Development behaviour* is based on suggestions that elicit further explanation or advice.
- *Reasoned negative behaviour* can create a downward spiral in response unless the behaviour is conducted in a very reasoned manner.
- *Emotional negative behaviour* such as attack leads to an attack response.
- *Clarifying behaviour* checking the current position leads generally to supportive responses.
- *Seeking information behaviour* is a good shaping tactic.
- *Giving information behaviour* depends on the context as it is usually given in response to some other prompt for information.

How the negotiations are conducted will depend on the type of relationship desired with the supplier. The organisation will have to decide the extent to which the relationship is based on an adversarial or collaborative approach. If a more collaborative style is to be developed then this will involve a number of characteristics:

- commitment to the relationship and the seeking of best solutions
- agreement to common objectives
- open communications – research has suggested that even if weaknesses are self-evident this can lead to a collaborative approach from the other party
- strong ethical behaviour
- a reduction of total life cycle cost.

In particular there will be a need for a high level of communication skills.

The style of the relationship will also be determined by the time available to the parties. If deadlines are tight then competitive strategies will have to be used which will be time-intense if the parties are of similar bargaining strength. In such circumstances conflict will necessarily arise, and its resolution will be a reflection of the management style employed.

One of the more well-known models is by Blake and Mouton (1964, 1978) who show extremes on a continuum of care for the task and care for people.

Figure 13.1: The managerial grid

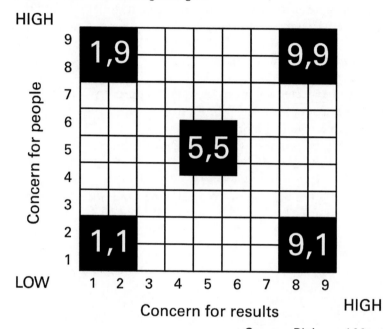

Source: Blake and Mouton (1964, 1978)

Blake and Mouton created a two-dimensional 'managerial grid' that has become a classic way to diagram the best way or universal approach model. This grid diagrams two basic dimensions of an effective leader. They are the *concern for results (task)* and *concern for people*. This managerial grid model has a numerical rating for each cell depending on the degree or amount of concern a manager demonstrates for results *and* for people. These two 'concerns' are considered to be independent of each other. The ideal is considered a 9.9-oriented manager who integrates a high concern for *both* the task and people to produce outstanding performance. Failure to integrate this style can lead to negotiation problems. For example a low integration will lead to relationship suffering because of the apathetic style of the manager, whereas too strong a focus on the task will lead to the opinions of other individuals being disregarded.

Negotiators can fall into four types.

The logical negotiator will be good at:

- knowing all the facts relating to the negotiation
- asking factual questions
- covering all bases so that no facts are left out
- providing information.

Logical negotiators tend to leave aside emotional criteria which may have an effect on the supplier if there is no attempt to build trust or be aware of sensitivity in any of the issues discussed.

13

The relationship negotiator will be better at:

- establishing relationships with the other party
- being sensitive to the other party's emotional issues
- building trust
- perceiving the position of the other party.

There is a danger that sight is lost of the purpose of the negotiations and the objectives in the anxiety to build good relationships.

The intuitive negotiator tends to be better at:

- coming up with unexpected solutions or ways of approach
- sorting out the key issues from the minor ones
- visualising the implications of a proposal
- accurately assessing the progress of the negotiation
- seeing the whole proceeds.

Their biggest weakness is the willingness to break ranks and not stick to the objectives.

The tough negotiator will tend to:

- be focused
- be unconcerned as to whether or not people are upset
- be adversarial and suppress arguments
- will give little to reason or pressure.

A tough opponent, but one who will have difficulty in building a relationship and runs the risk of the supplier walking away.

Many of these styles will be included in the make-up of all negotiators. The lead negotiator will have to ensure the best approach for the situation is put forward and weakness in the make-up of negotiators improved through training and development.

13

Self-assessment question 13.2

Outline what negotiating style you might adopt when buying.

Feedback on page 217

13.3 The importance of culture in dealing with overseas suppliers

As international sourcing continues to develop as organisations seek to achieve a competitive advantage, the buyer will need to possess knowledge of the determinants of suppliers' national and regional culture. Many, if not all, will have some impact on the trading relationship and are important if the buyer is to secure a successful commercial agreement.

Learning activity 13.3

Explain the research you would carry out on the cultural background of key suppliers.

Feedback on page 218

Determinants of culture include:

- social structure
- religion and religious history
- political output
- language
- education
- economic philosophy.

A buyer cannot afford to be badly informed and needs sufficient market intelligence on the cultural value systems and norms as this may have a significant bearing on how contracts are ultimately negotiated.

Organisational culture

Recent observations on the relationship between business, society and culture include two influential studies of the dimensions of acculturation in a transnational corporation by Hofstede; and a later study of managers in various developed countries by Trompenaars. Cultural differences may extend to negotiating styles, decision-making processes, problem-solving techniques and ethical issues. It is important for the buyer to learn these cultural cues and respond effectively.

13

Self-assessment question 13.3

Geert Hofstede personal website: http://www.geert-hofstede.com is the website of Geert Hofstede, whose research into national cultural differences has been regarded as a seminal work. Identify the cultural differences of your key suppliers as defined by the Hofstede research and listed country by country on his website.

Feedback on page 218

13.4 Successful negotiations

Successful negotiations need thorough planning, including market intelligence, and an awareness of the supplier's culture and organisational needs. The buyer should be fully informed of the strengths and weaknesses of the respective negotiating positions, and have at their fingertips all the relevant data on costs, production, sales, and so on. Some of this data should be available as part of a formal presentation.

Research suggests that setting the right tone at the beginning of the negotiation will avoid any unnecessary tension between the parties. For example, the importance of providing refreshments should not be underestimated. Small talk is also important in breaking the ice and assessing the other side's negotiating style and language style, which can then be mirrored in the formal discussions.

There should always be some express respect for the other side's experience and expertise.

The task should wherever possible be framed positively as a joint endeavour.

There should be some awareness expressed as to issues on the supplier's side. Open-ended questions will assist in gaining further information of the other side's goals, interests and concerns.

Good listening skills will enhance the buyer's performance and include:

- keeping eye contact with the speaker
- taking notes as appropriate
- focusing on the speaker's points at all times
- responses are not formulated until the speaker has finished
- pay attention to the speaker's body language
- repeat what has been stated so as ensure that all has been understood.

Empathy and sensitivity is important throughout the negotiations including acknowledgement of any thorny issue that may cause tension between the parties.

Exploiting differences between the parties

By concentrating on dealing with the differences between the parties in a positive way, it may be possible to bridge the gaps in the negotiations. By trading on differences, value is created for both parties. For example, if there is a resource issue, it may be possible for the buyer to make a contribution to warehouse, transportation, and even administrative assistance if this is something that would not unnecessarily add to the cost structure. Future expectations from a close and long-term relationship are a strong factor in achieving short-term concessions on price and delivery etc. Risk is another factor that needs careful discussion, and if the risk is greater to one of the parties it may be possible to move aspects of the risk to the party least affected.

A buyer should not be tempted to close a deal too quickly before all aspects are considered. It is worthwhile spending a bit more time to conclude a satisfactory deal.

The negotiations should remain within a clear framework so that the parties remain focused. The buyer can assist this framework approach by constantly restating the key issues on which a successful negotiation will be based,

13

for example, quality of supply, the need for zero defects and prompt and accurate delivery.

Buyers should also be prepared to evaluate the negotiating process on an ongoing basis, as new information comes to the table and requires assimilation. A slower-paced negotiation allows the buyer to reflect on progress and style and who might be dominating the proceedings and perhaps restore some equilibrium.

Learning activity 13.4

From your own organisational experience list the factors that have contributed to successful negotiations.

Feedback on page 218

Now try self-assessment question 13.4 below.

Self-assessment question 13.4

Examine what personal skills and strengths you might bring to negotiations.

Feedback on page 218

13.5 Assessment of the risk in negotiations

The major supply risk of failed negotiations can be assessed in terms of the profit margin of the business.

Barriers to agreement

There are many reasons why negotiations fail, including tough negotiators who fight for every scrap of value. The response to this is to walk away if the other side should see the benefit in reaching agreement. A strong BATNA will enhance the negotiating positions.

Few agreements are possible if there is lack of trust. Insecure agreements will not last long as parties seek better relationships with others. Transparency in the negotiations is an important part of the process, as is the structure of the agreement which includes benefits in the long term, subject to compliance and performance. A good specification and detailed but fair contract is part of the structure of negotiations which can build stability into the relationship.

Trust is built with clear open communication lines.

Informational vacuums in which both parties are not forthcoming with information about their needs and business situation is a dilemma which must be resolved if there is to be successful agreement completion.

13

Differences in culture may bring unspoken assumptions to the negotiating table. Buyers must look for patterns in any failure to understand or dealing with the supplier and seek intelligence to overcome the barriers.

Communication is at the core of the negotiation and can cause relationships to turn sour if the parties are not engaged in the right tone and at the right level. This points to the need to have skilled and sensitive negotiators who also possess the ability to use effective dialogue in all situations, no matter how tense.

Technical difficulties which cannot be overcome in the short term, including having a strong BATNA available to combat tough opponents who are demanding too much. A clear communicative style is a strong asset. Good specifications also are important. Above all there is a need to develop a strong feeling of trust within the relationship and the selling of the benefits to both parties over the long term.

Learning activity 13.5

Sony delayed its launch of the long-awaited PlayStation 3 until November 2006 instead of spring 2006, confirming months of growing speculation of a delay. Sony was still trying to finalise with content producers and other electronic organisations, the copyright-protection technology and other standards for the Blu-ray DVD disc, the high-definition video format for PlayStation 3 and other next-generation DVD players.

What is the risk in this scenario for the Sony organisation?

Feedback on page 218

13

Now try self-assessment question 13.5 below.

Self-assessment question 13.5

How would you minimise risk in your own negotiations?

Feedback on page 218

Revision question

Now try the revision question for this session on page 342.

Summary

Negotiations are a skilled activity which requires a professional approach to the whole process, considerable personal and intellectual skills and an acute awareness of the business world.

Suggested further reading

Read the chapter on negotiation in Lysons and Farrington (2006).

Feedback on learning activities and self-assessment questions

Feedback on learning activity 13.1

It should be recognised that most negotiations are rarely win-win (where both parties meet their objectives) or win-lose (where one party meets their objectives and the other doesn't) situations. Instead, negotiations are mixtures of common and conflicting interests and objectives and call for a mixture of negotiating strategies. It is the complexity that needs to be recognised and will relate to the importance of the negotiations and also the bargaining strength of the parties.

However, the following would normally be part of all negotiations:

- attention given to preparation
- structuring the negotiation to get the best possible outcome
- managing the timeline so that there is a correct degree of urgency
- managing the information exchange so that one party does not dominate.

Feedback on self-assessment question 13.1

The list would contain the typical MIL points: a categorisation of what the organisation:

- Must achieve
- Intend to achieve
- Like to achieve.

In addition there would be some indication as to the BATNA.

Feedback on learning activity 13.2

Much depends upon the style of negotiations decided upon by the organisation, whether it is adversarial or partnership. If it is the latter then the long-term relationship with the supplier will be important, especially if the supplier is a major supplier. However, negotiations should still achieve the key objectives in terms of cost savings, price, delivery schedules and performance after taking into account the reasonable requirements of the supplier.

Feedback on self-assessment question 13.2

Negotiators may vary their style according to the circumstances, and the culture of the business. However, their personality may result in an entrenched style – which could be the logical negotiator, the relationship negotiator, the intuitive negotiator or the tough negotiator.

13

Feedback on learning activity 13.3

Research will be essential to appreciate the strong cultural differences of the supplier's country so that as an important early issue offence is not caused by the style of negotiations, words or tactics used. By understanding a supplier's cultural background in terms of business ideology, religious, philosophical and educational influences, political structure and social structure, it will be possible to shape the communications within negotiations to have maximum impact.

Feedback on self-assessment question 13.3

Differences between people within any given nation or culture are much greater than differences between groups. Education, social standing, religion, personality, belief structure, past experience, affection shown in the home, and a myriad of other factors will affect human behaviour and culture. Awareness of these cultural differences is important if negotiations are to be effectively managed.

Feedback on learning activity 13.4

Planning and knowing the strengths and weaknesses of the other party is essential for successful negotiations, as is the background and issues that the other party may bring to the negotiating table. An outline of the extent and content of the planning process would be useful. Using the right tone, establishing friendly relationships, working on the differences between the parties, plus an assessment of the extent to which relationships with suppliers have contributed to the successful negotiations.

Feedback on self-assessment question 13.4

Confidence and enjoyment in the proceedings so that they are not hurried, the ability to build trust, the skills to move positions, good listening skills and an ability to know when a win of successful position has been secured. In addition good knowledge about the products and processes under discussion and a breadth of view about the industry in general.

Feedback on learning activity 13.5

The delay in market terms means that rivals such as Microsoft have a longer period to establish their new Xbox as the current market leader. It is also a good example of the risks involved in collaborative decisions on advanced technology. Negotiations are complicated and take time when there are more than two parties. In addition there needs to be some assessment as to whether or not the insistence on such advanced technology, which will be expensive, will be purchased by discerning customers.

Feedback on self-assessment question 13.5

The major risk in negotiations is that they will not be concluded satisfactorily for the benefit of the organisation. Sometimes negotiations fail,

13

sometimes relationships are damaged which may affect future performance of the supplier.

There are a number of strategies that can be adopted to minimise the risk.

- Adopt a clear communication style. Listening is a key aspect of effective communication. The ability to listen on multiple levels – what is and what isn't being said – is key during negotiations and in building rapport with others.
- Build early cross-functional alliances. Invest upfront time in building relationships across the organisation, as well as with external partners and customers who may be directly or indirectly impacted by your proposed project.
- Be prepared to identify the buyer's risks to the supplier.
- Adapt to the risk styles of others.
- Work hard to build early rapport with your counterpart. People negotiate with people, not tactics, and therefore it's important to establish early rapport with the supplier.
- Understand your supplier's issues and problems.
- Assume more of the risk.
- Pace the flow. The more risk-averse the environment, the greater the need for you to manage the pace and flow of negotiations.
- Close the negotiations properly.

13

Aligning negotiations with strategy

Introduction

Negotiation is more than securing the best price at the right price. It is also about the alignment of the purchasing function's activities with the overall strategic position of the business.

Session learning objectives

After completing this session you should be able to:

14.1 Design a negotiation campaign in line with business strategy.
14.2 Apply negotiating tactics to specific organisational objectives.
14.3 Relate negotiating strategies with ethical policy.

Unit content coverage

Learning objective

3.2 Manage the negotiation process in line with organisational objectives and its relation to policy, general strategy and internal strategy for the purchasing and supply process.

Prior knowledge

Study session 1.

Timing

You should set aside about 5 hours to read and complete this session, including learning activities, self-assessment questions, the suggested further reading (if any) and the revision question.

14.1 To design a negotiation campaign in line with business strategy

Introduction

Organisations need to be able to align their procurement strategies not only to their corporate or business unit objectives, but also to the dynamic demands of the marketplace. In most industries, it is rather unusual that a single company performs all activities from product design, production of components, and final assembly to delivery to the final user by itself. Usually organisations are elements of a value system or value chain and therefore analysis should cover the whole value system in which the organisation operates. The strategic objectives set by the organisation have

'Activities within the organisation add value to the service and products that the organisation produces, and all these activities should be run at optimum level if the organisation is to gain any real competitive advantage'.
Porter (1998b)

14

to be delivered by the specialist functions within the organisation and assisted by the major players within the supply chain. Within the whole value system there is only a certain value of profit margin available. The final margin is determined by the price the customer pays set against the costs incurred.

The purchasing function must use its market position and negotiating skills to improve the margin and to cooperate to improve efficiency and reduce costs.

Learning activity 14.1

Produce a report showing how your procurement negotiating objectives align with the overall strategy of the business.

Feedback on page 228

The **value chain** as described by Michael Porter (1985) categorises the generic value-adding activities of an organisation. The value chain analysis describes the activities the organisation performs and links them to the organisation's competitive position.

Figure 14.1: Porter's value chain

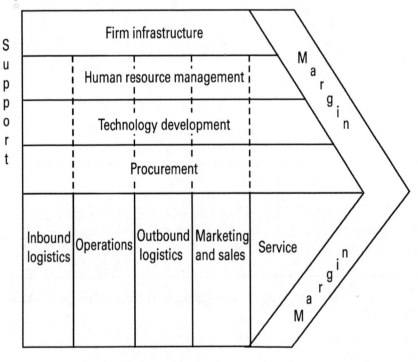

Primary activities

Source: Porter (1985)

Value chain analysis describes the activities within and around an organisation, and relates them to an analysis of the competitive strength of the organisation. Therefore, it evaluates which value each particular activity adds to the organisation's products or services. This idea was built upon the insight that an organisation is more than a random compilation of

14

machinery, equipment, people and money. Only if these things are arranged into systems and systematic activities will it become possible to produce something for which customers are willing to pay a price. Porter argues that the ability to perform particular activities and to manage the linkages between these activities is a source of competitive advantage.

The 'primary activities' include: inbound logistics, production, outbound logistics, sales and marketing, maintenance. The 'support activities' include: administrative infrastructure management, human resources management, R&D and procurement. The costs and value drivers are identified for each value activity. It is a powerful tool for strategic planning the margin and will influence, according to Lynch (2000), decision making in areas such as:

- market adaptability
- taking on the competition
- adding value through enhanced performance or value
- achieving low costs through manufacture
- delivering human resource objectives
- establishing a link between manufacturing and marketing.

Whatever the decision making, the buyer is required to ensure the supply. Suppliers have become critical players in the success of the business, and their failure to deliver on any of the key results areas will have a major impact on the effective management of operations.

Negotiations will have to reflect the strategic direction of the business and consider the concerns over the increased risk associated with aggressive outsourcing and relationship management models.

The increasing trend of suppliers designing, building and often directly delivering complete subsystems has seriously diminished options of splitting contract awards and managing second sources. Such interdependence makes the penalties for failure an additional relationship problem. Increasingly purchasing and senior management must negotiate on a tightrope which balances conflicting strategies and tactics that simultaneously reduce cost and risk.

14

Self-assessment question 14.1

Examine how business strategy can be out of line with supplier reality.

Feedback on page 228

14.2 Applying negotiating tactics to specific organisational objectives

The planning process and objectives

The purchasing function will need to respond to operational objectives that flow down from the strategic planning at senior level. The negotiating plan that will incorporate these objectives will inevitably have elements of cutting costs, reducing inventory and sharing basic demand forecast data with established trading partners. The use of e-commerce technology has begun to facilitate the more efficient management of the supply chain operations; the strategic cost drivers are generated from senior management in response to stakeholder demands – shareholders or lenders – in an attempt to optimise supply chain efficiency and effectiveness.

Meeting these customer needs without increasing supply chain costs through rising inventory levels requires work on closing the gap between the traditional supply chain approach and the customer. In some industries this may involve connecting supply chain planning processes with customer relationship management (CRM) software. CRM is about influencing demand through promotion and brand value, and that information needs to be fed back into the supply chain to improve planning.

Learning activity 14.2

In a reverse auction, buying organisations post the items they wish to buy and the price they are willing to pay, while suppliers compete to offer the best price for the items over a period of time. This is, of course, a good cost strategy but there are potential problems.

Critics of reverse auctions argue that online reverse auctions rarely deliver savings that are as great as advertised by auction service providers. In addition, they contend that savings from reverse auctions are difficult to measure and that they do not teach buyers and sellers how to solve problems jointly. They conclude that reverse auctions are damaging for buyer-supplier relationships.

Some of the savings from using reverse auctions disappear because of factors such as errors in supplier data, post auction negotiation, and changes in specifications or quantities. In addition, it does not account for extra expenses resulting from problems such as poor quality, late deliveries and supplier non-performance. When these losses are added up, net savings from reverse auctions look far less appealing than buyers expect.

Even more dangerous is the deterioration of buyer and supplier relationships when reverse auctions are used to simply attack suppliers on price.

How do you account for the developing activity in reverse auctions with the literature expounding closer supplier relationships?

Feedback on page 228

Now try self-assessment question 14.2 below.

Self-assessment question 14.2

A cost reduction approach to buying is a feature of many of the major supermarkets. The benefits have been seen in falling prices for the consumer. As a strategy can this be maintained?

Feedback on page 228

14

14.3 The ethical impact on negotiating strategies

The importance of ethics

Ethics is often defined as a concern 'with the moral principles and values which govern our beliefs, actions and decisions'.

Lysons and Farrington list the importance of ethics for purchasing:

- Purchasing staff are the representatives of the organisation in its dealings with suppliers.
- Sound ethical conduct in dealing with suppliers is essential to the creation of long-term relationships and the establishment of supplier goodwill.
- Purchasing staff are probably more exposed to the temptation to act unethically than most other employees.
- It is impossible to claim professional status for purchasing without reference to a consideration of its ethical aspects.

Discussion has already taken place on negotiation style and the rejection in most circumstances of the adversarial style. Whether or not it is unethical will be dependent upon the viewpoint of ethics. For example, the *individualist* view of ethics suggests that conduct is good which promotes my personal interests as well as those of my organisation, irrespective of how this affects the interests of other people or organisations.

Learning activity 14.3

Explain the ethical stance in your own organisation to purchasing within a competitive market.

Feedback on page 229

The Chartered Institute of Purchasing and Supply have issued a code of conduct that members should respect, as follows.

Introduction

1   Members of the Institute undertake to work to exceed the expectations of the following Code and will regard the Code as the basis of best conduct in the Purchasing and Supply profession.
2   Members should seek the commitment of their employer to the Code and seek to achieve widespread acceptance of it amongst their fellow employees.
3   Members should raise any matter of concern of an ethical nature with their immediate supervisor or another senior colleague if appropriate, irrespective of whether it is explicitly addressed in the Code.

Principles

4   Members shall always seek to uphold and enhance the standing of the Purchasing and Supply profession and will always act professionally and selflessly by:

14

(a) maintaining the highest possible standard of integrity in all their business relationships both inside and outside the organisations where they work;

(b) rejecting any business practice which might reasonably be deemed improper and never using their authority for personal gain;

(c) enhancing the proficiency and stature of the profession by acquiring and maintaining current technical knowledge and the highest standards of ethical behaviour;

(d) fostering the highest possible standards of professional competence amongst those for whom they are responsible;

(e) optimising the use of resources which they influence and for which they are responsible to provide the maximum benefit to their employing organisation;

(f) complying both with the letter and the spirit of:
   (i) the law of the country in which they practise;
   (ii) Institute guidance on professional practice;
   (iii) contractual obligations.

5 Members should never allow themselves to be deflected from these principles.

Guidance

6 In applying these principles, members should follow the guidance set out below:

1 Declaration of interest – Any personal interest which may affect or be seen by others to affect a member's impartiality in any matter relevant to his or her duties should be declared.

2 Confidentiality and accuracy of information – The confidentiality of information received in the course of duty should be respected and should never be used for personal gain. Information given in the course of duty should be honest and clear.

3 Competition – The nature and length of contracts and business relationships with suppliers can vary according to circumstances. These should always be constructed to ensure deliverables and benefits. Arrangements which might in the long term prevent the effective operation of fair competition should be avoided.

4 Business gifts – Business gifts, other than items of very small intrinsic value such as business diaries or calendars, should not be accepted.

5 Hospitality – The recipient should not allow him or herself to be influenced or be perceived by others to have been influenced in making a business decision as a consequence of accepting hospitality. The frequency and scale of hospitality accepted should be managed openly and with care and should not be greater than the member's employer is able to reciprocate.

Decisions and advice

7 When it is not easy to decide between what is and is not acceptable, advice should be sought from the member's supervisor, another senior colleague or the Institute as appropriate. Advice on any aspect of the Code is available from the Institute.

This Code was approved by the Council of CIPS on 16 October 1999.

It is clear from the Code that before, during or after negotiations it is important that purchasing staff do not accept gifts or hospitality that is more than trivial or, in the case of hospitality, in the normal course of commercial business. Indeed, any inducement that can be construed as an inducement or reward for entering into a contract would amount to a criminal offence under the Prevention of Corruption Act 1906, or the Prevention of Corruption Act 1916 (which are concerned with public sector corruption).

The general benefits of having a code are the following:

- It provides guidance as to the cultural values of the business and the expected style of managers and employees.
- It signals expectations of proper conduct to those dealing with the organisation.
- It nurtures a business environment of open communications which is essential in building the sort of relationships necessary for flexible supplier response.
- It prevents possible legal proceedings.

Are codes enough?

There is no guarantee that an individual's dealings with suppliers will not stray into unethical conduct. Organisations may decide to take a tougher line in an increasingly competitive world and the result is that sometimes people are mistreated. However, the tough-guy negotiator may not win many friends but it is also questionable if it is unethical if this becomes the accepted management style of the organisation.

Training and development will inculcate what is expected as behaviour in negotiating situations.

Negotiations could engender a socially responsible spirit if practical help and advice is given to suppliers where appropriate, for example, giving feedback when they have failed in their bid to become a supplier, or giving advice and assistance with design and production. Prompt payment is also a good strategy for building trust and loyalty. If relationships are to become closer then the buyer may enter into a partnership supply relationship.

14

Self-assessment question 14.3

Undertake a self-assessment of how ethical standards are maintained during negotiations.

Feedback on page 229

Revision question

Now try the revision question for this session on page 342.

Summary

All purchasing decision making must be closely aligned to the business purpose. As part of the value chain, fulfilment of the business objectives by procurement contributes to the ultimate margin to the benefit of all those in the organisation.

Suggested further reading

Read the chapter on negotiation in Lysons and Farrington (2006).

Feedback on learning activities and self-assessment questions

Feedback on learning activity 14.1

Most business strategies require the purchasing function to deliver the right goods and services at the right time and at the right price, and in addition negotiate for continuing improvement in the supply chain. Linked in with this is the constant drive to secure a lean operation and flexibility in operations so as to deal quickly with changing customer demands. The report should reflect this general strategy and also assess the contribution that the purchasing function can make to the final margin.

Feedback on self-assessment question 14.1

The business strategy may set unrealistic goals which create undue pressures down the supply chain to conform to unobtainable targets of real-time delivery, substantial cost reductions, contributions to design and contributions to promotions.

Feedback on learning activity 14.2

The use of e-auctions is increasingly common where the buyer can exploit a dominant position in the market. They are certainly effective in driving down prices in competitive markets, and are effective for large orders. The potential downside is that the considered negotiation element is largely missing plus the resulting agreement after the conclusion of give-and-take negotiations. Subsequent involvement of the supplier in purchasing operations will be more difficult if the contracts are awarded purely on the auction. It is about cost, not relationships.

Feedback on self-assessment question 14.2

The recent investigations by the Office of Fair Trading suggest that the dominant position of the major supermarkets is not beneficial to all sectors of the business community. Customers are pleased with the price reductions and many suppliers are guaranteed substantial contracts. The long-term impact of this strategy in terms of future tactics, diversity of supply and customer choice is yet to be seen.

14

Feedback on learning activity 14.3

Compliance with the CIPS ethical code would be a good benchmark in terms of some of the values expressed, namely integrity in relationships, setting high standards of ethical performance, rejecting inappropriate business behaviour and complying with the letter and spirit of the law.

In addition there would be specific rules in place to ensure that there is no restrictive practice activities, or personnel are gaining from their position as buyers.

Feedback on self-assessment question 14.3

Buyers will be aware of the ethical issues by which they must abide as a result of the own contracts and training on ethical policy. Awareness will extend to the consequences of breaking their contractual contacts and organisational rules of behaviour, and on a positive note they will appreciate that an ethical and trustworthy stance is better for long-term customer relationships.

14

14

Advanced negotiation techniques

Introduction

Skilled negotiators seek to learn a little more about the tactics of those with whom they negotiate. The ability to influence is an important skill, as is the understanding in basic psychological terms what is behind the actions, words and body language.

Session learning objectives

After completing this session you should be able to:

15.1 Assess the contribution of transactional analysis to negotiating styles.
15.2 Evaluate the psychology behind game theory.
15.3 Explain the techniques behind influencing skills.

Unit content coverage

Learning objective

3.4   Understand advanced negotiation techniques.

Timing

You should set aside about 5 hours to read and complete this session, including learning activities, self-assessment questions, the suggested further reading (if any) and the revision question.

15.1 The contribution of transactional analysis to negotiating styles

Transactional analysis

It is thought that in developing negotiating techniques and skills, some adherence to psychological theory will aid the contractual negotiations. Transactional analysis, developed by Eric Berne in the 1950s, has relevance to understanding negotiating behaviour. The 'transaction' is a unit of social interaction. People interact and speak and by acknowledging the presence of others provide a *transactional stimulus*. The transactional response is the reaction of the other person to the stimulus. These responses tend to proceed in chains and are influenced by the frames of mind or ego types, namely parent, adult and child, which influence behaviour. Transactional

'Regardless of whether a person intends to take a line [verbally or nonverbally], he will find that he has come to do so in effect. The other participants will assume that he has more or less wilfully taken a stand...'
Goffman (1981)

15

analysis is a contractual approach. A contract is 'an explicit bilateral commitment to a well-defined course of action' (Berne, 1970). This means that all parties need to agree:

- why they want to do something
- with whom
- what they are going to do
- by when
- any fees, payment or exchanges there will be.

Contracts need to be outlined in positive words – what is wanted, rather than what is not wanted. Our minds tend to focus on the negative and so this encourages failure. Contracts need to be: measurable, manageable and motivational. Measurable means that the goals need to be tangible, that each party involved in the contract will be able to say in advance how they will know when the goal has been achieved. The goal will be specific and behavioural and clearly defined. The contract will also need to be manageable and feasible for all those concerned.

Parent ego state

In simple terms this state reflects the influence of the parent carer. In negotiations we have to be aware that some of our attitudinal perceptions are based on the character of our parents, and we end up expressing ourselves as they did.

Adult ego state

The Adult ego state is about direct responses to the here and now. We deal with things that are going on today in ways that are not unhealthily influenced by our past.

The Adult ego state is about being spontaneous and aware with the capacity for intimacy. When in our Adult state we are able to see people as they are, rather than what we project onto them. We ask for information rather than stay scared and rather than make assumptions. Taking the best from the past and using it appropriately in the present is an integration of the positive aspects of both our Parent and Child ego states. So this can be called the Integrating Adult. Integrating means that we are constantly updating ourselves through our everyday experiences and using this to inform us. Experience combined with positive behaviour can improve the negotiation outcomes. It can be used to balance the Parent and Child states, to remove, where possible, feelings of negativity or inadequacy, and to take from earlier Parent state experiences something positive.

The Child ego state is a set of behaviours, thoughts and feelings which are replayed from our own childhood.

Perhaps the boss calls us into his or her office; we may immediately get a churning in our stomach and wonder what we have done wrong. If this were explored we might remember the time the headteacher called us in to tell us off. Of course, not everything in the Child ego state is negative. Equally we might go into someone's house and smell a lovely smell and remember our grandmother's house when we were little, and all the same warm feelings we had at six years of age may come flooding back.

Both the Parent and Child ego states are constantly being updated. If this updating can concentrate on positive elements, then the person's character and behaviour patterns will become more positive. Negative memories in the Child state can hamper personal growth.

All these states can become contaminated where people inculcate something as a fact when it is merely a belief. Stubbornness and intransigence could then be the result.

The process of analysing personality in terms of ego states is called *structural analysis*. It is important to remember that ego states do not have an existence of their own; they are concepts to enable understanding. People who understand their personality determinants may be able to make adjustments and thereby be a more practical and more sensitive negotiator.

Learning activity 15.1

Reflect on recent negotiations in which you have been involved, and explain how preparation could achieve a positive adult state.

Feedback on page 238

Now try self-assessment question 15.1 below.

Self-assessment question 15.1

List a couple of factors from the child state that might hamper productive negotiations.

Feedback on page 238

15

15.2 Game theory and other approaches to negotiation

Game theory

For those who are mathematically minded, game theory which was developed by Neumann, Morgenstern and also Nash has as its purpose a strategy to secure the most favourable game value in the long run. It is an attempt to balance achieving the best position but also dealing with issues of uncertainty. A mirroring strategy, in which the player responds to a given move with a similar move, is the most common. A mixed strategy involves randomly choosing among one's best strategies according to some proportions in order to maximise favourable game value. This is the strategy that would work best in the long run, as it keeps the opponents guessing, whereas a pure strategy in repeated games would give the opponent an advantage of predictability (von Neumann and Morgenstern, 1947).

A classic game in the theory of games literature is what is called the Prisoner's Dilemma. There are two actors or participants in the game, and while each has the incentive to maximise personal gains at the expense of the other, in the long run both participants would be better off in cooperating against the other factors entering into their world. The result is that they are both better off, compared to a total loss if both carried on in their individual strategy to outwit the other.

In the 'Prisoner's Dilemma' two prisoners, A and B, have been convicted of a minor crime and are serving a month's jail term but they are jointly suspected of having committed a more serious offence, for which the penalty is a year's jail sentence. Each of them is individually offered immediate release from prison if he alone admits to having committed the second crime, while there will be a sentence of only six months' imprisonment if both confess. Without confessions from either, there can be no prosecution for the second offence. The dilemma facing each prisoner is then whether it is in his own interests to confess to the second crime: the table below shows the consequences for both prisoners in the four sets of circumstances which could arise (see table 15.1).

Table 15.1

	A keeps silent	**A confesses**
B keeps silent	• A: imprisoned for one month • B: imprisoned for one month • Total imprisonment: two months	• A: free • B: imprisoned for one year • Total imprisonment: one year
B confesses	• A: Imprisoned for one year • B: Free • Total imprisonment: one year	• A: imprisoned for six months • B: imprisoned for six months • Total imprisonment: one year

The rational, utilitarian course of action is to minimise the total amount of imprisonment for the two men together, which is achieved by both keeping silent and not confessing. Tactical ethics requires them both to be rogues together; open honesty does not pay in the long run. However, this extends the dilemma further. If both prisoners realise that it is not in their joint interests to confess, each may assume that the other is not going to confess. There is then a real temptation for each one to break ranks and win immediate freedom at the expense of the other.

This is not, however, a one-time stance. Game theory understands that most games are repeated rather than single-shot. Repetition means each player has additional information based on past game decisions of the other player. This complicates calculation of choices and changes the equilibrium point. Thus if the Prisoner's Dilemma is repeated a sufficient number of times, players may learn to take a strategic view and cooperate.

In terms of negotiation, some rough parallels can be drawn from the repeated dealings between buyers and suppliers, and because of the growing knowledge of each other's situation and tactics, the benefits of cooperation soon become apparent, and an adversarial or win-lose strategy is less attractive. It links once more to the question of power and the extent to which an organisation wishes to engage in a long-term relationship.

15

Body language

In all negotiations there is an element of assessment of the other side's feeling towards the negotiations as they progress. For example, whether the negotiations are being conducted in an open and honest way, whether the supplier is happy or not with the current state of affairs.

Body language may play a small part in revealing the feelings of the other side to the negotiations and a skilled negotiator may become attuned to these factors.

Baily et al (2004) list the possible interpretations (see table 15.2).

Table 15.2

Posture	Possible meaning
Leaning forward when making a point	Interested, wants to emphasise a point
Avoiding eye contact	May be embarrassed, not telling the truth
Arms folded, body turned away	Defensive, no compromise, not interested
Body turned towards you, leaning forward	Interested, warming towards your comments
Looking at a watch or window	Wants to leave or avoid any further discussion
Hands supporting head and leaning back	Confidence
Stroking nose regularly, avoiding eye contact	May be lying
Good eye contact, fingers stroking face	Interested in what you are saying

Use of ploys

In some negotiations ploys are used to win ground. These can include standards such as:

- *Nice guy/hard guy.*
- *Add ons*, in which a basic deal is negotiated and additional issues cost more money.
- *Deadlines*, where the other side is pressurised to complete or the deal is off.
- *Russian front*, in which two choices are offered with one so bad that the other is accepted.
- *Empty larder*, where one party suggests that they have so little to offer in an attempt to reduce demands.

It can be seen that this becomes part of a 'game' that is soon recognised by an experienced negotiator and is soon countered. They also run the risk of damaging long-term relationships.

Learning activity 15.2

To what extent do the various models or ploys suggested in this study session have relevance in modern negotiations?

Feedback on page 238

Now try self-assessment question 15.2 below.

Self-assessment question 15.2

Reflect on your own negotiating style and identify any body language traits that might reveal how you are feeling.

Feedback on page 239

15.3 Influencing skills

Influencing styles

A skill that is needed in all negotiations or discussions is the ability to persuade others to see your point of view. Much influence stems from the power residing in the individual wielding it. In negotiations that power may come naturally from being the representative of an organisation that is in the stronger economic position. Other power sources come from knowledge and expertise.

Learning activity 15.3

Undertake observational research on organisational key players and extract pertinent examples of successful influencing strategies.

Feedback on page 239

A good influencer is able to:

* work collaboratively in changing environments, respond to pressure and achieve goals and objectives
* establish rapport and gain buy-in, support and commitment
* motivate others to 'do more with less'
* dissolve or overcome resistance
* create positive partnerships critical for success in the future.

The Margerison-McCann Influencing Skills Model identifies a number of influencing techniques:

* *Pacing* is the technique of varying your communication style to match that of other people.
* *Inquiry* is listening carefully to what people are saying and asking questions to fill in the gaps. Knowing when to use closed-ended inquiry or open-ended inquiry and when to focus on the facts or the feelings are the skills associated with this sector.
* A joint *diagnosis* of the root cause of a problem is essential before any discussion on solutions is attempted.

15

- When discussions or negotiations are complex and long, everyone will lose track of the important points. *Summarising* is therefore essential to ensure that everyone has the same understanding.
- *Leading* is one of the most critical solution-centred skills as it can focus the conversation on the important issues. It is a process of transmitting information in a way that leads people to talk about possible solutions rather than your imposing solutions upon them. Leading can be done overtly (simple leading) or covertly (complex leading) and can involve advanced techniques such as story-telling.
- *Proposing* involves presenting possible solutions as a choice of options. The number of choices will often depend upon the various role preferences of the team.
- *Directing* is the technique that managers use without thinking. It involves telling others what to do and can be used in collaborative partnerships with suppliers.

Huczynski (2004) identified influencing as a person's ability to affect another's attitudes, beliefs or behaviours. Influencing is a process that is not always observable but is understood. It will happen naturally during negotiations as benefits are proposed and exchanged, if the norms of obligation and reciprocity are followed. People generally respond positively if they feel acknowledged, understood and appreciated. Influencing skills require a strong combination of interpersonal, communication, presentation and assertiveness techniques.

It is a good alternative tactic to threats or aggressive behaviour and will help sustain long-term relationships. Kipnis (1986) and Forsyth (1993) studied influencing techniques used by managers on others. Many of these strategies are useful for the negotiations, although some such as bullying, manipulation, use of sanctions and assertiveness may damage relationships. Successful strategies might include:

- *reason*, in which there is reliance on data and information as the basis for logical argument
- *friendliness*
- *higher command*, whereby extra power is referred to in an attempt to impress the other side
- *making promises for the future*
- *discussion* on complex issues
- *use of expertise and knowledge.*

15

Self-assessment question 15.3

Undertake an assessment of the personal skills that you require for successful negotiating.

Feedback on page 239

Revision question

Now try the revision question for this session on page 343.

Summary

Negotiating at an advanced level is not just about standard negotiation approach – opening, exploring issues and inventing options, making offers, offering concessions, reaching closure – it is also about techniques of influencing and the understanding and playing of mind games to ensure the best advantage is obtained.

Suggested further reading

Read the chapter on negotiation in Lysons and Farrington (2006).

Feedback on learning activities and self-assessment questions

Feedback on learning activity 15.1

A good negotiator will not be influenced by the mind games of others and will also be able to dispel any negative thought they may have which reduced them to child state by reinforcing in their mind the positive experiences, thus restoring the adult state. The Adult ego state is about being spontaneous and aware with the capacity for intimacy. When in our Adult state we are able to see people as they are, rather than what we project onto them. We ask for information rather than stay scared and rather than make assumptions. Taking the best from the past and using it appropriately in the present is an integration of the positive aspects of both our Parent and Child ego states. So this can be called the Integrating Adult.

Feedback on self-assessment question 15.1

The child state of mind tends to be any disturbance or distortion of a positive image caused by negative experiences in the past whether as a child or an adult, and which creates, for example, nervousness and affects the ability to perform at the right level.

If a negotiator is not confident of their own abilities and purpose, there might be a tendency in negotiations to be subordinated by the more dominant parent style of the supplier's negotiating tactics. Negotiators cannot afford to be other than effective and positive adults when dealing with complex and sometimes emotionally involved proceedings.

A child state of mind may lead to emotional outbursts (similar to a child) which may cause the buyer to lose credibility or weaken their negotiating position.

Feedback on learning activity 15.2

Ploys are of limited value to all but the inexperienced negotiator, and are easy to spot and block. Also they run the risk of damaging long-term relationships. For example, the nice guy/hard guy ploy is familiar to most people from the world of police interrogations.

Feedback on self-assessment question 15.2

There is scope here for some mild self-analysis, in particular in picking out any obvious nervous signs that might be obvious to the other negotiating side. Some consideration of identifiable body language traits will assist in being able to control any giveaway behaviour.

Feedback on learning activity 15.3

This is an opportunity to look, listen and learn from experienced negotiators to work out how they establish credibility and win points in complex situations, how they establish rapport, motivate others to concede and do more for less and create positive relationships with those in the supply chain.

Feedback on self-assessment question 15.3

There are many skills for a successful negotiator.

The Margerison-McCann Influencing Skills Model identifies a number of influencing techniques such as pacing – varying the communication style, inquiry – the ability to listen and respond, plus the intellectual ability to diagnose and respond to complex issues.

15

Developing supplier relationships

Introduction

As organisations continue to strive for competitive advantage, cross-functional internal working, collaborations and partnership agreements with suppliers are becoming more essential. The difficulty lies in integrating such collaborative arrangements and ensuring that they deliver results over a long period of time.

'Unless ... cooperative relationships become increasingly collaborative in nature, no changes will occur in the service delivery system.'
Melaville and Blank (1991)

Session learning objectives

After completing this session you should be able to:

16.1 Describe the importance of developing relationships within the organisation.
16.2 Explain the theory behind the establishment of collaborative and partnership agreements with suppliers.
16.3 Describe the impact of developing relationships throughout the supply chain.

Unit content coverage

Learning objectives

3.3 Plan and develop appropriate techniques for managing effective supplier relationships so as to foster trust and commitment in the negotiation process.
3.6 Describe the formation and co-ordination of a cross-functional negotiation team.

Timing

You should set aside about 5 hours to read and complete this session, including learning activities, self-assessment questions, the suggested further reading (if any) and the revision question.

16

16.1 The development of relationships with suppliers

Most organisational structures are organised along functional lines. Weber's bureaucratic hierarchy is designed to allow for minor economies of scale within the specialist functions, and the learning effects of these functions help them to solve problems as they arise. In other words 'you do your job and I will do mine'.

Purchasing as a specialist function fits neatly into this model in that it can use its combined power to develop strategies for supplier contract and negotiation, undertake research for new supply contacts and effectively tackle problems that arise with such supplies.

There is a great deal of sense behind this approach. The basis of economics as elucidated by Adam Smith in *The Wealth of Nations* (1776) is based on the specialisation of labour.

Specialism, however, can lead to demarcation and many organisations become dysfunctional because of the rivalry and jealousy that can exist between specialist groups – each claiming to be the 'centre of the universe'. This causes a loss of common purpose and makes effective coordination very difficult.

Supply chain management is seen by many other functions as primarily outward-looking, about creating and maintaining external relationship with the supply base. As we saw at the outset of this unit, an effective organisational strategy depends upon the effective management of the interface between the different internal functions.

The increasing competitiveness of the external market, higher expectations and demands from customers and the drive for differentiation and cost savings require a more coordinated effort.

Any form of cross-functional working involves a complex set of factors. Different individuals and groups have diverse, often conflicting perspectives and insights on the process.

Supporting intra-organisational relationships

The success of cross-functional working involves a number of challenges which need addressing:

- Policy deployment.
- Resistance is often encountered from other organisational functions who fail to see the importance of policies and procedures for procurement, and regard it as obstructive. The ever-changing nature of these policies is also a further barrier to understanding.
- The use of desktop electronic systems that control spend limits, for example, can assist in getting across the message.

Cross-functional teams

The operational stimulus for collaborative working needs to be clear and the objectives prioritised. Some potential points for focus may be:

- customer service
- product or service innovation and design
- costs reduction
- quality
- delivery improvements
- improvements in product or service flexibility.

16

Without a focus and direction there would be the danger that cross-functional discussions fail to reach the depth required to gain greater insight and meaning.

Collaborative working tools

Unless there is a centralised policy on data sets and data collection, information is often stored by organisational functions in a disparate manner. In addition, the discipline-specific information is often presented in an inflexible or impenetrable manner which slows comprehension and can be time-consuming to decipher. There is often little thought given to diverse sources of information that may appear at a meeting.

Communities of practice

The communities of practice idea rests upon the notion that individual relationships support group relationships and vice versa. Rather than sharing information from one whole team to another, it's more effective to link individual team members with people from other teams and networks and communities of practice. Communities of practice can help create the levels of trust and understanding that allow people to share mistakes as well as accomplishments,and half-baked ideas as well as brilliant insights.

However, such communities are often long-term projects which rely on a stable operating system and long-term relationships within the organisation. If organisations have a high turnover or are constantly restructuring, such relationships are difficult to build.

Service level agreements

Service level agreements can be used where the purchasing function operates as an internal consultancy service. Although an agreement as to the type and scope of service to be provided can easily be constructed, the major limitation is in devising sustainable penalties for non-compliance.

Training

A possible solution to integration is to offer specialised training to key workers in other areas so that 'intelligent customers' are created who have a range of procurement competences in sourcing, acquisition, or managing contracts.

Policy deployment

Policy is perhaps the most popular way of coordinating the relationships within organisations. The complexity and detail of some purchasing systems means that a number of good business functions arise.

Policy procedures carry out a number of functions to:

- record and store existing knowledge about what works and what doesn't in purchasing within particular organisations
- create a set of rules to replicate best practice

16

- ensure that purchasing activity produces best value within an ethical and possibly environmental context.

The disadvantages

As noted above, purchasing policies can become outdated very quickly and it is, therefore, important that such policies are introduced and reviewed effectively. Where purchasing policy is not implemented effectively, the cost of maintaining and policing the policy can be very high. Skills in communication between the various departments and functions become more important.

Implementing policy

There are a number of steps in introducing a purchasing policy within an organisation including:

- Objective setting: Policy objectives should always be SMART.
- Analysis: Procurement specialists, having identified the basic facts related to the issue at hand, will analyse and identify the key elements that will lead to a diagnosis of the problem, a clarification of the goal or objective and an understanding of the constraints on any proposed solutions.
- Development: In some organisations the general opinion held by staff is a key factor in any policy decision even though senior managers are often prepared to take decisions that the 'majority' does not support. Policy is not created in isolation; consequently different groups should be extensively consulted throughout the whole process of policy development and implementation. Is the organisation ready for a purchasing policy? What issues are current within the firm or organisation? How are these likely to change? Have the issues been considered from a number of perspectives, the alternatives considered, different views sought and ideas exchanged? There will also be some consideration of the costs involved in sustaining cross-functional relationships.
- Implementation: The implementation of purchasing policy will vary from organisation to organisation, so there are no fixed rules. Generally speaking, as well as consultation in developing a policy, there also needs to be a considerable amount of training and consultation during the implementation process.

Consultation involves actively seeking information or views before making a recommendation or decision. It normally involves providing information about a particular issue or proposal to stakeholders, and gathering their input or feedback. The information circulated often includes options or proposals that are being considered.

The background information that the purchasing department communicates in a consultation process advises interested parties of what is under consideration, how an issue is being defined by policy or decision makers (the intellectual or philosophical framework), and even which issues are considered high priority by policy or decision makers. Stakeholders may wish to have input at this level of issue definition in addition to any questions posed by policy or decision makers on a specific, narrower issue.

16

Approaches to the development of an sustainable policy

The options to development should be a set of realistic choices:

- paradigm shifts
- conventional substantive options
- process options.

Cross-functional teams

Cross-functional teams can make it much easier to coordinate activities and information. Where such teams share the same physical location, team members can informally stop by and discuss the timing of key aspects of a project, the interpretation of results or the logic behind a conclusion. Team members can immediately communicate information they used to have to wait for team meetings to share.

But they also lose some of the advantages of functional organisation. When team members are located with other specialists in a particular field, they can discuss a whole range of discipline-specific issues, which can be difficult to achieve in cross-functional working.

Cross-functional teams can focus on a single output and the connected processes. This may be a major subassembly in the production of a car or the management of a merger between two multinational corporations. This focus can help teams develop a real sense of common purpose and focus. By working together in close proximity over an extended period, they can develop a rhythm, a rapport and a common identity. This, in turn, leads to higher levels of trust, which vastly improves their ability to build on each other's ideas and solve business and technical problems.

Teams can be excellent vehicles for learning. To learn effectively, people need both time to reflect and a safe environment. They need time to think about their experience and its implications and incorporate new insights into their current mental models. They need safety to explore new ideas and challenge their own assumptions. Within the trust and rapport created in a team, people can feel safe enough to share their thinking, the reasons behind their conclusions, the questions they have about their conclusions and even their half-baked ideas. When they take time to collectively reflect on their experience, they can build on each other's ideas and deepen the richness of their thinking and insights.

16

Disadvantages

All of the above rests upon proper team selection and effective team leadership. However, in some cases this cannot take place, for instance, where expertise within a team is required but the people involved are unable to work together.

Teams can also become new 'silos'. People in team-based enterprises often complain that they have trouble getting information from other teams. They find out too late or not at all about work done by people in their own discipline who are assigned to other teams. They reinvent tools, analyses or approaches developed by their peers on other teams. They waste time searching for information they know is held by one of their colleagues. The very thing that makes teams work well – common goals, shared focus, physical proximity and working rapport – can easily lead to two related learning disabilities: isolation and team myopia.

Teams can get isolated. Team members naturally focus inward, concentrating on team goals and connecting with fellow team members.

Isolation can lead to team myopia. When teams have very little contact with other teams or are isolated for extended periods, they can get into the habit of rejecting ideas from outside and lose their ability to generate new ideas, that is, they can become myopic. Research in creative thinking has long shown that new ideas usually come from the intersection of disciplines, perspectives or ways of thinking. When they lose touch with colleagues from their own discipline, they have trouble keeping up with developments in their field.

These are often symptoms of what has been called 'groupthink' and include:

- overestimation of the group where the team members believe that the team can do no wrong
- closed-mindedness where the team refuse to listen to new ideas
- rationalisation where failure is blamed on factors outside the team
- self-censorship as people refuse to say anything that will disturb the team image of itself.

Teams can also easily neglect long-term capacity building. Most organisations need to balance the tension between short-term production goals and long-term capacity building. On an organisational level, this is the tension between production and product development. On an individual level, it is the tension between focusing on current projects and taking the time to develop and share knowledge. Because teams are typically tasked with output goals (producing a product or service) they tend to pull people toward the production side of this tension. They tend not to see the value of building capacity beyond their team. Frequently, they even have trouble preparing their members for the next generation of technical development.

Collaborative technology

We have seen that cross-functional teams may be located in the same physical location or 'co-located'. However, increasingly teams may be located at very different geographical points and may sometimes work many thousands of miles from each other. In some multinational companies central purchasing may be based in one country, while each factory has a local purchasing unit. Coordination between these units, and production, distribution and finance requires more than just an enterprise resource planning (ERP) system. It requires a range of computerised collaborative working systems (CCWSs).

If the system can be designed so that everyone using it benefits somewhat (by its improving their work problems), then acceptance and adoption will be far more likely to be successful.

16

Communities of practice

Some enterprises are trying forge cross-functional relationships in a way that blends policy, teams and computer-supported working. One way in which this can be carried out is through the development of communities of practice (COPs). Each COP focuses on a topic or discipline important to the organisation.

They are responsible for sharing knowledge and standardising practices. This approach links the organisation in two ways. Cross-functional teams focus on outputs, typical products, major processes or market segments. COPs focus on learning within functions or disciplines, sharing information and insights, collaborating on common problems and stimulating new ideas. Communities of practice are a way to preserve a discipline or technical focus, while cross-functional teams unite disciplines around common products. Teams weave the organisation together in one direction. Communities weave it together in the other.

Starting and supporting communities of practice is very different from team building. Since communities of practice are organised around knowledge, not outputs, traditional team-building activities of setting goals, dividing tasks and developing workplans are not appropriate. Start with a few communities of practice focused on topics important to the organisation. Focusing on strategically important topics will make it considerably easier to expand beyond the original communities.

Service level agreements

In the former examples of tools and approaches that can be used to manage internal relationships, we have looked at the way in which policies, cross-functional working, collaborative technology and COPs can be used to bring about improvements in those relationships. There is another way of improving internal relationships which can involve changes in the purchasing and supply function itself. This involves the use of internal service level agreements (SLAs).

SLAs allow internal customers to state their service level needs clearly and unambiguously. In turn, suppliers are enabled to focus their resources into providing services at the required level. Key performance indicators (KPIs) measure the quality of the service provision to allow for remedial action where necessary.

Where services, over time, are not delivered to expected levels of quality and efficiency, two courses of action can be taken. Either the service capacity can be increased (often accompanied by a cost increase), or the customer's expectation as to the level of service can be decreased. This decision should be taken transparently so that both customer and supplier are aware of new expectations and/or service targets. Any additional costs would also have to be negotiated.

Strengths of SLAs

An SLA can significantly improve the ability of purchasing to manage the expectations of internal customers. They can also help to establish service

16

standards and to document and communicate them. In this sense, a service level agreement can be an extremely effective communications tool for creating a common understanding between two parties regarding services, expectations, responsibilities and priorities.

Indeed, the process of SLA development can be incredibly useful. The process of information gathering, analysing, documenting, educating, negotiating and consensus building can, in some cases, do away with the need for an SLA altogether.

Weaknesses of SLAs

Many people complain that SLAs have no 'teeth'. Penalties are difficult to identify and implement. The development of SLAs is also time-consuming. Often SLAs are introduced after a relationship has begun to fail and there is little time or patience for a proper introduction process.

Learning activity 16.1

Explain why it is important for the purchasing function to become involved in intra-organisational relationships.

Feedback on page 261

Recognising cross-functional working

There are a number of ways of recognising an integrated, coordinated commitment to cross-functional working. Coherence is a word that pertains to arguments and means both internally consistent and easy to follow. Organisations now need to operate in a coherent way. Operating in this way, as opposed to a fragmented way, means that:

- Customer needs and requirements are clearly understood in every corner of the organisation.
- Work is viewed in terms of the whole of a business process, not merely as one department passing work from it to another department.
- Business processes are clearly linked to customer-critical outcomes.
- Work groups with employees from several different functional areas take responsibility for making sure that all business processes are coordinated, and serve the customer and the enterprise.
- Information is shared between work teams and functional departments.
- Technology supports information sharing.
- Policy and procedure changes are made only after consulting other functional groups to assess unexpected impacts on customers.
- Problems that arise are viewed as opportunities to improve the process of serving customers; there is less of a culture of blame, which may be replaced by collaborative working.

Evaluating intra-organisational relationships

Cross-functional teams, collaborative working and communities of practice are all ways of improving intra-organisational relationships. Just as we

16

might seek to improve the quality of our relationship with a supplier, we might also seek to improve the quality of our relationship with groups and departments within the enterprise.

However, in the same ways as the tools and methods that we choose to improve our relationships with suppliers need to be cost-effective, so do the tools and methods that we choose for intra-organisational relationships. This means subjecting all these methods to evaluation. Of course, the way in which we evaluate internal relationships may be different to the way in which we evaluate external relationships.

The criteria that we use to evaluate internal relationships will always contain some factors that are specific to the issue at hand. These may include asking questions such as:

- What is our primary objective? What is the key interest that we are trying to satisfy most?
- What is the absolute minimum that must be achieved?
- What are the desirable, but not essential, aspects that we want to satisfy?
- What are the key things to avoid?
- What are the consequences of continuing with the status quo, or doing nothing?

In working with internal stakeholders there are five general criteria that are usually helpful in determining the likely success or failure of a particular option. These are:

- legitimacy
- communication
- feasibility
- support
- affordability.

Legitimacy

Options for developing intra-organisational relationships will be explicitly, or implicitly, examined for their legitimacy by the key players involved. Legitimacy can be measured against a range of factors, including conventional knowledge – the way we do things around here or opinion. Being able to support a particular option with an objective standard or an expert opinion can be important.

Feasibility

The feasibility of various options is frequently not intuitively clear. Feasibility is affected by technology, demographic and geographic factors and organisational and administrative considerations. Feasibility changes over time, and is affected by factors within government, by the general technology in society and by the attitudes and behaviour of staff within the organisation. Feasibility issues include:

- Is the proposed option feasible from a technical, organisational and administrative perspective? Is the proposal supported by the current

16

theoretical and technical knowledge? Is it feasible with the financial and human resources that we have? If not, can they be acquired?
- What is the time frame required to implement the option? Is it consistent with the 'political' requirements?
- Will staff willingly cooperate in the implementation of the policy or programme?
- Can we force action on unwilling participants?

Affordability

At the heart of most choices is money. How much will it cost? Who will pay for it? Will the benefits outweigh the costs? These are essential issues that must be addressed in an analysis of the various options.

Communication

A large part of relationships is about communication: listening to what staff are saying and effectively communicating senior management's policies and intentions. The key question is: 'should a particular option be communicated by the department, by senior management or by external consultants to staff and other key stakeholders in particular?'

Self-assessment question 16.1

How does your own organisation seek to establish better internal relationships?

Feedback on page 261

16.2 Establishing collaborative and partnership agreements with suppliers

When relationships are described, we use dimensions in order to differentiate one type of relationship from another. Purchasing and supply staff will often describe their relationships with suppliers as 'good' or 'bad'. This might be useful to the purchaser involved, but because these measures are so subjective, it is much less useful to anyone else.

Nature of relationship

Once we turn from the type of relationship and the exchanges within it, we can then begin to consider the nature of the relationship. This is when things become a lot more confusing. There are a number of different terms used to describe the nature of relationships. These include:

- collaboration
- commitment
- communication
- trust
- openness
- cooperation

- power use and power sharing
- intimacy
- mutual investment
- gain sharing
- responsiveness
- flexibility
- adaptability
- speed
- joint total asset visibility
- real-time management
- process synchronisation
- partnering
- nurturing
- symbiosis
- risk assessment
- risk management.

Although many or all of these terms are instinctively appealing, they are less than useful when we try to use them in analysing a relationship, and even less useful when we set them as a contract term. As we have already seen, there are a number of processes which may support these outcomes.

Learning activity 16.2

Identify the organisational processes behind relationship development within your own organisation.

Feedback on page 262

Classifying relationships

As well as describing relationships we also need to classify them. Understanding the differences between relationships is useful. Mostly we classify relationships in terms of what the participants do together and how they do it, but there are exceptions such as holding enterprises where relationships are classified by means of the ownership of assets. There are a number of models for classifying relationships, one of which was developed by Robert Fiske, who suggested four classes of relationship:

- Communal sharing: In which individual needs are subsumed into a greater objective. Elements of this model are incorporated into the idea of 'shared destiny' across the buyer and supplier organisations, and which originated within some Japanese models of partnership sourcing.
- Equality matching: Based on reciprocity and fair exchange between the parties involved in the relationship so that fair value is always given in return for what is received, and no single party obtains advantage from the other party. Elements of this model are used in the employment of open book costing approaches and joint asset visibility exercises.
- Authority ranking: This is an approach where the relationship is based on the hierarchical status of the parties involved and where one party may be dominated by the other. Elements of this type of relationship

16

can be found where large-scale buyers can use leverage to dominate smaller suppliers.

- Market pricing: Where the relationship is based on calculations of cost and benefit and optimising return from activities. Elements of this type of relationship might be seen in a completely free market where supply and demand interactions are not influenced by buyer power. The internet was seen originally as a free market of this type, where small enterprises could trade across market boundaries. This has, of course, not yet come to pass.

Within the specific field of supply chain management a number of models of commercial relationships have been developed which seek to define relationships by the use of a range of approaches placed along a continuum from adversarial/transactional/short-term through to so-called co-destiny approaches. Research into these models is far from complete and there can be a great deal of overlap between them. For example, an adversarial/short-term relationship may be repeated over time and a series of short-term contracts turn into a longer one. Partnership relationships may have periods when they are challenged and adversarial techniques are used. Co-destiny approaches may shift into partnerships.

It is important to remember when considering relationships that the relationship is not always the starting point of the analysis and that we may need to start with the context and type of interactions that create the relationship.

Adversarial/transactional relationships

The focus of traditional purchasing was to build a large competitive supply base. This supply base was managed using short-term contracts and win-lose negotiation strategies where the objective was to obtain the best possible price, safeguarding budgets and maximising revenues.

Advantages

There are a number of advantages to this strategy including:

- offering an abundant potential supply base to encourage competition which the purchaser can exploit to negotiate favourable terms
- providing a shelter against supply interruptions due to unforeseen circumstances, for example industrial action or plant failure
- offering flexibility in sourcing without the need for a longer-term commitment.

Disadvantages

Adversarial relationships have received a great deal of criticism in many industries including construction and automotive assembly. Reasons for this adverse comment can be seen in a number of business drivers which demonstrate:

- The increasing share of purchased goods and services as a proportion of the manufacturing costs. In many industries this could be between 60 and 80% of the cost of manufacture.

16

- The current trend of focusing on the core capabilities of the organisation. This, in turn, results in more outsourcing and increasing reliance on suppliers.
- The dependence of successful implementation manufacturing techniques such as just-in-time (JIT) on acceptable purchased inputs of consistent quality.
- The shortening of a product life cycle and increased need for rapid product development and introduction.
- Consumer pressure for increased production variety and thus complexity.

Disadvantages include the amount of resource used in vetting and contracting with suppliers, other administration costs in managing a large supply base and the lack of accurate information sharing across organisational boundaries to permit effective planning and coordination.

Implementation

Short-term transactional approaches to purchasing may, however, be useful in a number of circumstances. One of these is in the field of indirect purchases – those not directly associated with end products or services. These may include a number of major expenditure clusters such as: advertising and marketing, technology, overheads, human resources and those specific to the business such as store fixtures or collection agencies. Three problems prevent most enterprises from managing these purchases effectively:

1 inadequate information: enterprises have confusing, inaccurate data about indirect purchases
2 insufficient resources: the people negotiating purchases lack skill or have other incentives in making purchasing decisions
3 improper techniques: few enterprises gather sufficient information or solicit competitive proposals.

Short-term approaches for improving purchasing in this area may include:

- Measuring pragmatically: Managers should be extremely selective and focused when defining pricing data for purchasing.
- Assigning resources selectively: Enterprises should increase the resources assigned to indirect purchasing and clearly define the roles of people assigned to administer supplier relationships.
- Demystifying business requirements: Enterprises must establish precise quality requirements for indirect purchases.
- Clarifying the pricing basis: Lax pricing practices work to the buyer's disadvantage. In order to compare prices, the buyer must establish discipline in pricing by creating and enforcing a standard vocabulary.
- Leveraging the free market: Buyers must be willing to use free-market competition to reduce costs and must take business away from suppliers if necessary.

Such approaches, however, run counter to the prevailing 'partnership' purchasing model. In a supplier partnership some authorities suggest that enterprises give up their right to investigate alternative sources by

16

making a commitment to work with a partner through good and bad. Such partnerships may be appropriate when there are few viable alternatives or when changing suppliers would be difficult. In many cases, enterprises could establish free-market competition as their standard operating procedure and form partnerships only on an exception basis.

Partnering relationships

Increasingly, in many sectors enterprises are considering, or have ventured into, a partnership agreement with suppliers. In the face of rapid changes occurring in drivers, such as cost management and increasing competition, suppliers have made drastic changes in the way they conduct business. Changing regulations, a consolidation of the supply base and changing consumer demands are some of the market forces that have played a role in the growing number of partnerships between an enterprise and its trading partners.

Partnership models

Supplier partnerships are either defined as a formal partnering activity or a more informal partnership arrangement. Formal partnerships include such ventures as mergers, acquisitions, joint ventures and licensing agreements. More informal partnerships include strategic alliances. Although many suppliers have formed relationships with other suppliers, truly strategic alliances are characterised by:

- synergy, whereby customers and suppliers seek to identify opportunities that arise from joint activities
- collaborative strategy development
- risk and gain sharing
- joint problem-solving activity
- mutual incentive to improve products and processes
- creation of common goals
- trust
- a long-term commitment
- increased information sharing
- increased communication.

Forms of partnership

Partnership can take a number of different forms and can, in itself, be used as a tool for the management of relationships. One method of managing relationships through partnering is to create different levels of partner (or classes of contractor) and incentivise progression through the different levels.

In setting up such a programme the lowest level of partner might be a commodity supplier. In this pre-partnering relationship, which is on the borders of the transactional relationship, bid specifications and requests for quotations are the norm within a normal framework of contractual and legal requirements.

The next level up might be the preferred supplier, typically on a shortlist of enterprises recognised for providing superior competences to other suppliers. However, the framework for this relationship remains framed by administrative processes and legal requirements.

Next is the value-added supplier which is recognised for distinctive competences which are particular to the customer's own needs or capabilities. Customising a service may be value-added parts of such a relationship. An enterprise might outsource functions like telecommunications or information systems to such a supplier. Product performance may be required as opposed to product features. However, contracts are still an important feature of these relationships.

Advantages

Partnerships have a number of advantages including:

- better information exchange for improved planning
- reduced costs in administration and sourcing
- potentially decreased risk as purchasers are able to focus on and manage risk more effectively
- increased potential responsiveness from suppliers with whom a long-term relationship helps increase reciprocity.

As we have seen, in some cases, partnerships are 'need to have' because they allow the introduction of new technology for integration.

Disadvantages

Partnerships also have a number of disadvantages including:

- The fact that longer-term relationships can lead to less flexibility where suppliers are unable to respond sufficiently quickly to changing needs
- Problems where customers may find that partnerships reveal many more problems within the supply base than were previously thought to have existed. Sometimes supply base reduction can concentrate problems that were previously hidden. In other cases, partnerships can hide problems by pushing non-partnership suppliers into lower tiers.

Implementing partnerships

As already noted, it is very difficult to 'implement' a relationship. Relationships are co-created by two or more entities (people, organisations and departments). Nonetheless, some organisations have experienced significant success in implementing effective partnerships with their suppliers. Some of the factors which seem to lead to success are:

- Enterprises involved in partnerships, where partners have equal decision-making control, tend to report a higher level of success
- Effective and frequent communication among partners (a critical element in a partnership agreement)
- Enterprises with distinct cultures and managerial styles. The key is the ability to manage and monitor these differences prior to and during the partnership. It is also important to position these differences as strengths to complement the other partner's weaknesses

16

- Partnerships can be formed between traditional rivals who have approached the partnership with 'cautious trust'
- Enterprises who form partnerships to expand their product line, increase their global capabilities or become full service suppliers report the highest success rates
- Enterprises involved in successful partnerships tend to conduct thorough upfront research on their potential partner(s)
- Enterprises taking on the additional workload that often comes with a partnership
- Successful partnerships tend to have top executives who actively support the partnership
- Successful partnerships often have core groups to manage and monitor the partnership.

Obviously, when market competition is eliminated in a longer-term relationship, cost management may take a different form. One element sometimes found within partnerships is so-called 'open book' costing approaches. This is more often linked to target and activity based costing approaches which are designed to optimise the trade-off between cost and the benefits of partnership.

Co-destiny relationships

So far we have talked about adversarial and partnership approaches to the management of relationships. Both of these approaches have utilised contracts and negotiation to obtain resources which can be specified. The style or nature of the tactics used will vary on a contract-by-contract basis, but there is another level of approach where desired resources cannot be specified, and where environmental uncertainty means that the risks and benefits cannot be easily quantified as to the skills and competences required. In such cases, there is room for considering what might be called a group of co-destiny approaches.

Types of co-destiny approach

Alliances

Alliances call for a higher level of performance which cannot be specified by a contract. Here the relationship may consist of two or more enterprises, who may decide to partner together on a single product or project. Although alliance partners share goals and information, the relationship is typically limited by the project, which has an end point. However, an alliance might be spun off or integrated into a new enterprise. This has happened often in the computer industry.

Cooperation

Cooperation implies a more open-ended relationship. Partners jointly understand certain market requirements and are committed to joint problem solving and joint growth or co-evolution. The partners share information and ideas and commonly coordinate activities for mutual benefit. Intel and Microsoft are a notable example. United Airlines and SAS are another.

16

Strategic partnership

Strategic partnership is the most mature, valuable and difficult type of these relationships. The partners have a broad understanding of each other's needs and visions and share important values. There is a high level of trust and mutuality with open information sharing, gain sharing and concern for mutual wellbeing. Because the partnership shares so much, it is adaptable to change and transcends tactical difficulties.

Characteristics of co-destiny approaches

Within the above relational structures, members often state that the relationships between the partner firms are based on trust and co-destiny (that they cooperate because they have some common goals). This is probably true, but is not very helpful for someone trying to start up or manage a relationship. There are still major questions to be answered. How is trust created? What types of partner should be contracted? How do you manage within this relationship? How long should the contract last and what type of contract can be used?

We saw earlier in this course book, when we looked at the types of exchange within a relationship, that equity acquisition or exchange might be one approach which the purchaser might use. Share ownership and mutual directorates are one way in which Japanese enterprises have achieved co-destiny within their supply networks.

However, as well as ownership mechanisms, co-destiny also relies on 'softer' elements such as culture. Toyota, the automotive maker, for instance, relies heavily on cultural aspects of the relationship, some of which we identified in talking about partnership, and some of which we will look at in more detail.

Co-destiny

Partners in a co-destiny relationship find themselves in a situation in which they are so closely tied that they win together, but also lose together.

Shared vision and shared goals

If no bureaucratic mechanisms for integration exist, an implicit coordination by shared goals and, even better, by a shared vision allows the partners to move in the same direction.

Equity

A co-destiny relationship relies on a specific code of conduct and on a specific professional sense of fairness whereby one party does not feel that it is unfairly controlled or dominated by the other.

Advantages and disadvantages of co-destiny and co-makership approaches

Co-destiny approaches provide many of the same type of advantages and disadvantages as a partnership, but perhaps more intensely. This often

16

means that parties to the relationship can experience the type of cultural problems experienced within enterprises seeking to complete a merger. Co-destiny relationships may often have a huge impact on the people and organisations involved. Many fail to deliver their potential value because the motivation of staff and workplace culture suffers during the integration process.

Implementing co-destiny and co-makership

Although organisations often speak of aiming for a co-destiny culture which is the 'best of both worlds', there is rarely a successful strategy in place to make this happen. Successful management of the integration process requires careful examination of a wide range of issues relating to corporate strategy, industry analysis, finance, accounting and post-integration management.

Integration strategy and value delivery activities are the activities associated with determining the level of integration and establishing exactly how the value from the relationship will be created. These are closely related to the processes of identifying the overall deal logic and determining where the value will be derived.

In many cases, the purchasing and supply function may well be focused on improving access to and control of the manufacturing facility. There may, however, be other elements which accompany the relationship. For example, where the logic for an acquisition is to obtain a new technology, the core focus will be on integrating the team that has developed the new technology with the acquirer's own R&D team.

In many cases the setting of integration objectives is a process that requires close contact between the two companies and will span the planning and execution phases of integration. This ensures consensus between the two organisations on objectives and early buy-in and leads to more realistic and achievable targets.

Self-assessment question 16.2

Outline how resistance to collaborative working with suppliers might be overcome.

Feedback on page 262

16.3 The impact of developing relationships throughout the supply chain

Relationship development with suppliers and internal customers will assist in meeting several organisational objectives including:

- managing some of the risks linked to supplier failure or poor performance

- improving quality by reducing waste and rejection rates so as to manage indirect costs
- improving innovation and the success of new product development projects
- increasing agility and flexibility within the supply base so as to configure to fast-changing customer needs
- reducing cycle time so as to manage indirect costs and improve customer retention
- managing risk and cost through effective inventory management
- providing leadership for the whole of the internal and external supply chain through the use of a wide range of tactics and operational initiatives.

Apart from the critical points suggested above, the very nature of the buyer/supplier relationship has changed over the years. A new breed of suppliers has emerged. For example, in cases of integrated product design, suppliers often become heavily involved in the process of development, even at times becoming the design team.

It is critical for all organisations to obtain assured supply. More outsourcing, higher levels of productivity and operations such as the use of vendor-managed inventories have all increased the risk that a critical component may not be available when it is time to make an original equipment manufacturer's shipment. Aggressive outsourcing for cost and efficiency reasons means that unless there are split contracts, or some other form of secondary supply, the organisation is increasingly vulnerable to missed deliveries. There is always the possibility that failure on product lines may mean failure to achieve the financial targets with the resultant impact on annual performance and profitability.

If a supplier fails to deliver competitive features or maintain an adequate supply then this can have serious consequences for an equipment manufacturer.

The balance of power in the relationship has also been shifting with suppliers owning intellectual capital and increasing intellectual property in supplied goods. The use of contractual penalties and other control mechanisms will maintain some form of control over the supply process, but in interdependent relationships this cannot be used too often.

Internal impact

A number of contributions can arise from closer relationships within the internal supply chain. These include:

- Spend aggregation: Where the strategy is to determine the spend across the whole organisation, broken down into suppliers and commodities. Once this information is gleaned then better contracts can be negotiated to cut costs. Although this is a fundamental issue, many larger organisations find it difficult to collect such information because of unnecessary administrative complexity.
- Materials consolidation and standardisation: Looking inwards to determine the numbers of a part of commodity purchased, the

16

purchasing function can select a preferred supplier of one variety and find a way to ensure it is used for all part requirements. The challenge is to establish an effective description of what an organisation buys and then analyse functional equivalents to determine best value varieties. This avoids the cost of duplication and attendant costs in handling, storage and maintenance.

- Demand and forecast deviation: Purchasing functions need to anticipate future demands. This is based on past spend trends and future product plans. The more variability in the business and lack of planning may lead to missed opportunities for lower unit prices from established and new suppliers.
- Contract performance: Linkages to other parts of the production operations may enable the purchasing function to flag anomalies that occur with usage against volumes ordered. Systems must be put in place that allow for actual transactions to be recorded and monitored, a difficult process without collaboration amongst the functions, when the organisation may have thousands of contracts and dozens of procurement systems with inconsistent administration.
- Early product design involvement: Close liaison with all those involved in design will ensure that new suppliers are sourced ahead of decisions to go into production with a new product or innovation.

External impact

- Supply chain mapping: With sound relationship management, the purchasing function will be able to identify some of the problems that arise from the supply chain configuration. In particular, problems from the suppliers in the lower tiers will surface undetected without a good early warning system. Software programs exist which assist in the analysis of lower tier suppliers.
- Supplier market analysis: Informed knowledge of the supply chain will enable the purchasing function to look quickly at alternative sources if required by the organisation.
- Supplier risk analysis: Analysing supplier weaknesses in terms of costs, cycle time, quality or other performance measures is a vital role for the purchasing function that is aided by strong performance management and sound relations.
- Supplier performance management: The management of the supplier base is essential to avoid the damaging of the organisation's prospects as a result of poor supplier performance.

16

Learning activity 16.3

Describe the processes by which an organisation can implement a sustained collaborative adventure.

Feedback on page 262

Now try self-assessment question 16.3 below.

Self-assessment question 16.3

List the potential security issues of collaborative sharing.

Feedback on page 262

Revision question

Now try the revision question for this session on page 343.

Summary

There are a number of ways of recognising an integrated, coordinated commitment to cross-functional working. Organisations now need to operate in a coherent way internally and externally if they are to achieve a competitive position.

Suggested further reading

Read the chapter on sourcing and supplier information in Lysons and Farrington (2006).

Feedback on learning activities and self-assessment questions

Feedback on learning activity 16.1

It is important for an organisation to obtain a competitive advantage with alliances and interrelated working so that the process of making and delivering a product or service becomes better than that of rival organisations. Collaborative working within the organisation will assist that process, but it will not be an easy process to establish and maintain. There have to be clear objectives, and these will be formulated from the purchasing position in terms of being able to best advise suppliers on customer needs, design changes, and of course new product developments. Close working together will not occur across disciplines unless there is a commitment within the organisation because it appears to be feasible and cost-efficient, with the end results clear and transparent.

Feedback on self-assessment question 16.1

There is scope in this question to examine the way in which the purchasing function integrates with the other business functions. There needs to be some evidence of the formal structure and who are the key players and initiators. Some consideration of the benefits, issues raised and solved will be evidence of the type of results needed to sustain cross-functional working.

16

Feedback on learning activity 16.2

An internal scan of the purchasing function and wider environment is required to establish the culture of the business and its stance towards suppler relationships and involvement within the business. Much will depend upon the structure of the supply chain and the ranking of tiers and who are regarded as the most important suppliers. Where bottlenecks occur frequently there may be a source of closer linkage. The pace of the industry, the complexity of the products purchased, the demands for lean operations will all be factors in deciding how close the relationship should be with suppliers. There will also be some comment on the style of purchasing negotiations.

Feedback on self-assessment question 16.2

Much will depend upon the depth of relationships that the organisation desires. Establishing closer working relationships is not easy and requires management skill and investment in time and energy. Some of the factors discussed in the text include:

- synergy
- collaborative strategy development
- risk and gain sharing
- joint problem-solving activity
- mutual incentive to improve products and processes
- creation of common goals
- trust
- a long-term commitment
- increased information sharing
- increased communication.

Feedback on learning activity 16.3

A clear management vision is required and a belief in long-term relationships, commitment to first tier suppliers, partnership working, involvement in decision making and the flow of information between the businesses are all examples of the process towards greater involvement and participation of the supply base. This does involve considerable commitment and skills in the management of complex relationships and processes.

Feedback on self-assessment question 16.3

The stealing of ideas and other intellectual property is the key factor. Organisations should be clear as to how they are to protect their intellectual property. There will always be issues of organisational learning as they become more closely involved.

16

Avoiding disputes

Introduction

Successful dispute settlement is an important part of maintaining relationships. Conflict is an inherent part of business because of the differences in objectives between the organisational players. What is important is how the conflict is resolved to the benefit of the businesses involved.

'The goal of the basic conflict resolution process is to improve communication and reduce losses associated with conflicts.'
businesslistening.com

Session learning objectives

After completing this session you should be able to:

17.1 Demonstrate how skilled and effective negotiating can influence the outcome of minor disputes between suppliers.
17.2 Describe how a sound negotiating and influencing style can contribute to positive supplier relationships.
17.3 Explain how the contract contributes to dispute resolution.
17.4 Give examples of how outside agencies can contribute to dispute resolution.

Unit content coverage

Learning objective

3.5 Understand the role of negotiation to mitigate major contractual disputes and/or supplier relationship breakdown issues, including the use of contractual escalation clauses, the role of third party mediators and techniques for alternative dispute resolution.

Prior knowledge

Awareness of dispute settlement issues.

Resources

Access to organisational material on contracts and contract resolution.

17

Timing

You should set aside about 5 hours to read and complete this session, including learning activities, self-assessment questions, the suggested further reading (if any) and the revision question.

17.1 The settlement of minor disputes between suppliers

Dealing with conflict

Disputes will arise with suppliers because of the inherent conflict within the relationship, if each party to the agreement is seeking to maximise their return on the contract in pursuit of higher margins. In addition there will be the usual issues surrounding performance, quality, cost and perception of timescales.

> 'Conflict is a process, which begins when one party perceives that another party has negatively affected or is about to negatively affect something the first party cares about.'

(Mullins, 2002)

Conflict is a sign of active ongoing, forceful relationships. It can be a problem:

- if it becomes disruptive
- if it takes away time and energy from the real task at hand
- if it alters judgement as emotions run high
- as a result of loser effects, if one party feels they are being exploited
- if future co-operation may suffer.

Often it is not dealt with seriously as an organisational issue (Johnson and Scholes, 2002), or simply treated as a micromanagement issue. However, the correct handling of any dispute should leave the parties satisfied with any resolution.

The benefits of conflict to the relationship could be:

- motivating energy
- making underlying issues explicit
- sharpening people's understanding of real goals and interests
- enhancing mutual understanding
- stimulating a sense of urgency
- discouraging engagement in avoidance behaviour
- preventing dangerous and premature resolution problems.

Some of the conflict with suppliers will be attributed to the organisation's own internal conflicts as each function strives to achieve its own goal orientation which should be complementary but in practice will not necessarily be the case.

17

Learning activity 17.1

Your organisation has recently received quotations for a number of components for a proposed new product launch. Overall you are unhappy about their pricing strategy as you want to gain an advantage over leading competitors.

(continued on next page)

Resolution of disputes

Resolution of disputes through an integrative negotiating style will generally seek to achieve positive outcomes for the parties and secure long-term relationships. Both parties have to be open with their concerns, trust each other and be willing to be as flexible as appropriate to the circumstances.

Successful win-win bargaining strategies as proposed by Johnson and Scholes (2002) include:

* define the conflict as a mutual problem
* pursue joint outcomes
* find creative agreements that satisfy both groups
* use open, honest and accurate communication of group needs, goals and proposals
* avoid threats
* communicate flexibility of position.

Conflict resolution methods

Negotiators should not attempt to resolve conflict in the same way each time as it will eventually lead to unsuccessful conclusions. A range of different approaches is useful.

A well-known study (Thomas, 1976) identified five approaches to conflict resolution – competition, accommodation, avoidance, compromise and collaboration. We covered these in the context of negotiation in a previous study session, and you should now re-read the text under these five headings in section 13.1.

17

17.2 A negotiating and influencing style that can contribute to positive supplier relationships

Establishing a relationship

The relationship between the parties in terms of history and timeline and how much time is available for the negotiation will determine the strategy.

The buyer has to decide whether this negotiation is a one-off or will there be a need to maintain a long-term relationship.

An understanding of the relationship with the supplier is essential, in particular:

- Have you negotiated with this supplier before?
- How does it typically approach doing business with my organisation?
- What is the state of the current relationship between the parties?
- Are there any particular political or community sensitivities that may arise as a result of this negotiation?
- How skilled and experienced is *your* negotiating team?
- How skilled and experienced is *their* negotiating team?

Prepare to negotiate by:

- forming a team (if appropriate), specifying roles, rehearsal
- reviewing your own position and underlying interests
- obtaining input and advice from key stakeholders
- reviewing the possible positions and underlying interests of the supplier
- developing some possible outline proposals which consider the needs and interests of both parties to use to start the negotiation rolling.

Learning activity 17.2

Examine a recent negotiation at your organisation and list the factors that made it successful including sustaining the long-term relationship of the parties.

Feedback on page 281

Objectives

Once the context for the purchasing negotiation is understood, a detailed plan for the negotiation should be in place. Controlling the negotiation is vital, and the first step in controlling the negotiation is to set clear, realistic and achievable objectives.

Knowing the overall objectives of the negotiation is essential, because this will help the negotiator decide the most appropriate strategy or approach to be used for the negotiation. Without broad goals or clarity of desired outcomes of the purchase, it is very difficult to control the negotiation. Once a strategy is clearly defined, it is possible to decide on consistent objectives for the negotiation and to develop a negotiation plan.

As we have discussed before, the plan should include, for example, details of negotiating objectives, team composition, time frames for the negotiation, negotiation styles to be adopted, strategies and tactics to be applied, limits on the negotiators' authority and process requirements.

The approach

We have already covered the approach to negotiating in an earlier study session and you should now re-read the text under the heading 'Introduction' in section 13.1 to refresh your memory.

17

Effective negotiation involves adopting a planning strategy that develops answers to the key negotiation questions:

- What is the context in which I must operate?
- What am I trying to achieve?
- What problems am I likely to encounter?

Understanding the context

Negotiation always takes place within a context. Some of the important issues to consider in understanding the context of a negotiation include:

- The *supply market* in terms of:
  - *competition:* Is the market fully competitive, dominated by a few larger suppliers, filled with unsophisticated suppliers?
  - *growth:* Is this a new market, a growing market, a mature market, a retracting market? What is the impact of new technology on this market?
  - *geography:* Is this a global market, a distributed market, a rural market? Is distance an issue?
  - *power:* Who owns the suppliers? What level of turnover do the suppliers have? What is their financial status? What proportion of their turnover does this contract represent?
- The procurement decision in terms of:
  - *purchasing risk:* What is the nature of the purchase you are making in terms of its level of risk, and level of expenditure?
  - *complexity:* How complex is the good or service that is being purchased?

Negotiation variables

In an earlier study session we covered the three critical variables that have a major impact on negotiation, and you should now re-read the text under the heading 'Negotiation variables' in section 13.1.

Measuring the effectiveness of negotiating performance and outcomes

This was covered in an earlier study session and you should refresh your memory by re-reading the final part of section 13.1.

Self-assessment question 17.2

Identify the factors that contributed to a recent successful negotiation.

Feedback on page 281

17

17.3 How the contract contributes to dispute resolution

When we consider contracts, it is important to remember that the role of contracts changes to meet changing business conditions and that, as well as different forms of contract, there are also different categories of contract.

For the purposes of this section we will consider four contracting categories:

1 incentive
2 relational
3 psychological
4 digital.

In business, the basic building blocks of commerce are contracts between two parties. There are other types of obligation, such as promises, but these are, by and large, not the core of business. Agreement is the basis of earning money.

However, contracts are, of themselves, necessarily incomplete. Agreements are made in particular contexts, and those contexts can change in unexpected ways. Forecast demand can shift, machines can break down, people can misunderstand complex instructions, wars can break out and so on. Maintaining an agreement in these circumstances can be difficult. There are two approaches to managing contracts in such circumstances. The first is to design incentive contracts that will motivate the parties to complete the agreement. The second is used where parties need flexibility in order to achieve their intended aims and objectives. This has led to the notion of relational contracts (also called 'hybrid', 'symbiotic', or 'cooperative'), which are designed to allow parties to fulfil elements of an agreement that were not specified in the original contract.

Key elements of relational contracting are the:

• identities and personal attributes of parties
• norms of indeterminate duration
• norms of behaviour, or shared codes of conduct, informing responses to new developments after the contract has been agreed
• written documentation which is treated as a record of what has been agreed
• norms of behaviour, or shared codes of conduct, overruling written documents in settling disputes.

Relational contracts provide the means to sustain ongoing relations in long and complex contracts by adjustment processes of a more thoroughly transaction-specific, ongoing administrative kind. This could include an original agreement, and, if it does, that may still not influence the relationships between the contracting parties.

These types of contract rely on a range of factors including the way in which the contract is perceived, the relationship between the parties, levels of trust and a wide range of other factors. Contracts of this type rely on effective relationships between the parties, but can also have drawbacks, as we shall see.

Underpinning relational contracts is the way in which contract perception impacts on contract performance. This involves considering how contracts are made, both between organisations and within organisations, and considers a concept borrowed from research into the employment contracts and looks at psychological contracts between parties.

17

In addition, we will also look at some of the issues arising from electronic trading and the way in which these contracts may impact on commercial relationships. Once an agreement is made, it rests upon good faith. This presumes that both contracting parties will complete their share of the agreement, but again circumstances change, as do the attitudes of the parties involved. One of the ways in which contracts can be used to deal with changing circumstances and changing motivations is through incentive- or performance-based contracts.

Performance-based contracts

As the scope of the goods or services contracted increases in size and complexity – whole sub-assemblies instead of bolts or facilities management instead of cleaning – organisations increasingly come to rely on incentive- or performance-based contracts. These contracts link part of the supplier's payment base to key performance areas and outcomes.

Although determining the type of contract to use is often the first type of incentive considered, it is important to understand that contract type is only part of the overall incentive approach and structure of a performance-based acquisition.

Setting objectives for performance

More complex contracts closely link performance and quality of service to profit and rewards to encourage good performance. When the buyer and supplier agree to the use of a performance-based contract, certain preconditions contribute to successful implementation (table 17.1).

Table 17.1

Objective	Process
Alignment of purchaser/supplier priorities	• Performance incentives that are aligned to the corporate strategy and direction of the organisation • Clear identification of risk • Flexibility to allow changes to incentives, key result areas, outputs and benchmarks during the term of the contract/agreement.
Incentives for improved performance	• Mechanisms that deliver mutual gain from achievement ('win-win') • Incentives to achieve improved performance • Incentives that add value to the purchaser's business and are based on performance • Incentives that are easy to administer and can be operated in a cost-effective manner.
Measurement methods that support performance improvements	• Results that are measurable and not based on perception only • Established and agreed minimum performance.

17

Ideally, if the purchaser is able to establish and agree with the supplier on the performance measures from the outset of the contract, the incentive scheme should then be negotiated during the tender/contract formulation period. A performance incentive scheme may apply after the first year or at the end of the original contract term in return for attaining high levels of service. A scheme may also commence in conjunction with granting an extension and/or continuance of the contract, thus providing a bonus in the form of continued service provision without the need to re-tender to obtain improved terms.

Incentive types

Alternatively, performance-based contracts can include sanctions for non-performance, such as a percentage fee for late completion or flat rate for substandard levels of performance. It is important that contract managers pursue fair application of any sanctions in accordance with the contract and, where 'trade-offs' are used, they be appropriate to the objectives of the contracted goods or services (table 17.2).

Table 17.2

Forms of incentive	Possible approaches
Extending the contract	If the original contract was for three years, an extension could be granted for an additional one, two or three years.
For a project where time is critical, the supplier is given financial incentive for completing ahead of time (or alternatively penalised for late completion)	Bonus payment amounts payable per day, week or month ahead of schedule (subject to quality checks).
Target costs established	Appropriate in a relationship where the scope of services is broad and requires reimbursement at cost (established using an external benchmark). If the target is achieved, the ratio for shared savings may be on 50:50, 60:40 or an 80:20 basis.
Part (usually 50%) or all of the supplier's potential profit placed at risk against achievement of performance	Appropriate when management fees are applied with 'transparent' pricing – alternatively, 100% of the supplier's potential profit may be placed at risk with an incentive of additional potential 'bonus' if performance targets are reached or exceeded.
A reward at the discretion of the purchaser	Contract- and performance-based statement of work linked to the purchaser's strategic plan would be used to measure performance, but not necessarily to the formal incentive – the bonus is then based more on total customer satisfaction.

Escalation and savings

When using a performance-based contract, organisations need to consider escalation or savings provisions. Escalation addresses the need for pricing increases over the term of the contract. In single-year contracts, escalation is not normally necessary. In longer-term contracts, a facility for escalation is needed and a method of dealing with it adequately should be considered. Lengthy calculations or complicated formulae are not generally checked effectively, as time or other constraints and day-to-day pressures often apply.

Performance measurement systems (PMSs)

The contract manager is responsible for ensuring measurement and monitoring of the actual performance in relation to the planned or required

17

performance as outlined in the performance-based contract. In order for the contract to be monitored, a performance management system (PMS) should be developed and applied for monitoring of service levels. The extent of the PMS, and the effort required to establish it, depends on the size and complexity of the contract and the number of contracts being managed by the contract manager. The PMS should recognise the dependencies between the performance of the supplier and purchaser.

There is some evidence showing that incentive contracts can have a negative effect on supplier flexibility, driving out the very flexibility that it seeks to achieve. This appears to be a downside of incorporating flexibility into a contract. Suppliers sometimes tend to treat it as another contract term, which reduces their autonomy, and therefore stick to the letter of the contract.

Relational contracts

As we have seen, transactional contracts define a single transaction. Most business operations rely on either a series of contracts or a single long-term contract. When we looked at partnership relationships earlier in the course book, we saw that longer-term involvement timescales are seen as one of the key elements in establishing such a relationship. It is important to note that relational contracts do not necessarily need to be longer-term contracts and that, indeed, in some cases, relational contracts may be a series of shorter-term contracts or a long-term contract with clauses allowing significant variance.

Relational contracts involve a number of informal agreements and unwritten codes of conduct that powerfully affect behaviour, both within and between enterprises. Such relational contracts are often the 'lubrication' that keeps the enterprise moving. They may consist of informal quid pro quos between co-workers, as well as unwritten understandings between bosses and subordinates about task assignment, promotion and termination decisions. Even ostensibly formal processes, such as compensation, transfer pricing, internal auditing and capital budgeting, often cannot be understood without consideration of their associated informal agreements.

Business-to-business dealings are also supported by relational contracts. Supply chains often involve long-term collaborative relationships through which the parties reach accommodations when unforeseen or uncontracted-for events occur. Similar relationships also exist horizontally, as in the networks of firms in the fashion industry or the diamond trade, and in strategic alliances, joint ventures and business groups.

Whether vertical or horizontal, these relational contracts influence the way enterprises deal with other enterprises. Both within and between enterprises, relational contracts help circumvent difficulties with formal contracting (that is, contracting enforced by a third party, such as a court or an arbitrator). For example, a formal contract must be specified ex ante in terms that can be verified ex post by the third party, whereas a relational contract can be based on outcomes that are observed by only the contracting parties ex post, and also on outcomes that are prohibitively costly to specify ex ante.

17

A relational contract allows the contracting parties to make use of their detailed knowledge of their specific situation and to adapt to new information as it becomes available. For the same reasons, however, relational contracts cannot be enforced by a third party and therefore must be self-enforcing agreements.

The success of relational contracts depends upon a number of factors. When considering contracts, it is important to remember the effect of reputation, that is, the effect that failure or breach would have upon the party's future business activities. Each party's reputation must be sufficiently valuable that neither party wishes to renege on the contract.

This means that relational contracting rests on repeated interaction within a particular well-defined group together with a set of norms governing the behaviour of the group members.

In addition, two principles of behaviour are important:

1 solidarity
2 reciprocity.

According to MacNeil, an authority on relational contracting:

> 'Getting something back for something given neatly releases, or at least reduces, the tension in an enterprise desiring to be both selfish and social at the same time; and solidarity, a belief in being able to depend on another, permits the projection of reciprocity through time.'

For longer-term relational contracts, contract law faces the dilemma of, on the one hand, offering a means of commitment and, on the other, allowing for sufficient flexibility to adjust to changes in the environment. This tension between the need to fix responsibilities at the outset and the need to readjust them over time permeates the long-term contractual relationship.

Repeated contracting involves achieving cooperation through self-enforcing (possibly tacit) agreements. Repeated interaction may enable cooperation, because of the potential for a current deviation to be punished in the future. For this to work, four conditions must be met:

1 Any deviation must be observable.
2 Any deviation must be punishable.
3 This punishment must be credible so that it is clear that, when required, the punishment will be carried out.
4 The parties must be patient in the sense that the future matters to them.

One way of exploring some of the issues in relational contracting is through the use of game theory. Cooperation is usually analysed in game theory by means of a non-zero-sum game called the 'Prisoner's Dilemma'. The two players in the game can choose between two moves, either 'cooperate' or 'defect'. The idea is that each player gains when both cooperate, but if only one of them cooperates, the other one, who defects, will gain more. If both defect, both lose (or gain very little), but not as much as the 'cheated' cooperator whose cooperation is not returned. The whole game situation

17

and its different outcomes can be summarised as shown in table 17.3, where hypothetical points are given as an example of how the differences in result might be quantified.

Table 17.3

Action of A	Action of B	
	Cooperate	*Defect*
Cooperate	Fairly good [+ 5]	Bad [- 10]
Defect	Good [+ 10]	Mediocre [0]

Table 17.3 shows outcomes for actor A (in words, and in hypothetical points) depending on the combination of A's action and B's action in the Prisoner's Dilemma game situation. A similar scheme applies to the outcomes for B.

The game got its name from a hypothetical situation involving two criminals who have been arrested under suspicion of having committed a crime together. However, the police have insufficient evidence to convict them.

The two prisoners are isolated from each other and the investigating detective visits each of them and offers a deal. The one who offers evidence against the other one will be freed. It is clear to both that if neither of them accepts the offer, they are in fact cooperating against the police, and both of them will receive only a small punishment because of lack of evidence. In these circumstances both gain.

However, if one of them defects by confessing to the police, the defector will gain more, because he is freed and the one who remained silent, on the other hand, will receive the full punishment, since he did not help the police, and there is now sufficient proof.

If both prisoners defect, both will be punished, but each one less severely than if they had refused to talk. The dilemma resides in the fact that each prisoner has a choice between only two options, but cannot make a good decision without knowing what the other one will do.

Such a distribution of losses and gains seems natural for many situations, as the cooperator whose action is not returned will lose resources to the defector, without either of them being able to collect the additional gain coming from the 'synergy' of their cooperation. For simplicity we might consider the prisoner's dilemma as zero-sum insofar as there is no mutual cooperation: either each gets 0 when both defect, or when one of them cooperates, the defector gets + 10, and the cooperator - 10, in total 0. On the other hand, if both cooperate, the resulting synergy creates an additional gain that makes the sum positive: each of them gets 5, in total 10. The gain for mutual cooperation (5) in the prisoner's dilemma is kept smaller than the gain for one-sided defection (10), so that there would always be a temptation to defect.

The problem with the Prisoner's Dilemma is that if both decision makers were purely rational, they would never cooperate. Indeed, rational decision

17

making means that you make the decision which is best for you, whatever the other actor chooses.

The Prisoner's Dilemma has been used to study cooperative behaviour, and computer programs have shown that the winning strategy over time is to open with a cooperative choice and thereafter mimic the strategy of the other player. These theoretical approaches do not, however, necessarily work in the real world and we will now consider why that might be.

Psychological contracts

Relational contracting is an attempt to obtain a change in the type of behaviour that purchasers require from suppliers. This is often discretionary, not directly or explicitly linked with contract terms, but in aggregate, promotes the efficient and effective functioning of the relationship.

It means that the purchaser and supplier spontaneously go beyond the formally prescribed limits of the contract and create some type of partnership agreement. It should be noted, in passing, that alternatives to contracts may come about for unusual reasons. In certain cultures such as the Japanese and Vietnamese, low numbers of lawyers and an unwieldy or incoherent legal system make legal enforcement unfeasible.

What are psychological contracts?

The traditional focus of purchasing has been on the nature of the paper contract and ensuring the right sets of terms and conditions and the right clauses for variation and payment. All of these things are important. However, in an environment where purchasing is increasingly trying to incorporate better risk management and improved flexibility into contracts, they are much more than pieces of paper.

A contract needs to be underpinned by changes in the individuals and groups that are going to fulfil the contract. These changes may include loyalty, commitment, positive attitudes, responsiveness, participation, risk sharing, innovation, 'going the extra mile', 'putting the relationship first' and cooperation.

In order to obtain these changes, contracts need to be effective at behavioural, cognitive and affective levels. That is to say that contracts need to achieve changes in what the supplier does (building your rear axle assembly or delivering your financial package), shifts in the way in which they think (for example, 'We need to make sure this product or service is right first time'), and in the way in which they feel (for example, 'This relationship is important to us; let's make sure we don't mess it up').

The most effective contracts are made at all of these levels. Contracts are made over time or at one moment in time, but they do change over time, and these changes are rarely tracked. In addition, contracts may not be enforced across the whole of the organisation, which can lead to misunderstandings due to contracting parties receiving multiple and conflicting messages.

17

The stages of a psychological contract

Contracts shift markedly over time and a contract can consist of a number of stages. These stages may not always be clearly defined. Different approaches, such as social exchange theory or social economics, identify different stages but there seem to be a number of areas where these stages overlap:

- Needs or problem definition: when the contractor becomes aware of the problem or need which they face and becomes able to communicate that need.
- Prospecting: where the contractor actively seeks other entities with whom it can seek to contract itself. The next stage in the process may be decision making to enter into the contract.
- Negotiation: in this case, negotiation is the next stage of contract. Morley offers a useful view that negotiation is a tool which is designed to position a relationship.
- Entry: this stage involves the fulfilment of the need or the resolution of the problem identified in stage one. This fulfilment may range from a single action at one point in time to a series of complex actions over an extended period. The entry stage and the negotiation stages of a contract are often blurred, particularly when need is not known or clearly communicated.
- Termination: the final stage in the contract. Termination may come about for a variety of reasons and may be caused by one or both contracting parties. Just as the entry stage of a contract may be fraught with difficulty, so may the termination stage, as one party may seek to engage in harm-reducing or benefit-gaining behaviour. This has been called 'end game strategies'. Termination may also be difficult because either one of the contracting parties may still be involved in the contract at a behavioural, cognitive or affective level.

It should be noted that these stages are rarely clearly defined and one party may believe itself to be at one stage when the other party believes itself to be at a different stage. The stages often become confused in themselves with negotiation, termination and entry often blurring.

Who contracts?

It is very easy to perceive contracts as being between two contracting parties, despite the multiple constituencies within those parties. Where transactional or relational contracts might be between two or more enterprises, psychological contracts are more often between two people or one person and a number of others. Although TQM initiatives are designed to involve the whole of the organisation in a contract (as are other customer-focused initiatives), they may often fail to involve all staff. In such cases, supplier development initiatives, workforce communication programmes and comprehensive performance management systems can be used to affirm the contract.

As we have seen, one of the objects of contracting is to reduce harm to the parties involved. As a consequence, individuals and groups will seek to establish the credibility of a promise before entering into a contract.

17

Promises which are made publicly (to a group) would seem to have more credibility than promises made to an individual.

There is a cultural aspect to contracting. Psychological contracts are also controlled, to a greater or lesser degree, by social norms as to the expectations contained in a particular social setting. Where traditional buyer supplier relationships have been adversarial, the organisation that wishes to change the nature of its contracts will find that social norms may work against the change.

Learning activity 17.3

Undertake a review of your organisation's contractual agreements and identify how they assist dispute resolution.

Feedback on page 281

Now try self-assessment question 17.3 below.

Self-assessment question 17.3

How does your contract deal with a late delivery?

Feedback on page 281

17.4 The use of mediation and other techniques to assist dispute resolution

There are a number of informal types of dispute resolution without course to the law.

Mediation

Mediation involves bringing in a third party to assist in resolving the dispute. In a negotiation situation the behaviour and feelings of the parties can become polarised and the negotiations become deadlocked.

A mediator can be used to make contact with the parties in dispute. Their strong communication skills do not control the agreement but help resolve the dispute process. The mediator's duty and expertise lies in assisting the parties in exploring the range of settlement options and coming to a mutually acceptable outcome. They guide the two parties to discover the solution to their problem.

The mediator cannot compel the two parties to resolve the dispute in any way, because the parties retain absolute control over the situation. Mediators meet jointly with the parties in order to gain a thorough understanding of their needs and interests. The confidentiality allows the parties to test their perception of the facts and the law. Even if there is not a resolution of the dispute some form of streamlining of the issues is completed.

17

Conciliation

Whereas conciliation is used in employee relations disputes it is rarer in commercial disputes. It tends to be very open-ended and focuses on restoring communications between the parties rather than the resolution of the dispute. Conciliators employ an approach which focuses on the parties as a system rather than allocating blame to one party.

Formal means of dispute resolution

Adjudication

This has an element of formality to it and some industries such as construction have procedures built into their agreements (regulated by the Housing Grants Construction and Regeneration Act 1996). Either party has the right at any time to refer the dispute to adjudication, even, sometimes where the contract has ended. There is evidence that such an approach tends to end in the right decision, which is usually confirmed if parties then proceed to litigation. There is also evidence of considerable cost savings by taking this route of alternative dispute resolution.

The benefits of this informal approach are:

- reduced costs
- reduced time
- increased flexibility
- expertise is neutral
- preservation of relationships
- greater control over the process
- improved confidentiality
- enhanced ability to manage resources.

Arbitration

An alternative to civil proceedings is arbitration, which allows parties to bring their disputes before a non-legal independent expert so that he or she may decide the case. In 1979 the Royal Commission on Civil Liability found that less than 2% of cases in which an attempt was made to recover damages for personal injury reached the stage of a hearing in court.

Arbitration has been argued to be the commercial world's alternative to the slow, expensive, inconvenient High Court litigation. It is based on the inquisitorial rather than adversarial system, with the arbitrator taking an active role in the proceedings.

It is governed by the **Arbitration Act 1996**, which has now repealed the Arbitration Acts of 1950 and 1979. The new Act changes little of the principles but stresses the power of the parties to determine in their contract exactly how and when the arbitration will take place. The powers of the parties do not extend to excluding court interference entirely.

An independent arbitrator is usually chosen after the dispute arises, although not always. For example, an insurance policy usually contains a clause providing for this method of settling any disputes which may arise.

17

The arbitrator is appointed to hear arguments presented by the parties. The type of arbitrator chosen will depend on the nature of the case. The arbitrator's main role is to try to effect a settlement between the parties rather than to impose a judgment as to who is right or wrong.

The rules of natural justice apply. Some control may be exercised by the courts. An order known as *certiorari* can be used to bring before a higher court those cases from 'inferior' courts and tribunals that have already been decided to determine whether they have exceeded their jurisdiction or if there has been any denial of natural justice, for example, the right to be heard.

Arbitration may arise in different ways:

* By contract: The parties may by contract include a clause agreeing to refer any dispute to an arbitrator; this person may also be named in the contract. Almost all vehicle insurance policies have such a clause.
* By ruling of the court: The judge may decide to refer the dispute to arbitration.
* By statute: For example, under the Marine Insurance Act 1905, maritime disputes are to be settled by arbitration. London is an international arbitration centre, with 70–80% of all disputes being referred to it.

The Arbitration Act 1996 and judicial review

Prior to the Arbitration Act 1979, the English courts were able to review an arbitrator's decision by requiring him to state a special case for consideration by the court. The commercial community found this led to delays and caused much dissatisfaction.

The 1996 Act therefore limits the rights of parties to apply to the court to review an arbitration award.

The arbitration will only be reviewed under the Act in the following circumstances:

* As an appeal on a question of law – s1(2): Both parties must have consented to this being permitted or there must be leave of the court. Leave will only be granted where the interests of justice or the integrity of the arbitration process demand it, or where the question is one of general public importance (*Antaios Compania Naviera SA* v *Salen Rederierna AB* [1985]).
* To ask the arbitrator to give his reasons in greater details – s1(5): Leave must be obtained from the court first. The criteria for this are laid down in the *Antaios* case mentioned above. The court will ensure that this procedure is only used for its proper purpose, and not as an indirect way of obtaining a review of the arbitrator's award.
* To determine a preliminary point of law – s2: All parties must agree to this or else the leave of the court must be obtained under s2(2).

In addition to the rights of the parties being limited to seek judicial review, the 1996 Act allows the parties to insert a provision for 'exclusive agreements'. These agreements remove the jurisdiction of the courts entirely.

If it is a domestic arbitration, then such a clause can be included after commencement of the original arbitration. However, if it is non-domestic arbitration (that is, one not held in the UK and the parties are not resident in the UK) then such a clause and agreement would only be effective if it was entered into by the parties before the arbitration proceedings started.

It is possible for the parties to insist that there be no application to the court until after the arbitrator has made a decision. This is called a Scott/Avery clause, after the 19th-century case of the same name, and as seen earlier in this section. The advantage here is that the decision of the arbitrator on the facts of the case will usually not be undermined by a court. The court therefore will only consider the application of the law to those decided facts (*Balfour Beatty* v *Channel Tunnel Group* [1993]).

When a dispute arose, the contract allowed for this to be referred to a panel of experts chosen by the parties to conduct arbitration under the international construction rules. The courts refused to interfere in any way with the operation of the clause until after the arbitration panel had made their decision.

Arbitration has definite advantages and disadvantages over court action, some of which are listed here.

Advantages

- It is *less formal* – the informal atmosphere and straightforward procedure is often preferred by parties involved.
- It is *flexible* – it avoids the rigidity which the doctrine of judicial precedent imposes on the traditional courts.
- There is *greater specialist knowledge* – for example, more commercially aware expert staff are involved.
- It *avoids publicity* – proceedings are held in private.
- It is often *less expensive* – the procedure is cheaper. Although the costs of the arbitrator may be quite high, the time spent on arbitration is often less than on a civil litigation case in the commercial court. If legal representation is discouraged, there is the potential for reducing the fees further.
- It is *quick*.
- Parties can *select and stipulate* the identity of the arbitrator. If the parties cannot agree on who is to be appointed, then the Arbitration Act gives the courts the power to do so.
- It is *regulated* by statute – Arbitration Act 1996.
- An arbitrator's award may be *enforced* in the same way as a High Court judgment. This means that the courts allow the parties to settle their own disputes, but at the same time maintain a supervisory role.

Disadvantages

- Arbitrators are often not skilled in applying or interpreting the law, although increasingly, commercial arbitrators are also senior lawyers.

17

- There are no formal rules – discretion can lead to inconsistent and unpredictable decisions.
- The parties may still end up in a court of law, though at least they must go to arbitration first, especially if there is a Scott/Avery clause.
- Appeal is only possible on a point of law, not a point of fact.

Learning activity 17.4

If your organisation was in dispute with a supplier why would arbitration be the preferred method of dispute resolution?

Feedback on page 281

Now try self-assessment question 17.4 below.

Self-assessment question 17.4

List the advantages and disadvantages of avoiding court disputes.

Feedback on page 282

Revision question

Now try the revision question for this session on page 343.

Summary

Conflict will occur occasionally within the business relationships. Resolving the conflict can be achieved effectively and with minimal damage to the parties if they have negotiating skills that can seek out and resolve the differences. Failing this the use of a clear and fair contract will often suffice. If litigation is the only way then the use of arbitration will ensure confidentiality.

Suggested further reading

Read the chapter on purchasing procedures in Lysons and Farrington (2006).

Feedback on learning activities and self-assessment questions

Feedback on learning activity 17.1

A review of the skills of the negotiator, influencing skills and working through the problem in order to reduce conflict and achieve a sustainable solution. The techniques listed below the learning activity, as described by Thomas (1976), show the different methods by which a result can be achieved, with emphasis given to collaboration.

Feedback on self-assessment question 17.1

An opportunity to review the theories on conflict resolution where the more effective strategies based on competition, compromise or collaboration will assist in achieving the desired result.

Feedback on learning activity 17.2

The organisation should have a philosophy towards long-term relationships, plus skilled negotiators that follow that philosophy, seeking to resolve disputes informally and formally. The review of a negotiation will look at how power has been exercised, the planning and preparation stage, and whether there was sufficient information about the capabilities of the supplier's organisation. The team performance during the negotiations will also have to be discussed. Finally, there should be an analysis of the closure and whether all objectives have been achieved.

Feedback on self-assessment question 17.2

Skilled negotiators who are well prepared and understand the context and the power involved in the negotiation will have a better chance of achieving a successful outcome. It is also a question of preparation, the state of the relationships between the parties that will have been established over a period of time, individual personal and intellectual skills brought to the negotiation and a clear communication strategy.

Feedback on learning activity 17.3

An examination of the standard contract will reveal the written obligations, but there are also the hidden aspects to explore as to how far the contract is used to achieve supplier performance. There should be some indication of the clauses used to ensure compliance with specifications, delivery, risk and also how damages may be claimed.

Feedback on self-assessment question 17.3

A simple examination of the contract will reveal the scope for the right to reject, terminate or cancel.

Feedback on learning activity 17.4

Arbitration between businesses is usually preferred to a court action as it allows for selection of an arbitrator skilled in the industry's affairs. It is *less formal*. It is *flexible* – it avoids the rigidity which the doctrine of judicial precedent imposes on the traditional courts. It *avoids publicity* – proceedings are held in private. It is often *less expensive* – the procedure is cheaper. It is *quick*. An arbitrator's award may be *enforced* in the same way as a High

Court judgment. This means that the courts allow the parties to settle their own disputes, but at the same time maintain a supervisory role.

Feedback on self-assessment question 17.4

Although court hearing will lead to professional detailed examination of the merits of the case, relationships will suffer because of the exposure to the public gaze and the adversarial approach.

17

Information flows and competitive advantage

Introduction

This unit looks at the importance of knowledge management and how it contributes to a competitive advantage.

Session learning objectives

After completing this session you should be able to:

18.1 Assess the contribution to business efficiency of improved information and knowledge systems.

18.2 Show diagrammatically models of communication flows and the reduction of 'noise'.

18.3 Give examples of how computer technology contributes to speedier business solution flows internally and externally.

18.4 Evaluate the contribution of knowledge sharing to the long-term benefit of the business.

Unit content coverage

Learning objective

4.1 Develop and implement appropriate information and knowledge sharing systems between purchasing departments and suppliers to provide benefits to both parties.

Prior knowledge

Awareness of information technology systems.

Timing

You should set aside about 5 hours to read and complete this session, including learning activities, self-assessment questions, the suggested further reading (if any) and the revision question.

18.1 Knowledge management and information systems

Achieving a competitive advantage through knowledge

Organisations can obtain a competitive advantage by developing their products, people and processes in a meaningful way. In addition the exploitation of their intellectual property also provides scope for a competitive edge, seeking to provide access to ever-increasing markets,

'The business world has enthusiastically adopted the idea that knowledge has become the most strategic of corporate assets, the principal basis for competitive advantage.'

Marr and Spender (http://managementfirst.com/knowledge management/articles/knowledge assets.php)

18

283

making a significant contribution to end-use value and being difficult to imitate.

Learning activity 18.1

If you were asked to report on the key areas of knowledge within the purchasing function of your organisation, what would be included in that report?

Feedback on page 291

The resource-based view of an organisation combines the internal core competences that are dynamic in its behaviour and are based around:

- a strong portfolio of competences, including communications, involvement and a deep commitment to working across organisational boundaries
- products that should be based on competences
- organisations that should continue to invest in core competences and capabilities
- good companies that should try to incrementally develop their competences by bringing in new ones through major project development.

One of the difficulties of knowledge management is in determining exactly what that means. Much of knowledge management is concerned with systems that capture that knowledge or information.

> 'Drucker… scoffs at the notion of knowledge management. "You can't manage knowledge," he says. "Knowledge is between two ears, and only between two ears." To that extent, Drucker says it's really about what individual workers do with the knowledge they have. When employees leave a company, he says, their knowledge goes with them, no matter how much they've shared.'

The actual knowledge of a business is contained in the sum of its human capital. Explicit knowledge can be captured in a variety of paper and electronic means. Explicit knowledge can be captured and protected in the various intellectual property devices such as copyright, patents and trademarks. A person's skills and expertise that is contained in tacit knowledge is more difficult to capture. This knowledge appears in individual and group performance when the individual is involved in complex tasks. More straightforward, routine or standardised knowledge can be reduced to systems and processes. This form of knowledge is easier to share but is also easier to copy and imitate.

18

Self-assessment question 18.1

Assess the controls that are necessary on knowledge flows because of confidentiality and business risk.

Feedback on page 291

18.2 The importance of good communication flows

Communicating and adding value

Communicating with others in the supply chain should, whether it is about the availability of materials or equipment, information about quality standards, about the pricing philosophy or about the ordering process, add value.

We have seen in the previous section the growth and importance in what is known as knowledge management, where information needs to be processed and communicated effectively. Most organisations seem to have problems in communicating despite the advances in technology that have assisted the process. The human contribution to maintaining effective relations with suppliers is still important, irrespective of the technology involved. The sending of messages between members of the supply chain can be more effective if an efficient computer-based information system is used, but in terms of the less structured tacit information or knowledge, these systems are less efficient.

The transmission of data needs to be conveyed and interpreted clearly if people are to work together effectively. Achieving understanding can be difficult if the message is not made clear to the recipient.

Learning activity 18.2

In relation to the models of communication flows, examine areas of poor communications within your own organisation and identify the causes.

Feedback on page 291

Good communications are essential if value is to be added within the supply chain. This is important in several areas:

* *Innovation* which requires all those in the supply chain as well as the specialists within the organisation to be able to relate scientific and technical discoveries with customer demands and expectations.
* *Quality* involves everyone in the supply chain playing their part and understanding its importance to customer value and cost reduction.
* *Delivery* requires everyone communicating about orders, capacity and potential bottlenecks.
* The removal of *waste* needs good communication systems.

In order to communicate effectively it should be understood that the sending of a message is subtle and complex.

The Shannon and Weaver model (1949) (see figure 18.1) gives a good interpretation of what happens when a message is sent, received and then feedback given. The use of coder and decoder terminology is so that the

18

message givers understand the possible reasons for failure. Distractions and disruptions that disturb any stage of the communication process are known as *noise*. Noise can be a combination of individual psychological filters, message semantic filters or context mechanical filters. Feedback is essential otherwise the sender cannot know if the message has been received and understood.

Figure 18.1: The Shannon and Weaver model

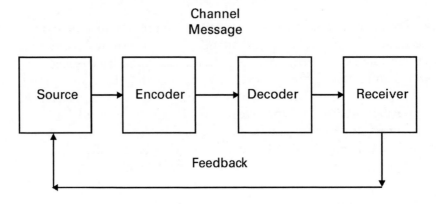

The sender must assume that the message will fail and put time and effort into preventing that failure.

Heltriegel and Slocum (1988) suggest five principles for coding a message accurately:

- *Relevancy:* Make the message meaningful and significant with careful selection of words, symbols and gestures.
- *Simplicity:* Put the message in the simplest possible terms, reducing the number of words, symbols or gestures.
- *Organisation:* Organise the message as a series of points to aid understanding.
- *Repetition:* Restate the key parts of the message at least twice.
- *Focus:* Concentrate on the essential aspects of the message.

Self-assessment question 18.2

Research within your organisation what training and development is available for the improvement of communication flows.

Feedback on page 291

18

18.3 The use of computer technology to speed up business solution flows

Intelligent information

As we saw earlier, there are many computer systems and software available to assist business, strategy planning and operations.

Learning activity 18.3

Research how your organisation collects and stores knowledge, data mining and access levels.

Feedback on page 291

Examples of technology-driven systems that can improve the efficiency of supply chain management are listed below.

Supplier management relationship software

Managing relationships with suppliers can be complicated, but it is also important to the overall performance of the company. Software programs have features and tools that can help manage supplier relationships, inventory costs, and multi-organisational collaboration, as well as other key elements of the vendor/buyer connection.

Usually the product allows buyers to communicate with their vendors in real time via web-based programs. The tools often also automate much of the negotiation process and simplify online bidding for projects so it is easier to form an initial relationship for both parties.

E-procurement

E-procurement is more than just a system for making purchases online. A properly implemented system can connect companies and their business processes directly with suppliers while managing all interactions between them. This includes management of correspondence, bids, questions and answers, previous pricing, and multiple emails sent to multiple participants.

A good e-procurement system helps a firm organise its interactions with its most crucial suppliers. It provides those who use it with a set of built-in monitoring tools to help control costs and assure maximum supplier performance. It provides an organised way to keep an open line of communication with potential suppliers during a business process. The system allows managers to confirm pricing, and leverage previous agreements to assure each new price quote is more competitive than the last.

E-marketplaces

An e-marketplace is a location on the internet where companies can obtain or disseminate information, engage in transactions, or work together in some way. Most of the e-marketplaces provide two basic functions: they allow companies to obtain new suppliers or buyers for company products, or they develop streamlined trading networks that make negotiating, settlement and delivery more efficient. Currently e-marketplaces exist in many different industries.

18

E-tendering

E-tendering systems are designed to eradicate the need for cumbersome hard copy documentation being sent by the normal mail. It facilitates the despatch of invitations to tender, specifications and other documents such as pre-qualification questionnaires through a secure electronic service through the internet.

Reverse auctions

Companies today need to shave expenses wherever possible and that includes the purchase of goods and services needed to keep their businesses running smoothly and efficiently. Previously, the process of finding vendors was extremely limited and was very time-consuming. Many businesses simply found it easier to pick one company and continue doing business with them indefinitely instead of hunting around for the best provider for each new project. Today, technology has changed that completely thanks to reverse auctions and the internet.

Reverse auctions are simply auctions where the bidder is the seller not the buyer. The bid reflects how much the buyer is being asked to pay, not how much the good or service is being sold for. Web-based reverse auctions have become extremely popular for purchasing everything from accounting services to securing raw materials.

Buyers' benefits involve cutting costs and time expenditures. In the past, buyers who needed work done had to send out a complete project description to potential sellers. With reverse auctions, buyers create a project description and post it online. Invitations are then sent out to potential vendors who place a bid and briefly describe their qualifications and the details of what their bid includes. Because all of the bids are lined up beside each other in a chart formation, comparing them is simpler for the buyer. Additionally, buyers can eliminate certain bids based on criteria such as price or deadlines, which makes the final selecting even easier. Most reverse auction software also allows buyers to communicate with bidders so that they can refine their bids or offer clarifications. All of these features combined allow the buyer to pick a quality vendor who can fulfil the needs at a good price and in less time.

Sellers also reap benefits from reverse auctions if they use them effectively. One of the benefits is that it makes projects and component supply more open to a wider number of sellers. Technology provides vendors from all around the globe with equal access to the invitation and an equal shot at winning the work. While this is a benefit, particularly to offshore and/or small vendors, it can also be a drawback and has resulted in many sellers bidding too low on projects just to try to win the auction. The competition may seem negative, but it does provide an incentive for sellers to add value to their fees by providing a variety of other services, which will benefit buyers who are willing to look beyond price alone.

Tracking contracts

In many organisations there is a tendency to lose track of active contracts. The organisation may struggle to keep track of critical actions that need to be taken after the contract is agreed. The software can flag up when the contract needs to be renewed.

Self-assessment question 18.3

When corresponding with suppliers, actual or potential, how do existing systems protect confidential information from getting into the wrong hands?

Feedback on page 291

18.4 How e-commerce technology contributes to the long-term benefit of the business

Business-to-business technological breakthroughs

As we have discussed, the pace of technological change has been phenomenal and the use of the internet has begun to change the way business is done.

Open-platform based technology that is both cheap and easy to install allows companies to use the internet to open up new distribution channels, create online markets, increase revenues and boost the bottom line and margins.

The availability of more information or knowledge enables sellers to bypass professional buyers who have some of the information required, reaching the product or service provider. This is creating new businesses and business structures, as the retailer is taken from the supply chain as a result of online catalogues and auctions. There is greater access to the marketplace.

Buyers must be alert to the increased number of potential suppliers that can enter the market because of lower entry costs. Market intelligence systems can source and compare a wide range of products and services available. Low prices will be easier to find, but the information may not eliminate the risk element including quality issues, which will require analysis by the buying professional.

The biggest growth area for optimisation technology is found in supply chain management (SCM) where intelligent algorithms supply the backbone for powerful advanced planning and scheduling (APS) applications, designed both as customer solutions or commercial packages.

APS solutions allow enterprises to optimise their supply chains to reduce costs, improve product margins, lower inventories and increase manufacturing input. Functional systems such as ERP and SCM are primarily concerned about making data accessible in order to improve productivity. Optimisation takes this further with business variables examined so that all the issues relating to the supply chain are examined. The relationships between business issues are formulated as constraints, and the desired objective such as maximising profitability is imposed.

18

B2B transactions are driven by the need to match supply and demand in real time, usually because of the increased inflexibility of product capacity. Interactions between buyers and sellers can be routine with repurchases or reorders, but often they are complex and involve considerable amounts of data to be transferred before, during and after any transaction, which must be shared between several departments. The information includes specifications, designs, drawings, purchase agreements, delivery schedules, inventory control price negotiations and so on. Technology has created the means for improved efficiency of this data interchange, but also the development of web portals has led to a more focused method by which exchanges can take place. Hubs have been created where all the interested participants congregate. This should lead to lower costs as efficiency is improved as the transaction cost is reduced. It also means that organisations have to change their way of doing business and act quickly if opportunities arise.

Learning activity 18.4

Research examples from industry of successful collaboration between suppliers and buyers.

Feedback on page 291

Now try self-assessment question 18.4 below.

Self-assessment question 18.4

Identify specific examples of improvements in lead times, problem solving, product development as a result of increased interdependence and the sharing of business information.

Feedback on page 291

Revision question

Now try the revision question for this session on page 343.

Summary

Organisations must have sophisticated systems that collect, store and manage their knowledge and information flows. The building up of a significant store of knowledge is important for innovation, problem solving and the resolution of problems within the supply chain.

Suggested further reading

Read the chapter on purchasing and information technology in Lysons and Farrington (2006).

Feedback on learning activities and self-assessment questions

Feedback on learning activity 18.1

All purchasing functions will have specific knowledge built into their operational systems plus the substantial knowledge of its personnel. This combination of resources, which includes the capital invested into the systems, constitutes the sum total of the function's knowledge.

Feedback on self-assessment question 18.1

Confidentiality agreements between the parties are the best protection along with the usual IP protection.

Feedback on learning activity 18.2

Identification of the communication 'noise' elements within the business and the causes is important if remedial action is to be taken. 'Noise' distorts the communication flows so that communications often break down.

Feedback on self-assessment question 18.2

Are there short courses on presentation skills, team briefings, influencing skills and so forth?

Feedback on learning activity 18.3

A technological question on databases, data mining and data warehouses. The storage of data and knowledge is important for market intelligence reasons and for the more routine data capture of salient information about its supply base, for example. If the organisation is to respond quickly to changes driven by customers, competitors of the supply chain, it requires substantial amount of data and information at its fingertips.

Feedback on self-assessment question 18.3

An examination of the defences against hacking and viruses is required.

Feedback on learning activity 18.4

There are many examples of alliances and collaborative ventures that have brought gains and benefits for the partnering organisations.

Feedback on self-assessment question 18.4

Research into historic performance and trends within the organisation. Suppliers will have contributed to reduction of costs as a result of collaboration on systems improvements.

18

Study session 19
Developing suppliers

Introduction

This module looks at the processes such as TQM, 6-Sigma, and innovation that can assist in delivering added value from suppliers.

Session learning objectives

After completing this session you should be able to:

19.1 Describe the contribution of TQM and continuous improvement to supplier development.
19.2 Demonstrate with examples the benefits of operational improvement through 6-Sigma to supplier development.
19.3 Explain the methods by which teamworking collaboration can be established and sustained.
19.4 State the techniques for the establishment of breakthrough value creation.
19.5 Examine how innovation throughout the supply chain can be sustained.

Unit content coverage

Learning objective

4.2 Identify the critical elements of supplier development.

Prior knowledge

Links back to relationship development in section 16.1.

Resources

Access to TQM and other quality-related documentation.

Timing

You should set aside about 5 hours to read and complete this session, including learning activities, self-assessment questions, the suggested further reading (if any) and the revision question.

19

19.1 The contribution of TQM and continuous improvement to supplier development

The importance of TQM

What is TQM?

TQM resists a simple definition for several reasons. TQM can be defined as:

- An approach
- What it is about
- An end product
- A system.

Examples of each *approach* include:

- TQM as an attitude: 'TQM is an approach to improving the effectiveness and flexibility of business as a whole. It is essentially a way of organising and involving the whole organisation … more of an attitude' (Oakland and Porter, 2004).
- TQM defined by 'what it is about': Total quality is about success through people.
- TQM defined as an end product: A British Telecom definition as seen by two facilitators of the program at Sheffield described TQM through a set of 15 vision statements summarising what the BT organisation and people would be like when TQM had been achieved.
- TQM defined as a system: 'TQM is a cost-effective system for integrating the continuous quality improvement efforts of people at all levels in an organisation to deliver products and services which ensure customer satisfaction' (*Personnel Management, Factsheet*, May 1990).

Additional difficulties in defining TQM arise because:

- TQM is a philosophy rather than a tangible product
- TQM reflects the mission, history and culture of a particular organisation – what works for one organisation may be ineffective in another
- TQM involves changing the organisational culture to a long-term commitment to quality requiring continuous improvement of inputs and processes.

Bearing in mind the above considerations, two acceptable definitions of TQM are:

1 TQM is a management philosophy and a methodology that work together to produce an organisation focused on customer satisfaction, continuous process improvement, employee participation, teamwork, leadership and recognition.
2 Total quality management is the integration of all functions and processes within the organisation to achieve continuous improvement of the quality of goods and services.

The development of TQM

TQM originated in Japan as a result of the efforts of a group of American management consultants and statisticians who helped to rebuild Japanese

19

industry after World War II. TQM transformed cheap and unreliable products labelled 'made in Japan' into goods now internationally known for their high quality, reliability and innovation. These consultants were principally W Edwards Deming, Joseph Juran and A V Feigenbaum. The DTI publication *The Quality Gurus* (Bendell, 1991) identifies 'three clear groups of quality gurus (a guru is an influential teacher) covering the period since World War II'. These are:

1 *The early Americans* who took the messages of quality to the Japanese.
2 *The Japanese* who developed new concepts in response to the Americans' messages.
3 *The new Western wave of gurus* who, following Japanese industrial success, have given rise to increased quality awareness in the West.

The early Americans

The Americans were themselves effectively responsible for making possible the miraculous turnaround of Japanese industry and for putting Japan on the road to quality leadership.

Much of this transformation was associated with the introduction of statistical quality control into Japan by the US Army over the period 1946 to 1950 and the visits by three key American quality gurus in the early 1950s. These were:

- W Edwards Deming
- Joseph M Juran
- Armand V Feigenbaum.

The Japanese

The Japanese adopted, developed and adapted the methodologies that the Americans brought in and by the late 1950s had begun to develop clearly distinctive approaches suitable for their own culture. The Japanese gurus emphasised mass education, the use of simple tools and teamwork and had a background in an educational role. Three important quality gurus are:

- Dr Kaoru Ishikawa
- Dr Genichi Taguchi
- Shigeo Shingo.

The new Western wave

Much of the increased awareness of the importance of quality in the West in recent years has been associated with a new wave of gurus who have well publicised some of the quality issues, through the 1970s and 1980s. Significant contributions were made by:

- Philip Crosby
- Tom Peters
- Claus Moller.

A brief account of each of the above is given below.

W Edwards Deming (1900–1993)

Deming is regarded as the 'father' of the TQM movement. Deming applied the statistical concept of sampling to the control of quality. He introduced the concepts of variation to the Japanese and later a systematic approach to problem solving which later became known as the Deming or PDCA cycle (see figure 19.1), namely:

1 plan
2 do
3 check
4 analyse and act.

Figure 19.1

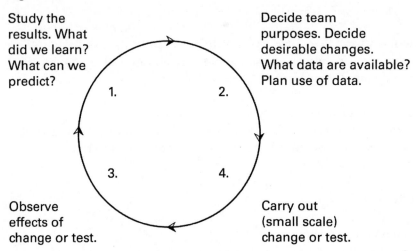

Study the results. What did we learn? What can we predict?

1.

Decide team purposes. Decide desirable changes. What data are available? Plan use of data.

2.

3.

Observe effects of change or test.

4.

Carry out (small scale) change or test.

Later, in the West, Deming emphasised that improvement in quality had to have managerial support. Changing the process (quality improvement) is management's responsibility. In his book, *Out of the Crisis* (1986), he expounded his famous *14 points for management*:

1 Create constancy of purpose to improve product and service.
2 Adopt new philosophy for new economic age by management learning responsibilities and taking leadership for change.
3 Cease dependence on inspection to achieve quality; eliminate the need for mass inspection by building quality into the product.
4 End awarding business on price; instead minimise total cost and move towards single suppliers for items.
5 Improve constantly and forever the system of production and service to improve quality and productivity and to decrease costs.
6 Institute training on the job.
7 Institute leadership; supervision should be to help do a better job; overhaul supervision of management and production workers.
8 Drive out fear so that all may work effectively for the organisation.
9 Break down barriers between departments; research, design, sales and production must work together to foresee problems in production and use.
10 Eliminate slogans, exhortations and numerical targets for the workforce, such as 'zero defects' or new productivity levels. Such exhortations belong to the system and are beyond the power of the workforce.

11　Eliminate quotas or work standards, and management by objectives or numerical goals; substitute leadership.

12　Remove barriers that rob people of their right to pride of workmanship; eliminate annual or merit ratings and management by objectives.

13　Institute a vigorous education and self-improvement programme.

14　Put everyone in the company to work to accomplish the transformation.

One criticism of the 14 points is that, though important, they do not in themselves provide tools for their implementation.

Deming also identifies what he terms the *'seven deadly diseases of management'*, namely:

1　Lack of constancy of purpose to plan product and service that will have a market and keep the company in business, and provide jobs.

2　Emphasis on short-term profits; short-term thinking (just the opposite of constancy of purpose to stay in business), fed by fear of unfriendly takeover and by the push from bankers and owners for dividends.

3　Personal review system, or evaluation of performance, merit rating, annual review, or annual appraisal, by whatever name, for people in management, the effects of which are devastating. Management by objective, on a go, no-go basis, without a method of accomplishment of the objective, is the same thing by another name. Management by fear would be better still.

4　Mobility of management; job-hopping.

5　Use of visible figures only for management, with little or no consideration of figures that are unknown or unknowable.

6　Excessive medical costs.

7　Excessive costs of liability.

Some of the above 'diseases' such as points 6 and 7 are peculiar to American industrial companies, but points 1 to 5 are universally applicable.

The steps in *Deming's seven-point action plan* are:

1　Management struggles over the 14 points, 'deadly diseases' and obstacles and agrees meaning and plans direction.

2　Management takes pride and develops courage for the new direction.

3　Management explains to the people in the company why change is necessary.

4　Divide every company activity into stages, identifying the customer of each stage as the next stage. Continual improvement of methods should take place at each stage, and stages should work together towards quality.

5　Start as soon and as quickly as possible to construct an organisation to guide continual quality improvement. Deming advocates the Deming or Shewhart cycle as a helpful procedure for improvement of any stage. The Shewhart cycle consists of a simple circle or wheel divided into four quadrants designated respectively: plan, do, study (or check) and act.

6　Everyone can take part in a team to improve the input and output of any stage.

7　Embark on construction of organisation for quality. (Deming sees this as requiring the participation of knowledgeable statisticians.)

19

Before his death in 1993 Deming synthesised his thinking over the previous 60 years into what he termed 'the system of profound knowledge' which comprises four interrelated parts:

1   Appreciation for a system. This stressed the importance of:
    • an understanding on the part of managers of the relationships between functions and activities
    • recognition of the importance of a long-term aim that everyone – shareholders, customers, employees, suppliers – and the environment should gain through innovation and cooperation.
2   Knowledge of statistical theory especially that relating to variation, process capability, control charts, interactions and loss function and their application to leadership and teamwork.
3   Theory of knowledge:
    • past experience facilitates prediction of future planning
    • an understanding of the underlying theory is fundamental to identifying why previous plans have achieved success.
4   Knowledge of psychology. This is indispensable to the understanding of human relationships, especially those that impinge on motivation and incentives.

Joseph Juran (1904–)

Like Deming, Juran is a noted quality authority. In the 1920s, he worked for Western Electric and for a time was quality manager at the Hawthorne Electric Works in Chicago. In 1951, the publication of his *Quality Control Handbook* established him as an international quality figure. Unlike Deming, Juran does not advocate a major cultural change in an organisation but rather seeks to improve quality by working within the system.

Again, unlike Deming who proposes no specific definition, Juran defines quality as 'fitness for use'. This is broken down as shown in figure 19.2 to four categories.

Figure 19.2: Juran's four categories of quality

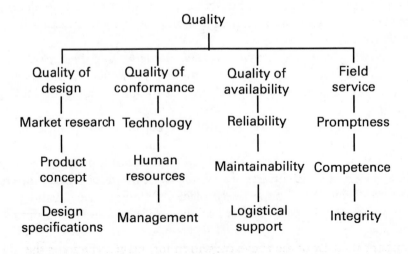

Juran suggests that the achievement of quality involves two levels:

1   The mission of the organisation as a whole is to achieve a high quality level.
2   The mission of each individual within the organisation is to achieve high production quality.

He also provides a *quality planning map* comprising the following steps:

1   Identify who are the customers. These are not just the end customers but also other internal and external customers.
2   Determine the needs of these customers.
3   Translate those needs into our language.
4   Develop a product that can respond to those needs.
5   Optimise the product features so as to meet our needs as well as customer needs.
6   Develop a process which is able to produce the product.
7   Optimise the process.
8   Prove that the process can produce the product under operating conditions.
9   Transfer the process to operations.

Juran, like Deming, recognised the futility of mere slogans and exhortations to quality. As he put it, 'The recipe for action should consist of 90% substance and 10% exhortation, not the reverse.'

His *formula for results* is:

1   Establish specific goals to be reached.
2   Establish plans for reaching the goals.
3   Assign clear responsibility for the goals.
4   Base the rewards on the goals achieved.

The *definition of TQM* framed by the Juran Institute founded in 1979 is:

'The set of management processes and systems that create delighted customers through empowered employees leading to higher revenue and lower cost.'

Armand V Feigenbaum (1920–)

Feigenbaum is known for three important contributions to the concept of quality:

1   His international promotion of the quality ethic.
2   His work as the originator of total quality control.
3   His development of the quality cost classification.

In respect of the first of the above contributions, Feigenbaum was the founding chairman of the International Academy for Quality. The second and third contributions were first presented in his book *Total Quality Control* which appeared in 1951 under the title *Quality Control Principles, Practice and Administration* in which he defines quality control as:

> 'An effective system for coordinating the quality maintenance and quality improvement efforts of the various groups in an organisation so as to enable production at the most economical levels which allow for full customer satisfaction.'

Quality in this definition means 'best for customer use and selling price'. *Control* represents a management tool with four steps:

1 Selling quality standards.
2 Appraising conformance to these standards.
3 Acting when standards are exceeded.
4 Planning for improvement in the standards.

Feigenbaum was also responsible for the categorisation of the four main costs of quality – prevention costs, appraisal costs, internal failure costs and external failure costs.

The *ten benchmarks of quality* identified by Feigenbaum are:

1   Quality is a company-wide process.
2   Quality is what the customer says it is.
3   Quality and cost are a sum, not a difference.
4   Quality requires individual and teamwork.
5   Quality is a way of managing.
6   Quality and innovation are mutually dependent.
7   Quality is an ethic.
8   Quality requires continuous improvement.
9   Quality is the most cost-effective, least capital-intensive route to productivity.
10 Quality is implemented with a total system connected with customers and suppliers.

Kaoru Ishikawa (1915–1989)

Evans and Lindsay (2005) state that:

> 'It may be safely said that without the leadership of Kaoru Ishikawa, the Japanese quality movement would not have enjoyed the worldwide acclaim and success that it has today.'

In particular, he was the pioneer of the Quality Cycle movement in Japan in the 1960s.

The cause and effect diagram (also called the 'Ishikawa' or 'fishbone' diagram) was invented by Ishikawa in 1950. A typical cause and effect diagram is shown in figure 19.3 .

Figure 19.3: The cause and effect diagram

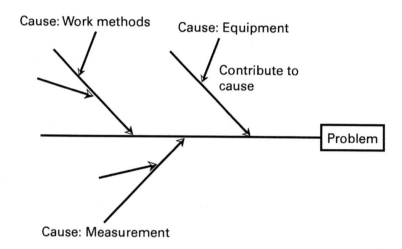

The problem is stated at the end of a horizontal line. Each branch pointing into this main stem represents a possible cause. The branches pointing to the causes are contributors to these causes. The purpose of the diagram is to focus on the causes rather than the symptoms of a problem. While typically done on paper, some computer programs have been created to make fishbone diagrams, which are one of the seven Japanese tools of quality management.

The causes and contributory causes are identified by group discussion and brainstorming sessions.

Ishikawa is also credited with the development of quality cycles although there is some disagreement as to whether the concept of the quality cycle started in the United States soon after 1945 with the Japanese adopting and adapting the approach through Ishikawa in the 1960s. A *quality cycle* has been defined as:

> A small group of work people who, under the leadership of their own foreman or supervisor, are trained to identify, analyse and solve quality-related problems on a voluntary basis and present their solutions to managers.

The main benefits of quality cycles are those of employee involvement and commitment in solving problems relating to quality improvement and productivity and ensuring that the agreed solutions are implemented.

Quality cycles are, however, only effective when:

- they are fully supported by top management
- the environment and technology are such that the quality cycle groups have plenty of scope for developing improvements

19

- the members of the quality cycle are trained in problem solving and analytical techniques
- cycles are properly coordinated and monitored.

Ishikawa also expanded Deming's four steps referred to earlier in this section into six as shown in figure 19.4.

Figure 19.4: Ishikawa's six steps

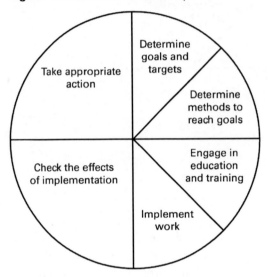

Ishikawa adopted a primarily statistical approach to quality and emphasised control charts, scatter diagrams and sampling inspection.

Genichi Taguchi (1924–)

We have already encountered Taguchi in section 4.3 of this course book and you should revise the information given.

Shigeo Shingo (1909–1990)

Shingo's principal contribution to quality was his development in the 1960s of Poka-Yoke (mistake proofing). This approach is based on the premise that the most effective approach to controlling quality is to stop the process whenever a defect occurs, define the cause and prevent the recurring source of the defect. This is the principle of the JIT production system. No statistical sampling is therefore necessary. Source inspection is therefore an active part of production to identify errors before they become defects. Such inspection constitutes 'zero quality control', which Shingo argues can achieve what may have been impossible using quality control methods.

Philip B Crosby (1926–)

Crosby is well known through his two best-sellers *Quality is Free* (1979) and *Quality Without Tears* (1984). In these books, he incorporates the ideas of some writers such as 'do it right first time' and 'zero defects'.

Crosby defines quality as: '**conformance to requirements**'. 'Requirements' in this context means those that the organisation has established for its products based directly on its customers' needs. He also assigns responsibility for quality to management. While employers are involved in

19

operational difficulties which they should draw to management's attention, the initiative for quality comes from the top.

Crosby laid down what he termed **five absolutes of quality**, namely:

1   Quality means conformance, not goodness or elegance.
2   There is no such thing as a quality problem.
3   There is no such thing as the economics of quality; it is always easier to do the job right the first time.
4   The only performance measurement is the cost of quality.
5   The only performance standard is zero defects.

Crosby also regarded **quality improvement** to be a 14-step process comprising:

1   Management commitment.
2   The establishment of quality improvement teams with senior representatives from every department/function.
3   Quality measurement aimed at determining where current and potential quality problems lie.
4   Evaluating the cost of quality and explaining its use as a management tool.
5   Raising the quality awareness and commitment to quality of all employees.
6   Taking corrective action to rectify problems identified through the previous five steps.
7   Establishing process monitoring for the improvement process.
8   Training supervisors to actively carry out their part of the quality improvement programme.
9   Holding a 'zero defects day' to communicate that there has been a change and to reaffirm management commitment to quality improvement.
10   Encouraging individuals to establish improvement goals for themselves and their groups.
11   Encouraging individuals to communicate to management the obstacles they encounter in attaining their improvement goals.
12   Recognising and appreciating those who participate in quality improvement.
13   Establishing quality councils to communicate on a regular basis.
14   Doing it all over again to emphasise that the quality improvement programme never ends.

Tom Peters (1942–)

In his book with Nancy Austin, *A Passion for Excellence* (1985), Tom Peters regards leadership as the fundamental element in quality improvement. His distinctive contribution to the concept of leadership is 'management by wandering about' (MBWA). He suggests that, while an effective leader wanders, three major activities take place:

1   Listening: suggests caring.
2   Teaching: values must be transmitted when face to face.
3   Facilitating: able to give on-the-spot help.

19

He also identifies 12 traits of a quality revolution based on the perceived characteristics of the quality improvement programmes of successful American companies:

1   Management obsession with quality: This stresses the importance of action to back up emotional commitment, for example halving the number of rework mechanics, never walking past shoddy goods.
2   Passionate systems: Failure is invariably due to passion without system, or system without passion, Peters believes. Both are necessary and an ideology is important whether based on gurus or not.
3   Measurement of quality: This should begin at the outset of the programme, should be displayed, and should be carried out by the participants.
4   Quality is rewarded: Quality-based incentive compensation can cause an early breakthrough in top management's attitude.
5   Everyone is trained for quality: Every person in the company should be extensively trained. Instruction in cause and effect analysis, statistical process control, and group interaction should be given to all.
6   Multifunction teams: Quality circles, or cross-functional teams such as Error Cause Removal of Corrective Action Teams, should be introduced. Based on his experience, Peters favours cross-functional teams.
7   Small is beautiful: There is no such thing as a small improvement. There is significance in the fact that a change has occurred.
8   Create endless 'Hawthorne' effects: This is the antidote to the 12-18 month doldrums. New goals, new themes, new events are the antidote.
9   Parallel organisation structure devoted to quality improvement: This describes the creation of shadow quality teams and emphasises that it is a route through which hourly paid workers can progress.
10 Everyone is involved: Suppliers especially, but distributors and customers too, must be part of the organisation's quality process. Joint improvement teams may be formed.
11 When quality goes up, costs go down: Quality improvement is the primary source of cost reduction; the elementary force at work is simplification, for example of design, process or procedures.
12 Quality improvement is a never-ending journey: All quality is relative. Each day, each product or service is getting relatively better or worse, but never stands still.

Claus Moller (1968–)

Danish business economist, Claus Moller, believes that the administrative process rather than the production process offers more opportunity for overall productivity gains.

In order to improve service to the customer Moller believes that the people who produce the goods must be inspired to do their best, and that huge cultural adjustment is required by all. Moller believes this will only be mastered by improving the personal development of the individual. This will lead to increased competence in the three vital areas of *productivity*, *relations* and *quality*. TMI (Time Management International – founded by Moller in 1975) sees these three areas as 'evergreens', not fads, but intrinsic to all people's lives and so closely interwoven that they presuppose each other. See figure 19.5.

Figure 19.5: TMI world – 1990

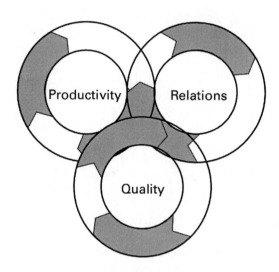

In his book, *Personal Quality* (1988), Moller sees personal quality as the basis of all other types of quality. Moller distinguishes between two standards of personal quality:

1   The ideal performance level (IP), which is the individual's personal quality goal.
2   The actual performance level (AP), which is influenced by the self-esteem of an individual.

Moller presents 12 golden rules to help improve the AP level. He also identifies 17 hallmarks of a quality company. For reasons of space, these are omitted from this course book.

TQM principles

The writings of the various gurus referred to above all emphasise one important principle: quality must entail a comprehensive approach involving all employees as well as suppliers and customers. It is therefore a 'total' approach.

Evans and Lindsay (2005) state that:

> 'TQM incorporates several dimensions: the design of products that meet customers' needs, control of processes to ensure their ability to meet design requirements and quality improvement for the continued enhancement of quality.'

The principles of TQM include:

* customer satisfaction – the customer is the driving force in TQM
* continuous process improvement
* teamwork

19

- recognition of all concerned with quality improvement
- integration of effort
- the importance of a cultural change that makes quality improvement an organisational norm.

The eight quality management principles defined in ISO 9000:2000 are also essentially TQM principles.

TQM techniques

A number of quality techniques have been identified. The original 'seven quality improvement tools' were:

Flow charts

Flowcharting is 'a graphical representation of all operations, movements, inspections, delays, decisions and storage activities involved in a process'.

There are three basic types of flow charts:

- Functional charts: used to describe how activities interact with one another within an organisation as well as with other organisations or systems
- Process flow charts: used to describe the sequence and relationship of tasks that make up an activity
- Process flow description charts: used to show the kinds of tasks such as those described in the above definition, performed within a process.

Flow charts use a standard set of symbols to represent the type of operations/processes being performed.

The basic symbols needed are as shown in figure 19.6.

Figure 19.6

Symbol	Graphic	Usage
Ellipse	⬭	Start or stop chart or section of chart
Rectangle	▭	Perform an action
Lozenge	◇	Ask a question
Line with arrow	→	Transportation
Negative answer	N	No
Positive answer	Y	Yes

There are also other symbols including:

Inverted triangle	▽	Storage
Large capital D	D	Indicates delay
Square	☐	Inspection

Checksheets

A checksheet is a special type of data collection form in which the information assembled can be interpreted without the need for additional processing.

Pareto diagrams

Pareto diagrams are named after the Italian economist Vilfredo Pareto (1848–1923) who, in 1906, observed that 20% of the Italian people owned 80% of their country's accumulated wealth. This has become known as the 80-20 rule. This principle has many applications, for example 80% of process defects arise from 20% of process issues; about 20% of purchased items account for approximately 80% of organisational expenditure. JM Juran referred to Pareto's Principle as 'the vital few and the trivial many'.

A Pareto chart is a specialised version of a histogram that ranks the categories in the chart from most to least frequent.

A typical Pareto chart is shown in figure 19.7.

Figure 19.7: Example of a Pareto chart

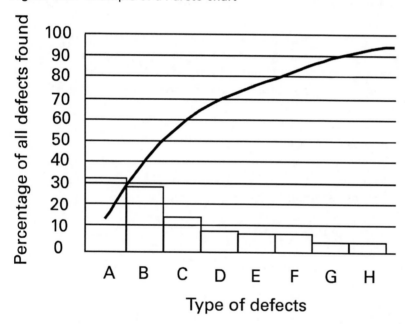

Histograms

These have been defined as 'graphic summary of variation in a set of data. The pictorial nature of the histogram enables people to see patterns that would be difficult to detect in a simple table of numbers.

Cause and effect diagrams

Reference to these diagrams has been made earlier in this section when discussing the contribution to quality of Kaoru Ishikawa.

Scatter diagrams

These diagrams provide a pictorial means of showing the relationships between two sets of data and how one variable causes change in the other. In a scatter diagram the horizontal (x) axis represents the measurement variable and the vertical (y) axis represents the measurements of the second variable. A scatter diagram from given data would appear as in figure 19.8.

19

Figure 19.8: A scatter diagram from given data

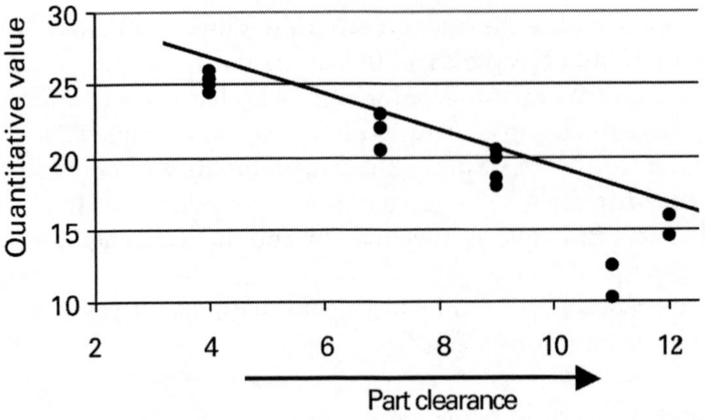

Seven new tools for quality management

These do not supersede the original seven quality improvement tools described earlier, nor are they extensions of these. They are rather interrelated systems and documentation approaches used to achieve design success by identifying objectives and the steps involved in quality improvement in enhanced detail.

These seven new tools are the:

1 affinity diagram
2 interrelationship diagram
3 tree diagram
4 matrix diagram or quality table
5 matrix data analysis
6 process decision programme chart (PDPC)
7 arrow diagram.

These are relatively advanced quality improvement techniques, probably beyond the scope of your examination. For that reason no explanation of these approaches is given. Should you be interested in learning about these 'tools', a good brief account will be found in chapter 9 of Oakland and Porter (2004) or in any modern text relating to TQM.

The benefits of TQM

These have been summarised by Evans and Lindsay (2005) as:

• improved customer satisfaction
• enhanced quality of goods and services
• reduced waste and inventory with consequential reduced costs
• improved productivity
• reduced product development time
• increased flexibility in meeting market demands
• reduced work-in-progress
• improved customer service and delivery times
• better utilisation of human resources.

Criticisms of TQM

- Blind preoccupation with TQM may result in a preoccupation with internal performance and technical specifications, which may disregard changes in the market. This is exemplified by the manager who said: 'Before we invested in TQM, we churned out poorly made products that customers didn't want. We now churn out well-made products that customers don't want.'
- TQM focuses on minimum standards – customers take zero defects for granted and expect far more from products.
- TQM creates a cumbersome bureaucracy of councils, committees and documentation relating to quality.
- TQM delegates the determination of quality to quality experts rather than people because TQM is a complicated entity beyond the comprehension of the average employee untrained in specialised statistical techniques.
- TQM calls for a cultural transformation which creates a cult in which the impression is given that only total commitment to TQM can save the organisation from ruin.

Learning activity 19.1

Identify how may of Deming's 14 points of quality management apply to your own organisation.

Feedback on page 330

Now try self-assessment question 19.1 below.

Self-assessment question 19.1

What problems surround the development and implementation of continuous improvement teams?

Feedback on page 330

19.2 Using 6-Sigma and other techniques to gain quality improvements

Continuous improvements

Achieving quality improvements requires a systematic approach to quality. Some manufacturing organisations have attempted to embed high quality standards through the adoption of 6-Sigma methodologies.

6-Sigma as used at many organisations simply means a measure of quality that strives for near perfection. 6-Sigma is a disciplined approach and methodology for eliminating defects.

19

The process of 6-Sigma describes quantitatively how a process is performing. To achieve 6-Sigma, a process must not produce more than 3.4 defects per million opportunities. A 6-Sigma defect is defined as anything outside of customer specifications. A 6-Sigma opportunity is then the total quantity of chances for a defect.

The fundamental objective of the 6-Sigma methodology is the implementation of a measurement-based strategy that focuses on process improvement and variation reduction through the application of processes linked to the 6-Sigma methodologies. This is accomplished through the use of two 6-Sigma sub-methodologies: DMAIC and DMADV. The 6-Sigma DMAIC process (define, measure, analyse, improve, control) is an improvement system for existing processes falling below specification and looking for incremental improvement. The 6-Sigma DMADV process (define, measure, analyse, design, verify) is an improvement system used to develop new processes or products at 6-Sigma quality levels. It can also be employed if a current process requires more than just incremental improvement. Both 6-Sigma processes are executed by 6-Sigma Green Belts and 6-Sigma Black Belts, and are overseen by 6-Sigma Master Black Belts.

Those buying organisations that use 6-Sigma successfully could encourage its implementation in first tier suppliers where quality is a particular KPI. This might be incorporated as part of the selection process or a condition on reapproval. The expertise gained by the organisation could be shared and cross-functional teams could be put together to work on implementation (including specialist training) and subsequent monitoring and evaluation.

Continuous improvement or Kaizen has been a feature of Japanese organisations for decades. This form of incremental improvements to quality standards has contributed to the competitive advantage gained by many of their international firms.

This has been driven by the formation of quality circles or task teams. Devised by Ishikawa in the 1960s, they are 'a small group of volunteers, usually from the same work area, meeting regularly, usually under the leadership of their immediate superior, to analyse and solve problems relating to their responsibilities and, where appropriate, themselves implement solutions agreed with management' (Lysons and Farrington, 2006).

The objectives of quality circles are:

- reduction of errors and the improvement of quality
- problem prevention rather than detection and correction
- reduction in product or service costs
- improved productivity
- increased employee involvement, motivation, job satisfaction and commitment
- improved teamwork and working relationships
- development of employee problem-solving ability.

Quality circles have not been adopted widely within the UK, which may indicate cultural environment from traditional employee relations perspectives. However, if planned properly with good, trained, QC facilitators and the support of senior managers and employee representatives, they would make a difference to organisational quality standards. If established, the experience and improvements gained could be transferred to the supply base where appropriate within the existing climate and culture. Again, as discussed earlier with 6-Sigma, trained teams from the buying organisation could offer advice and help in designing an implementation strategy.

Re-engineering techniques

Re-engineering and quality

Re-engineering is closely related to quality and TQM.

Many organisations adopt a step-by-step or 'incremental' approach to TQM. Re-engineering emphasises a 'socio-technical' approach in which a design team assesses the organisation's existing culture, systems and environment and makes recommendations for fundamental changes such as the introduction of self-directed work teams, profit-based pay, payment for knowledge and the reorientation of the organisation away from the 'functional stovepipes' of production, marketing, finance and HRM towards a more product, customer or geographically based outlook.

Quality tools are also applicable to re-engineering such as the establishment of quality standards, quality teams, cause and effect diagrams and control charts. Like TQM, re-engineering as a tool also shifts its focus from a leadership model of command and control to one of 'empowerment, commitment and trust'.

The principles of re-engineering

According to Hammer (2001), the seven principles of BPR are:

1 Organise around outcomes, not tasks. This principle calls for one person to perform all the steps in a process, thus providing job enlargement and enhanced job satisfaction.
2 Have those who use the outcome of the process perform the process – carry out the work where it makes most sense to do it. Having the work done by people closest to the process shifts tasks across traditional functional barriers. Employees, for example, can make some of their own purchases without going through the purchasing function or make simple repairs without calling on maintenance staff.
3 Subsume information-processing work into real work that produces information – the people who collect information should also be responsible for processing it, thus eliminating the need for another group to reconcile and process that information. Eliminating the need for invoices by processing orders and receiving information online eliminates much of the work done by traditional accounts departments.
4 Treat geographically dispersed resources as though they were centralised. The implementation of this principle has been facilitated by information technology. Centralised databases and telecommunications networks, for example, now allow companies to link with discrete units or individual field personnel, providing them with economies of

19

scale while retaining their individual flexibility and responsiveness to customers.

5   Link parallel activities instead of integrating their results. This principle is exemplified by the concept of concurrent engineering. In concurrent engineering, design and engineering personnel are brought together early in the design stage to develop the product and also the processes by which the product will be produced.

6   Put the decision point where the work is performed and build control into the process. With a better educated workforce and decision-aiding technology it is possible to devolve a considerable amount of decision making to the point where work is done. This makes for a flatter and more responsive organisation.

7   Capture information once. Information should be collected and captured on the organisation's online information once, at the source, thus avoiding mistakes in data and costly data re-entries.

Selecting processes for re-engineering

In deciding what process(es) to re-engineer, consideration should be given to the following:

- What processes will have the greatest impact on customer value and satisfaction?
- What processes offer the greatest potential for redesign in cost/benefit terms?
- What are the processes for which redesign is most urgent?
- What processes are known to be outdated in respect of the methods and technology used?
- What processes are most suitable to the strengths and expertise of the available re-engineering time and the interests of management?

Implementing BPR

Janson has identified three phases that apply to every re-engineering project:

1   Rethink: examining current practices and processes in relation to organisational objectives and strategies. Consideration of the extent to which customer satisfaction is being achieved and the extent or otherwise to which current processes provide competitive advantage.

2   Redesign: analysing existing process and deciding what elements need to be redesigned to enhance both customer and employee satisfaction.

3   Retool: evaluation of current advanced technologies to examine how they might be applied to improved existing processes.

Blair and Meadows (1996) suggest the following steps:

- Energise: this involves the vital steps of gaining commitment from management and employees to a shared vision which may be embodied in a mission statement.
- Prioritise: this involves selecting a process or processes to re-engineer which will give enhanced customer benefits. Such prioritisation involves the considerations referred to under 'Selecting processes for re-engineering' above and collecting information on cost, quality, service and time and the relative value placed on them by customers.

- Analyse: this will involve obtaining detailed information on who does what and why. A mapping of the existing system will expose problems and bottlenecks and indicate when improvements can be made immediately and in the future.
- Redesign: this involves building a process redesign project team comprising representatives from all relevant functions. There should also be consultation with suppliers and customers. Redesign may involve simplification of complicated processes, replacement of manual operations by technology, controlling work by exception, breaking down functional boundaries, reducing the number of managers/supervisors, multi-skilling, job enlargement and empowerment.
- Implementation: it is always advisable to test new processes before they are introduced generally. Once a redesigned process has passed this test, training or reorientation programmes will need to be developed and consideration given to issues of pay and incentives.

The benefits of BPR

These have been summarised as:

- Revolutionary thinking: re-engineering encourages organisations to abandon conventional approaches to problem solving and to 'think big'.
- Breakthrough improvement: the slow, cautious process of incremental improvement leaves many organisations unprepared to compete in today's rapidly changing marketplace. Re-engineering helps organisations make noticeable changes in the pace and quality of their response to customer needs.
- Organisational structure: through re-engineering, an insurance company, for example, was transformed from a factory-style organisation that was essentially rule driven and job centred to a marketing organisation that focuses directly on the customer. The current primary objective of the organisation is to identify real customer needs, rather than create products that ignore the needs and wants of the customers.
- Organisational renewal: re-engineering often results in radically new organisational designs that can help companies respond better to competitive pressures, increase market share and profitability and improve cycle times, cost ratios and quality.
- Corporate culture: perhaps the major accomplishment of the re-engineering effort is the change that occurs in the corporate culture and in the basic principles by which departments operate. Workers at all levels are encouraged to make suggestions for improvement and to believe that management will listen to what they have to say.
- Job redesign: re-engineering has helped create more challenging and more rewarding jobs with broader responsibilities for employees. Workers who are used to performing only one simple task continually repeated are now involved in the entire process.

Reasons for BPR failures

During the 1990s, there were just as many cases of BPR failures as there were success stories. Because of the high failure rate, estimated

19

313

at between 50% and 80%, the concept of BPR has become somewhat discredited, which is unfortunate because the underlying principles are fundamentally sound. Some reasons for BPR failures are:

- the high risk of changing what has been proved to work – 'if it ain't broke, don't fix it'
- inappropriate change management methods
- failure to take into account internal politics and entrenched interests
- the high cost of retooling and new technology
- a lack of participation and leadership
- a lack of commitment and motivation on the part of both management and employees
- inflexible software
- inadequate training in re-engineering processes.

Conversely, some critical success factors include:

- senior management commitment
- good project management
- the use of coaches and consultants
- consultation with employees.

Incentives to suppliers

Incentivisation or gain sharing, an example of a customer-led initiative, is when a prime manufacturer (OEM) manages a supplier improvement program. In this situation, the OEM is both the external improvement agent and the secondary target. As the agent, the OEM may share in the short-term financial benefits that an improvement yields. As the secondary target, the OEM may receive indirect benefits from the improvements in the long term.

Incentivisation is defined as:

> 'A process by which a provider is motivated to achieve extra "value added" services over those specified originally and which are of material benefit to the user. These should be assessable against pre-defined criteria. The process should benefit both parties.'

> HM Treasury

Incentivisation should always be considered from a practical point of view and is likely to be more relevant to contracts of sufficient scope and size to justify the investment in applying the technique where the anticipated benefits are assessed as being significant, and where, without incentivisation, improvements in performance would be unlikely to take place at a rate to match the business need.

Incentivisation creates a more proactive, cooperative relationship between the supplier and the buyer.

Good procurement requires:

- *a clear and precise objective* of what is to be achieved
- *a full understanding of the market* and of the suppliers within it

- *careful consideration when choosing suppliers* encouraging those suppliers most likely to deliver
- *effective contract management* by both parties and commitment to the incentives.

Incentivisation of a contract also requires:

- An *evaluation of the potential benefits* at the procurement planning stage.
- The creation, by buyers, of the *right culture of incentivisation* by sharing their contract strategy with suppliers. Suppliers must see the process as a positive one, be willing to collaborate on the performance of the contract and to share information in order to effect continuous improvement.
- *Effective preplanning* of payments (that is to say, that there is adequate provision to meet all potential incentive payments).

In addition, the following need to be taken into account:

- Incentivisation is more likely to be successful with large suppliers.
- Incentivisation requires time to achieve results so works better with longer-term contracts.
- Suppliers should be encouraged to propose innovative incentivisation schemes throughout the procurement process.
- Incentivisation will only work on the basis of trust between buyer and supplier.
- Use incentivisation only where appropriate – it should not be seen as 'an end in itself'.

Benefits

Some benefits that can be delivered by incentivisation in addition to those inherent in the base contract include:

- lower cost, faster or timelier delivery of service with no compromise on quality
- full understanding of the relationship cost, the quality of service delivery and the ability to deal more effectively with changes during the contract
- increased service levels
- greater price stability
- enhanced achievement of the desired outcome
- better utilisation of services
- improved management information
- improved management, control and monitoring of contract deliverables.

Learning activity 19.2

Analyse the potential for improvement in operational performance if techniques such as 6-Sigma, re-engineering or incentivisation are introduced within the organisation and in parts of the supply chain.

Feedback on page 330

19

Now try self-assessment question 19.2 below.

Self-assessment question 19.2

How does 6-Sigma deliver results?

Feedback on page 331

19.3 The extent to which teamworking collaboration can be established and sustained

Cross-functional teams and collaborative working

Cross-functional teams can make it much easier to coordinate activities and information. Where such teams share the same physical location, team members can informally stop by and discuss the timing of key aspects of a project, the interpretation of results or the logic behind a conclusion. Team members can immediately communicate information they used to have to wait for team meetings to share.

But they also lose some of the advantages of functional organisation. When team members are located with other specialists in a particular field, they can discuss a whole range of discipline-specific issues, which can be difficult to achieve in cross-functional working.

Teamworking

In many enterprises, teams are the building blocks of the organisation. In manufacturing, teams of multi-skilled operators may build a whole product or major subassemblies of a product. In new product development, people from sales, marketing, research, engineering and manufacturing team up to design products and bring them to market quickly and cheaply.

A team can be defined as a group of people with a common goal, interdependent work and joint accountability for results. In team-based enterprises, teams are composed of people from different professions or jobs so that all the knowledge and skill needed to manage a complete process to completion is represented. They are frequently responsible for producing key products or services. Their business directives, common goals and joint accountability tie them together into a cohesive unit. The team-based approach by an organisation can be adapted and the approach and skills transferred to collaborative working with suppliers.

Advantages

There are a number of advantages to teamworking. Because they are located together and share common goals, team members easily share the information and thinking that fell in the 'white space' between traditional functional 'silos'. Teams, irrespective of how they have been assembled,

19

improve focus. Cross-functional teams can focus on a single output and the connected processes. This may be a major subassembly in the production of a car or the improving of logistical problems between the suppliers. This focus can help teams develop a real sense of common purpose and focus. By working together in close proximity over an extended period, they can develop a rhythm, a rapport and a common identity. This, in turn, leads to higher levels of trust which vastly improves their ability to build on each other's ideas and solve business and technical problems.

Teams can be excellent vehicles for learning. To learn effectively, people need both time to reflect and a safe environment. They need time to think about their experience and its implications and incorporate new insights into their current mental models. They need safety to explore new ideas and challenge their own assumptions. Within the trust and rapport created in a team, people can feel safe enough to share their thinking, the reasons behind their conclusions, the questions they have about their conclusions and even their half-baked ideas. When they take time to collectively reflect on their experience, they can build on each other's ideas and deepen the richness of their thinking and insights.

Disadvantages

All of the above rests upon proper team selection and effective team leadership.

Teams can also become new 'silos'. People in team-based enterprises often complain that they have trouble getting information from other teams – this can easily lead to two related learning disabilities: isolation and team myopia.

Teams can get isolated. Team members naturally focus inward, concentrating on team goals and connecting with fellow team members. When PepsiCo expanded internationally, teams charged with building the business in Eastern Europe, Russia, the Middle East and the Pacific Rim had no planned way to share experiences, insights and ideas with teams working in other regions. The result was that every single team started anew, repeating the same mistakes and following the same blind alleys already explored by their predecessors. This sort of isolation is common for cross-functional teams. Even when team members fully intend to share insight and information with other teams, team goals often pull so strongly on people's time that they simply cannot find the time to do so.

Isolation can lead to team myopia. When teams have very little contact with other teams or are isolated for extended periods, they can get into the habit of rejecting ideas from outside and lose their ability to generate new ideas, that is, they can become myopic. Research in creative thinking has long shown that new ideas usually come from the intersection of disciplines, perspectives or ways of thinking. Scientists often do their most creative work a few years after they change fields. Small enterprises working at the edge of a field often develop new technologies. Teams' most creative ideas often come when they see how people in other enterprises or industries perform similar processes. When teams lose touch with other teams, they often get

19

into a rut of using the same approaches, tools and ideas repeatedly. This can be particularly hard for technical specialists on cross-functional teams. When they lose touch with colleagues from their own discipline, they have trouble keeping up with developments in their field.

These are often symptoms of what has been called 'groupthink' and include:

- overestimation of the group where the team members believe that the team can do no wrong
- closed-mindedness where the team refuse to listen to new ideas
- rationalisation where failure is blamed on factors outside the team
- self-censorship as people refuse to say anything that will disturb the team image of itself.

Teams can also easily neglect long-term capacity building. Most organisations need to balance the tension between short-term production goals and long-term capacity building. On an organisational level, this is the tension between production and product development. On an individual level, it is the tension between focusing on current projects and taking the time to develop and share knowledge. Because teams are typically tasked with output goals (producing a product or service) they tend to pull people toward the production side of this tension. They tend not to see the value of building capacity beyond their team. Frequently, they even have trouble preparing their members for the next generation of technical development.

Implementing teamworking

There are a number of models and approaches in implementing cross-disciplinary team building. This rests upon effective selection, an understanding of group processes, effective leadership, team membership and support. Skills which might be used to manage and work within effective cross-functional teams include the following.

Managing a team

- team selection: ensuring that the right blend of personalities and skills are selected; making sure that the recruitment process makes team members value the team
- management of conflict: understanding the uses of conflict; separating issues from people; understanding feelings and positions; using the right approach
- leadership: setting goals and standards; understanding processes; creating vision; communicating effectively
- development: helping the team grow and develop.

Working as part of a team

- initiating: proposing tasks, goals, or actions; defining team problems; suggesting procedures
- information sharing: offering facts; giving expression of feelings; giving opinions
- information seeking: asking for factual clarification; requesting facts pertinent to the discussion or activity

19

- opinion seeking: asking for clarification of the values pertinent to the topic under discussion; questioning benefits involved in the alternative suggestions
- clarifying: interpreting ideas or suggestions; defining terms; clarifying issues before the team; clearing up confusion
- orienting: defining the position of the team with respect to its goals; pointing to departures from agreed-on directions or goals; raising questions about the directions pursued in team discussions
- summarising: pulling together related ideas; restating suggestions; offering decisions or conclusions for the team to consider
- reality testing: making critical analyses of ideas; testing ideas against data to see whether the ideas would be likely to work
- participating: taking responsibility within the team; considering the ideas of others; serving as an audience in team discussion and decision making
- gatekeeping: helping to keep communication channels open; facilitating the participation of others; suggesting procedures that support sharing information
- harmonising: attempting to reconcile disagreements; reducing tension; getting people to explore differences
- compromising: offering compromises that yield status when his or her own ideas are involved in conflicts; modifying in the interest of team cohesion or growth
- encouraging: being friendly, warm and responsive to others; indicating by body language or remarks the acceptance of others' contributions
- consensus testing: asking to see whether the team is nearing a decision; sending up 'trial balloons' to test possible solutions
- standard setting: expressing standards for the team to attempt to achieve; applying standards in evaluating the quality of team processes.

Learning activity 19.3

It is often difficult to establish good working teams. What are the essential steps for effective team creation and management?

Feedback on page 331

Collaborative technology

We have seen that cross-functional teams may be located in the same physical location or 'co-located'. However, teams may be located at very different geographical points and may sometimes work many thousands of miles from each other. In some multinational companies central purchasing may be based in one country, while each factory has a local purchasing unit. Coordination between these units, and production, distribution, finance and suppliers requires more than just an enterprise resource planning (ERP) system. It requires a range of computerised collaborative working systems (CCWSs).

The world of CCWS is often described in terms of the time and space in which a collaborative activity occurs. Collaboration can be between people

19

in the same place (co-located) or different places (remote). Collaboration can be at the same time (synchronous) or separated in time (asynchronous).

The technology currently being used includes:

- video teleconferencing
- data sharing
- document sharing
- shared whiteboards
- chat
- instant messaging
- online presence (for example, ICQ, Ding)
- bulletin boards
- threaded news and discussion group systems
- email
- mailing lists
- voting/polling
- virtual communities
- virtual reality.

Implementing collaborative technology

The key to selecting or developing successful collaborative systems appears to involve an understanding of what is currently done, and designing systems that not only can mesh with that way of working, but can adapt gracefully as people change their way of working over time. One important lesson that has been learned from CCWS implementation is to pay close attention to the distribution of costs and benefits resulting from a change in work practice. Although a new system may be beneficial for an organisation as a whole it can still fail. If the new system imposes extra work for many people in order to benefit others, there will be a natural reluctance to use it.

Communities of practice

Some enterprises are trying forging cross-functional relationships in a way that blends policy, teams and computer-supported working. One way in which this can be carried out is through the development of communities of practice (COPs). Each COP focuses on a topic or discipline important to the organisation.

They are responsible for sharing knowledge and standardising practices. This approach links the organisation in two ways. Cross-functional teams focus on inputs, outputs, typical products, major processes or market segments. COPs focus on learning within functions or disciplines, sharing information and insights, collaborating on common problems and stimulating new ideas. Communities of practice are a way to preserve a discipline or technical focus, while cross-functional teams unite disciplines around common products. Teams weave the organisation together in one direction. Communities weave it together in the other.

A community of practice is a group that shares knowledge, learns together and creates common practices. Communities of practice share information, insights, experience and tools about an area of common interest.

19

Implementing COPs

Unlike teams, communities of practice rarely have a specific result to deliver to the organisation. They are typically driven by the value they provide to individual members. Individuals share information and insights and discover ideas which will save them money, time, energy and effort. The value individuals derive from the community is typically what keeps community members involved. While a team delivers value in the result it produces, a community discovers value in many day-to-day exchanges of knowledge and information.

Starting and supporting communities of practice is very different from team building. Since communities of practice are organised around knowledge, not outputs, traditional team-building activities of setting goals, dividing tasks and developing workplans are not appropriate. Starting and supporting communities of practice follows a different set of guidelines:

- Building communities around a few important topics: organisations frequently cast 'too wide a net' when initiating knowledge management approaches and end up building stockpiles of underutilised information – information junkyards. To leverage knowledge effectively, start with a few communities of practice focused on topics important to the organisation. Focusing on strategically important topics will make it considerably easier to expand beyond the original communities.
- Finding and building on natural networks: whether the organisation supports them or not, communities of practice arise naturally in most organisations. So don't create new communities. Once you have identified an important topic to form communities around, find the networks of people who already share knowledge about that topic. They are likely the seed of your community.
- Developing community coordinators and core groups: a key success factor for intentional communities is to have a coordinator who organises and maintains the community. This coordinator is usually a well-respected and well-connected community member. The coordinator invites people to participate, links people together, finds exciting topics for the community to address, connects outside the community and generally keeps the community vibrant. Coordinators usually rely on a core group of community members to contribute.
- Initiating some simple knowledge-sharing activities: since intentional communities of practice are a new approach to organisational structure, they are difficult for people to really understand. Nothing conveys what they are about better than the experience of sharing insights in a regular forum, supported by a coordinator and/or facilitator. Rather than explaining or extensively designing communities of practice, engage people in participating in them by starting a few in your organisation.
- Supporting communities: if the organisation values learning and sharing knowledge, it will provide a rich ground for growing communities of practice. But that means managers need to give people the time and encouragement to reflect, share ideas with other teams and think through the implications of other teams' ideas.
- Creating a community support team: because they are organised and supported differently from teams, community development requires a

19

different set of tools and approaches. Form a team to find, practise and use these new development tools.

Service level agreements and KPIs

In the former examples of tools and approaches that can be used to manage internal relationships, we have looked at the way in which policies, cross-functional working, collaborative technology and COPs can be used to bring about improvements in those relationships. There is another way of improving internal relationships which can involve changes in the purchasing and supply function itself. This involves the use of internal service level agreements (SLAs).

SLAs allow internal customers to state their service level needs clearly and unambiguously. In turn, suppliers are enabled to focus their resources into providing services at the required level. Key performance indicators (KPIs) measure the quality of the service provision to allow for remedial action where necessary.

Where services, over time, are not delivered to expected levels of quality and efficiency, two courses of action can be taken. Either the service capacity can be increased (often accompanied by a cost increase), or the customer's expectation as to the level of service can be decreased. This decision should be taken transparently so that both customer and supplier are aware of new expectations and/or service targets. Any additional costs would also have to be negotiated.

Self-assessment question 19.3

What are the weaknesses of team working and the solutions to overcome the problems?

Feedback on page 331

19.4 Breakthrough value creation

If an organisation can achieve a breakthrough change with its products or services this will create a distinct competitive edge. Inventions will drive the major technological breakthroughs, but the majority of innovations involve creativity in many areas, such as design, re-branding, service development, process improvement and new routes to market.

Customers are becoming increasingly demanding and have higher expectations of product, services and processes. Organisations must seek to continuously improve every aspect of their offerings if they wish to retain customer loyalty.

Technology is a key source of breakthrough innovation and has the power to force new standards on the industry. It drives the change and requires others to respond to the change. As competitors catch up with the technology then the organisation innovates again to find a new technological advance to go ahead again. It should also be remembered

19

that the implementation of new technological improvements can be slow because of initial problems with the technology and the sometimes daunting task of ensuring the workforce is fully trained in any desired new skills. There are also a requirement on occasions for other organisations within the supply chain to adopt some of the technology in order to respond to the new processes.

Also, as with all products, technology has a life cycle so that eventually it does not pay to spend more on improving the existing technology; new breakthrough technology is required.

Learning activity 19.4

What breakthrough innovation has your own organisation been involved with? Describe how the technology was transferred effectively down the supply chain without the intellectual property escaping to the outside world.

Feedback on page 331

Now try self-assessment question 19.4 below.

Self-assessment question 19.4

What processes are put in place in order that there is collaboration on technological advances?

Feedback on page 331

19.5 Innovation in supply chain management

Introduction

Innovation comes from a mixture of individual insight, collaboration, conflict between disciplines and, often, pure necessity. In this sense, innovation is often much more an art than a science. Innovation is important, both within the supply chain as a source of competitive advantage to enterprises, and to purchasing and SCM departments as they face new challenges, while working with limited resources.

This section looks at how innovation happens and whether innovation can be planned. Brainstorming, for example, is a very common process for creating innovation, and enterprises facilitate, often encourage, brainstorming. It brings collaboration and conflict together, triggers individual insights and elicits team creativity. There are many other means of stimulating innovation which range from the sublime to reading, meditation, taking a shower, foreign travel, facilitated meetings, basic research and prototyping.

Quite often, as with strategy, which can be a form of innovation itself, the challenge with all of these, and other means of innovation, is that

19

they result in multiple possibilities that must then be prioritised and evaluated. In a competitive market environment, with increasing demands for customisation, rising price pressures on suppliers and shrunken R&D budgets, the management of innovation introduces a process for evaluating innovations rapidly and determining which will provide the best value on investment.

Innovation challenges

Choosing how to compete through efficiencies is often seen as only a temporary source of competitive advantage for enterprises seeking to maintain a competitive edge and stay ahead of change purely through innovation. Innovative enterprises are those that scan the environment for change and opportunity, as well as for threats, and respond with ideas and actions that keep them growing and profitable.

Companies that compete through innovation know that new (or borrowed) ideas apply, not only to products, but also to processes. These processes include quality, productivity, service, financial discipline, employee attitudes and development. All are critical elements that contribute to competitive ability.

Broadly, innovation falls into two main areas: process innovation and product innovation.

Processes and innovation

There are two basic categories of innovation. These are:

1 Continuous improvements: innovations conceived and implemented by an individual or small group to make their job easier, better or more productive. Examples might include an improved form, a simplified ordering system or a slightly readjusted tool.
2 Organisational innovations: this may involve a range of different functions and levels within the enterprise.

The first, and often most difficult, step in creating process innovation is to develop an organisational culture that encourages, supports and rewards innovative ideas and effort. There are many barriers to developing an innovation culture. One of the most common is about enhancing confidence and encouraging employees to overcome their fear of being 'punished' for 'rocking the boat'. This may involve modelling innovative behaviour in management and/or introducing incentives in the form of rewards and recognition. Adding a sense of urgency by making innovation a key to security and growth can help emphasise commitment to new ideas.

It can be useful to develop a framework through which process innovation can be recognised and released. Components of such a framework may include:

1 Opportunity identification: competitive innovation is proactive so, instead of waiting for threats to make innovation a necessity, organisations can set up systems to scan for innovation opportunities. These systems can be internal and based on TQM principles that

19

empower employees or external people in the form of a company website that calls for ideas from the general public.

2 Prioritisation: obviously, not every innovation is a winner, nor does every good idea meet the needs and objectives of the organisation. Determining the general direction for innovative efforts, therefore, enables a company to prioritise and concentrate on opportunities most likely to make it more competitive. This often involves clearly communicating constraints, as well as goals and objectives, to guide innovative thinking.

3 Idea generation: generating ideas requires creativity. Creativity requires both a culture in which it is supported and time, resources and direction to grow. Creativity training can also help people think 'outside the box' in their day-to-day activities.

4 Analysis and implementation: a flood of ideas isn't, by itself, innovation. The organisation must ensure that these ideas are captured, analysed and, if deemed valuable, brought to reality. At each phase of innovation, different roles become central to the support process: the inventor is the individual (or group) who finds the opportunity or generates the idea. Inventors, however, are often not the best people to sell the idea through the organisation. That's the role of the champion, who can gather input and build backing for the proposal. Champions use advocacy skills to effectively 'sell' promising ideas to key individuals within the company. Those individuals, who become allies of the champion, are innovation supporters. Finally, in the case of the most complex organisational innovations, a sponsor from upper management is often essential to ensure that resources and attention are devoted to developing the idea.

Types of process innovation

A process is a series of activities, or steps, which are goal-oriented. Process activities or steps can be defined as:

- the operations or stages within the manufacturing cycle required to transform components into intermediates or finished goods
- the operations or stages within the service delivery cycle required to provide a level of service that meets customer needs.

Steps of any process should be specific and concrete. They tell 'how to …' make things, such as rear axle assemblies or gas turbine engines; or 'how to …' fill cans with ham or bottles with shampoo; or 'how to …' provide legal or travel services. Process management and process improvement are becoming increasingly important elements in day-to-day management in most organisations. Identifying, developing and improving processes is critical within SCM.

Processes are used to:

- support staff and enhance their efficiency and effectiveness
- support customers and help them interact easily with the organisation
- help control quality of service, monitor staff and business performance
- help achieve financial control
- help achieve management control.

19

Process innovation is often difficult. There is no one 'best' way of improving a process. Different approaches to process improvements have different goals and techniques. Business process re-engineering, for instance, seeks radical change and its techniques emphasise the use of industrial engineering tools to streamline and aggregate work flows. Total quality management seeks to implement continuous incremental improvement and its techniques focus on streamlining processes. The learning organisation aims to position a company for adaptation and innovation in an era of increasing change and flexibility; its process improvement efforts centre on collaboration and teams rather than work flows. All of these approaches are valid options in developing process innovation.

As we have already seen, opportunities for process innovation range from simple options that involve limited investment, change, effort and risk, to complex options that involve a high degree of all of these elements. Types of process innovation might include:

- Eliminating the process: for example, an oil company abandoned travel expense account reporting.
- Outsourcing the process to a firm for which it is an identity asset process (for example, a fashions manufacturing business may outsource inventory management and distribution to a logistics firm).
- Front-loading: leaving the major part of the process and supporting computer transaction processing systems as is, using computer workstations and telecommunications to add flexibility and new services at the front end and gradually erode the back end (for example, telephone companies front-load customer ordering systems to provide near-immediate installation of new services).
- Shifting responsibility for the process: have the customer or someone else do it. Or do it yourself (for example, Ikea created self-assembly furniture, banks installed ATMs and telephone banking, restaurants set up salad bars and carveries, management encouraged employees' use of laptop computers to produce presentation graphics and attractively formatted reports, reducing print costs).
- Streamlining: tighten linkages between activities to eliminate waste, number of steps, number of components needed, number of delays in place, other costs and people (for example, automotive assemblers used lean production manufacturing processes to reduce space requirements, investment in tools, engineering hours and on-site inventory by 50%).
- Integrating and locating work and information in a single customer contact point at which a process can be handled in its entirety (for example, insurance companies reduce processing time from around three weeks to two to four hours by having a case manager handle all the steps involved in issuing a new policy).
- Collaborating: cultivate a culture and an ethos of cooperation in order to coordinate smooth and effective interactions between interdependent workers (for example, team building across functional barriers such as sales and production staff can remove the barriers to understanding and functional priorities that impeded customer service).
- Networking: providing communications infrastructures that enable individuals, groups and outside firms to coordinate flexibly and collaboratively, and provide training, incentives and team support for them to do so (for example, router hardware manufacturers use

networks as the base for worldwide, rapid building of teams for special projects and problem solving).

- Importing: adopting a process or process infrastructure from another industrial sector (for example, a local government in the USA issued benefits cards that allow state benefits recipients to withdraw benefit payments from ATMs and buy food using credit card payment authorisation terminals in supermarkets, eliminating costly support services).
- Franchising: marketing a process, with supporting expertise, for someone else to turn into a business (for example, a burger company provided franchises with complete process capability under its organisational brand).
- Radicalising: raising awareness of a process in order to accelerate the degree and pace of organisational change, transform it or do both.
- Pre-empting: using a process infrastructure to capture another industry's traditional business at a customer moment of value (for example, an airline usurped international hotels' distribution channels by adding hotel reservations to its airline reservation system; and an electronics wholesaler taking on SCM for major customers).
- Inventing: creating a new process by thinking in new ways and breaking from conceptions of an industry 'core' process (for example, a retailer substituted catalogues for expensive store space; and a computer hardware manufacturer substituted catalogues, telephone ordering, customised assembly and UPS delivery for physical stores and inventory in the retailing of personal computers).
- Productivating: turning a process into a product that earns money (for example, a telecommunications company turned an internal customer invoicing process for long-distance phone calls into a $2-billion-a-year product, 'Friends and Family').
- Opportunities for process innovation are probably limitless. These are just a few examples. The product of process innovation can also be employed itself to improve organisational competitiveness.

Innovation and products

Although innovation is concerned with processes, it is also concerned with products. Many organisations and enterprises today are adopting strategies that treat intellectual property (IP) in a way that releases locked-up profits, acts as a catalyst for innovation and makes better use of existing assets.

For many enterprises this has meant recognising that intellectual property is much more than a set of legal documents and research results to be locked away in company vaults. Instead, employing a new approach to intellectual asset management, the companies have set up businesses to aggressively manage, market and sell a range of intangible assets including patents, trade secrets, chemical composition and product formulations, process technology, and even standard business practices.

Innovation for these companies has a product called intellectual property, which has value, and which can be profitably sold. In some organisations, profit margins on some sales of intellectual property average 78% after expenses. Some businesses in the chemical industry have developed an annual turnover of over $450 million in selling IP.

19

The management of intellectual assets can take a number of forms. The most obvious is selling or licensing intellectual property assets that fall outside the company's core business, or in a geographic region where the company has no plans to compete. Some of the biggest revenues earned by chemical companies come from licensing process technology, such as sharing how to build and operate a complex plant. For others, the value comes from tax write-offs gained by donating patents found to have no future value for the company. Still others simply downsize their IP portfolios to reduce patent-maintenance costs.

The shift in perspective to viewing intangible assets as products is often lucrative, but it doesn't come easily. One of the greatest challenges is changing the culture of protecting technology, know-how and intellectual property. Many people believe that licensing is just giving away know-how and valuable company assets. This is particularly true when the individuals or groups have made a major commitment to the development of the product, and feel a high degree of ownership. This process requires an effective management framework.

Some companies take an even more aggressive position with intellectual assets, and offer some technologies to the outside world before they are introduced into its own products. Such policies help reduce costs and spread the risk of getting new technologies up and running. In the past, if a company invented a new chemical for cleaning products or a part for an engine that required suppliers to build or add new facilities, that company often bore the full brunt of the cost, with volume guarantees based on take-or-pay type contracts.

This meant that the company carried the entire risk of building a new plant, which, if the product launch failed, was a cost that had to be written off. Increasingly, when a new chemical or part is taken to a supplier, companies will ask: 'Who else can this be sold to?' If suppliers find another customer, this has a dramatic impact on costs.

Adopting such an approach requires a fundamental shift in strategic thinking within an enterprise, and is based on the view that processes have become more important than the products that they create. This is a new concept of competitive advantage, which focuses on generating more shareholder value – even if this involves dealing with a competitor.

Such an approach requires a similar shift in the way that the success of the strategy is measured. It is important that companies measure value, not just revenues and royalties. For example, P&G invented a new packaging technology and negotiated a licensing deal with the supplier. Under the agreement, the supplier was allowed to sell the technology to other customers, but as part of the deal, any volume sold to those customers was credited to P&G, reducing the cost per unit P&G paid, based on volume incentives. In addition, P&G no longer had to pay mould changes for new designs. Such agreements are creative and win-win for both parties.

One chemical firm offers newly developed technologies directly to other chemical companies, where potential customers are well known, and/or places them on internet-based intellectual property marketplaces for wider audiences. Other companies approach venture capitalists, offering both technologies and entrepreneurs from the company to pursue the business opportunities, again spreading the risks and rewards of development.

Other companies are actively using the supply chain to market products and processes. This might involve selling process technology and plant engineering in emerging economies, such as enterprises in China and India who have close access to raw materials, such as gas and oil, but who want to move along the supply chain, beyond refining to manufacture polymers and intermediates. In the financial services industry, some banks are selling credit card services to their suppliers. To be successful at selling process technology, companies must demonstrate their know-how, with a full-service operation that works both technically and commercially.

Finally, another benefit of implementing intellectual asset management strategies is that they foster innovation. The supply chain often starts with innovation, and sometimes that innovation may be useful to other businesses, rather than being relevant to core activities. The most important thing for R&D is creativity and problem solving. Balance is important but if staff are always running into a wall that defines core business, and they are not allowed to look over the fence, this can often kill creativity.

Conclusion

The development and management of innovation is a major driver in competitiveness and therefore SCM. The opportunities for driving down costs and enhancing revenues can make a real difference to efficiency and effectiveness within the supply chain and the enterprise. Broadly, we can identify a framework for managers and employees seeking to foster innovation within their organisation. This framework dictates two types of innovation:

- process innovation
- product innovation.

These types are related, but can be treated separately. Both types of innovation have a place in the supply chain and both types of innovation require balance in order to maintain focus but not to stifle innovative projects.

Learning activity 19.5

Identify an innovative process that has occurred with your own organisation and explain the source and drivers of that innovation.

Feedback on page 331

19

Now try self-assessment question 19.5 below.

Self-assessment question 19.5

List the product or process innovations that have occurred within your own organisation over the last three years. How does this compare with competitors?

Feedback on page 332

Revision question

Now try the revision question for this session on page 343.

Summary

Collaborative working with the supply chain should increasingly be looking to raise the standards in terms of quality processes and encouragement to work jointly on new technological innovation.

Suggested further reading

Read the chapter on specifying and managing quality in Lysons and Farrington (2006).

Feedback on learning activities and self-assessment questions

Feedback on learning activity 19.1

A comparison with the Deming list should allow for critical comment on the progress of the organisation towards high quality standards plus a critical review of the value of the Deming agenda.

Feedback on self-assessment question 19.1

Continuous improvement is a systematic approach for an organisation to take to inculcate a quality culture and possible a competitive advantage. There is a management issue in making any cultural change towards a quality environment. It needs clear leadership, a champion, training of employees and a system that supports the quality culture.

Feedback on learning activity 19.2

Each of the suggested improvement techniques has value. It is suggested that a combination of all three would produce results. However, the organisation has to decide whether any new approach will reap benefits as against costs of implementation. Benchmarking with competitors would produce some research material for assessing the positive gains for a new approach. There are many examples of successes in the international market. Management of

19

all of these quality systems requires commitment from senior management, support of line managers and skills in implementation. Training will be required to ensure that the systems are embedded. Having an expectation that these systems are also part of the supply base is important but there will be barriers in persuading adoption. Making a bid criteria would be one approach but only if there is sufficient support within the industry and supply base.

Feedback on self-assessment question 19.2

Is 6-Sigma capable of producing genuine improvement results or is it a fad? A critical review of its history and take-up plus an assessment of the standards that it can impose on an organisation is required. There is no doubting the improvement in quality standards, but is this the best way of achieving high quality performance?

Feedback on learning activity 19.3

Good team selection is important plus the setting of clear goals and supported by sound leadership. Tuchman and Belbin theories should be recalled from former modules. Management and leadership is important in delivering sound team success, and the ability to handle conflict.

Feedback on self-assessment question 19.3

Usually linked to selection and management but there is also sometimes a drift towards groupthink. Teams should produce exponential results but they often underachieve because of lack of clear leadership and goal setting.

Feedback on learning activity 19.4

A review of key developments within the business which are essential if the organisation is to make progress. Some awareness of the difficulties in managing and implementing new technology, including training issues, costs, failures and so on should be mentioned. There is also a requirement to review the confidentiality procedures, both contractual and statutory, in place to protect IP.

Feedback on self-assessment question 19.4

Organisations should be looking to the supply chain to assist at some stage in the design and development of new technology. This question allows for an examination of the depth of that collaboration and the reasons behind it. It would be expected that suppliers make improvements on a continuous basis and some of these improvements would benefit those organisations further up the supply chain.

Feedback on learning activity 19.5

All organisations should have a stream of innovative products and processes coming into fruition if it is to sustain itself in the competitive arena. This

19

question calls for the identification of the different approaches to innovative development with the function and organisation.

Feedback on self-assessment question 19.5

Innovations within the process side of manufacturing could include: modifying or eliminating a process, streamlining the process, outsourcing or shifting responsibility to someone else. Product innovations might include: new material inputs, redesign, technical improvements, new uses for existing products, the development of new products and expansion of intellectual property right. In addition, organisations often use existing technological developments to expand their expertise into services whereby these can be sold on a consultancy basis.

A technological strategy

Introduction

A review of the impact that the internet has had on the development of supply chain management.

'A number of companies (Cisco, Dell, Adaptec, Zara, and Texas Instruments) have used the internet successfully to lower costs and add value to their businesses.'
Supply Chain Online

Session learning objectives

After completing this session you should be able to:

20.1 Explain the importance of sophisticated extranets as an aid to information flows.
20.2 Give examples from organisational life of e-sourcing and ordering.
20.3 Assess the value to the efficiency of the organisation of automated payment and accounting systems.

Unit content coverage

Learning objective

4.3 Appraise the application of technology to automate and streamline key operational processes within the supply chain (both internal and external to the organisation).

Prior knowledge

Awareness of the basics of internet technology.

Resources

Access to internet systems.

Timing

You should set aside about 5 hours to read and complete this session, including learning activities, self-assessment questions, the suggested further reading (if any) and the revision question.

20.1 The developing use of extranets

The use of extranets

When done correctly, extranets provide a safe way to allow transactional business-to-business activities and can save the organisation both time

20

333

and money. The automotive industry uses extranets to cut down on its redundant ordering processes and keep suppliers up to date on parts and design changes, allowing quicker response times to suppliers' problems and questions. Suppliers can receive proposals, submit bids, provide documents, and even collect payments through an extranet site. An extranet has restricted (password-protected) access, so it may be connected directly to each party's internal systems.

Does every company need one?

Many view extranets as the next era in web development. While other business-to-business communications, such as electronic data interchange (EDI), are out there, an extranet is more user-friendly because of its web interface and allows for less regimented and more ad-hoc inquiries. Before a company can make an attempt at harnessing the capabilities and profits gained from using an extranet, a fully functioning intranet has to be in place.

The benefits of extranets, such as reduced time to market and cost of doing business, and faster access to partner information, may be outweighed by the costs. Security, web servers and development, legacy systems integration, ongoing support and maintenance as well as a large amount of time and energy, may be more than setting up either a website or an intranet.

Learning activity 20.1

Research a good website design with a view to making critical comment as a business tool.

Feedback on page 339

Extranets generally have the following features:

- *The use of internet technologies and standards:* These include the standardised techniques for transmitting and sharing information and the methods for encrypting and storing information, otherwise known as the internet protocol, or IP.
- *The use of web§ browsers§:* Users access extranet information using a web browser such as Microsoft Internet Explorer. Browser software uses relatively small amounts of memory and resources on a computer and can be read on almost any computer. That makes an application developed for a browser easy to deploy. A browser on a user's machine is all the software he or she needs to take full advantage of the extranet application.
- *Security§:* By their very nature, extranets are embroiled in concerns about security. To protect the privacy of the information that is being transmitted, most extranets use either secure communication lines or proven security and encryption technologies that have been developed for the internet.
- *Central server/repository:* Extranets usually have a central server where documents or data reside. Members can access this information from any computer that has internet access.

In time, companies may be forced to use an extranet with their suppliers and customers. Even now, some large corporations say they will not do business with companies that won't be connected to a secure extranet in the coming years.

Self-assessment question 20.1

Examine your own organisational website and suggest an insert that would improve the visibility or effectiveness of your function.

Feedback on page 339

20.2 E-sourcing

We have already discussed the growth and benefits of e-procurement in earlier modules. E-procurement benefits are:

* improved information flow and service
* reduced transaction costs
* increased speed and efficiency
* removal of 'maverick' purchases made outside the organisational contractual arrangements
* the ability to aggregate purchasing across the organisation.

A summary of the key elements of e-procurement are:

* e-procurement, which now accounts for a significant amount of MRO (maintenance, repair and operating systems). Automating the paper-based system allows staff to focus on strategic supplier relationships and save costs and time
* hubs, where several networks can be connected together
* exchanges, B2B websites where buyers and sellers meet to transact business
* marketplaces, vertical or horizontal e-markets, either supplier/purchaser owned or neutral
* e-catalogues facilitate real-time, two-way communication between buyers and suppliers and allow for improved vendor relationships through improved vendor services and information to purchasers
* e-auctions
* reverse auctions.

Learning activity 20.2

Prepare a report on the latest technology assisting data transfer and payment systems.

Feedback on page 339

20

335

Now try self-assessment question 20.2 below.

Self-assessment question 20.2

Review your own organisation's purchasing practice and identify the integration with e-procurement.

Feedback on page 340

20.3 Automated processes

Electronic data interchange (EDI)

Purchasing systems such as EDI are now a standard feature of procurement operations. Organisations are moving towards the paperless office where routine communications such as orders, schedules and invoices go direct from computer to computer.

The main benefits of EDI are:

- *speed* as information moves rapidly between companies with little human interaction
- *accuracy*
- *cost efficiency* as there is a significant reduction in the cost of paper.

EDI is the transfer of data from one computer to another using agreed standards. Types of data transferred are according to Baily et al (2004):

- *trade data*, including all the purchasing documentation
- *CAD/CAM* data
- *query/response* to orders
- *monetary data*, which involves the electronic transfer of money computer to computer.

Learning activity 20.3

Identify the cost savings in using EDI in your own organisation.

Feedback on page 340

Bar coding

Bar coding is a form of automatic identification which has been adopted widely in the retail industry but is also used in warehousing, inventory control, production, operations management, distribution and quality control. The most prevalent system used in the UK is the European Article Number (EAN) system for the identification of goods, services and locations and automatic data capture. The information in the bar code is read by a laser scanner and sent to a computer. In retail organisations, the identification is returned immediately to the checkout where it is printed on a receipt.

In production operations it is used for several functions including:

- counting raw materials and finished goods inventories
- lot tracking
- automatic warehouse transactions
- package tracking.

The benefits are considerable, not least the speed of operation and accuracy. It has an impact on stock levels. Response times to customers and suppliers are faster as information is accessed quickly. Warehouse operations can be virtually automated. Fraud is also controllable.

Electronic point of sale (EPOS)

EPOS systems which are now familiar in almost all retail operations record the store sales by scanning the bar codes at the point of sale. Information on the detail of these sales is then immediately available further down the supply chain.

The benefits to the parties involved include:

- reduced checkout times
- the ability to pay by credit card
- smart shelves which indicate to management when stocks are low
- electronic article surveillance (EAS) which can assist in the detection and prevention of shoplifting.

Automated payment schemes

What are payment systems? A **payment system** is the shared part of an end-to-end process that offers an account-based transfer service between two final customers – and between two different banks. Payment systems sit at the heart of what is often referred to as the banking system. Transfers can occur between personal customers, between businesses, or between personal and business customers.

Payment systems are vital to the UK economy. In 2002 clearing systems processed over 5 billion clearing transactions, corresponding to a value of £86,025 billion.

Payment systems can be broadly divided into clearing schemes and plastic card networks. In terms of clearing schemes:

- Direct debits, direct credits and standing orders are cleared using Bankers' Automated Clearing Services (BACS).
- Cheques and paper credits are cleared via the Cheque and Credit Clearing Company (CCCL).
- Real-time gross settlement (RTGS) is cleared by the Clearing House Automated Payment Scheme (CHAPS).
- Plastic card networks cover debit, credit and ATM cards.

20

At the enterprise level, BACS can be integrated with an e-commerce B2B purchasing system to allow automated settlement of accounts between organisations.

As the BACS process is electronic, it removes the need to write cheques, which can be a costly process, subject to human error.

Electronic funds transfers

Banks can move money between one bank account and another electronically over computer networks. This is called electronic funds transfer or EFT for short.

BACS is one example of the application of EFT.

EFT is now a familiar feature of our daily lives. When a customer pays for goods in a shop or supermarket using a debit card, the customer and retailer accounts are updated electronically. If they pay at an electronic terminal, called an electronic point of sale (EPOS), then this is called EFTPOS, or electronic funds transfer at point of sale.

Although the processing could be completed in real time, the transactions in the UK are usually uploaded and processed as a batch overnight and then the customer and retailer accounts are updated.

SWIFT stands for Society for the Worldwide Inter-bank Financial Telecommunications network that allows member banks to send cross-border payment instructions to each other and effect cash movements using EFT.

CHAPS Euro is an electronic same-day payment system that enables the transfer of money in Euros. It was launched in 1999. Other similar systems exist outside Europe.

The internet has opened the way for e-commerce. To most of us this means selling goods and services over the internet. EFT is the means by which the transactions are authorised and completed online.

Selling over the internet offers many advantages for customers and retailers.

Advantages

- Can buy 24 hours a day, 365 days a year.
- No need to handle cash since all transactions are made using cards.
- The transactions are automatic, saving staff costs.
- The process is almost paperless.
- The customer can print off an onscreen receipt.
- The delivery process can often be tracked online.
- Goods are often discounted because of lower retail costs.

E-commerce can be more fully defined as a paperless exchange of business information using EDI, email, EFT and similar technologies.

20

Self-assessment question 20.3

Research how your company makes automated payment systems that are secure from fraud.

Feedback on page 340

Revision question

Now try the revision question for this session on page 343.

Summary

The internet has been developing quickly as a tool for buyers to purchase more effectively and efficiently through EDI transfers and the paperless office is around the corner.

Suggested further reading

Read the chapter on purchasing procedures in Lysons and Farrington (2006).

Feedback on learning activities and self-assessment questions

Feedback on learning activity 20.1

Scope is given here for some primary research on good business websites with critical comments on the design, information and accessibility, as well as an appreciation of its impact on the business fortunes of that organisation.

Feedback on self-assessment question 20.1

Websites need regular updating with pertinent, well-written inserts. Developing an understanding of the value of the website as a promotional tool is important.

Feedback on learning activity 20.2

There are a number of commercial systems available. This is an opportunity for seeking out the best. Data transfer will be in many forms and companies will specialise in providing solutions for a number of areas such as web integration used for data collection, adding significant value in areas such as:

- *Research and development support:* collection, standardisation and delivery of relevant research data typically from many different sources both generally available or behind a log-in page.

20

- *Competitor tracking and market intelligence:* gathering competitive product information, press releases, patent information and so on from competitor websites.
- *Information aggregation:* automated collection of large volumes of information such as job postings, credit information, news and so on.
- *Price information:* tracking of pricing information from sources like vendors, organisations and public institutions tracking such information.
- *Catalogues:* information gathering and dissemination.

Feedback on self-assessment question 20.2

Is the organisation fully technically integrated, and if not, what are the reasons?

Feedback on learning activity 20.3

The costs of implementing EDI have been expensive in many organisations. What cost benefits have accrued? There should be savings based on speed and accuracy for instance, plus the ability to extend the logistical supply chain around the world and to access and use large amounts of data.

Feedback on self-assessment question 20.3

There are three payments systems in UK banking, all overseen by the Association for Payment Clearing Services (APACS): (1) for clearing cheques (2) for clearing standing orders and direct debits and (3) the Clearing House Automatic Payments System – usually referred to as 'CHAPS'. The banks themselves will build in systems to prevent fraud on behalf of their customers.

Revision questions

Revision question for study session 1

Explain the importance of the purchasing function aligning itself with organisational objectives.

Feedback on page 345

Revision question for study session 2

Supplier selection has traditionally been described as being based on the 5 Rs (right price, right quality, right quantity, right time and right place). Is this still relevant today?

Feedback on page 345

Revision question for study session 3

Explain how an organisation effectively sets supplier KPIs.

Feedback on page 345

Revision question for study session 4

Describe the basis on which suppliers are assessed.

Feedback on page 345

Revision question for study session 5

Examine when an organisation would want to switch suppliers.

Feedback on page 346

Revision question for study session 6

Describe using practical examples how an organisation scans the environment to obtain useful market intelligence.

Feedback on page 346

Revision question for study session 7

List the advantages for an organisation in tiering the supply base.

Feedback on page 346

Revision question for study session 8

Good communications between two parties are important in maintaining their relationship. Explain how good communications are maintained.

Feedback on page 346

Revision question for study session 9

Low costs that can be transformed into something that customers see as value are a major competitive advantage. Explain how a buyer induces the supplier to lower their costs.

Feedback on page 346

Revision question for study session 10

Risk management is based on being able to distinguish between an event that is truly random and an event that is the result of cause and effect. Explain how organisations plan to minimise risk within the purchasing function.

Feedback on page 347

Revision question for study session 11

Research is about obtaining information that will provide a competitive advantage for the business. Explore the types of research that an organisation could undertake to improve its competitive position.

Feedback on page 347

Revision question for study session 12

E-business is seen by many organisations as an important factor in providing a competitive advantage. Describe how an organisation can use technology to achieve such a business lead.

Feedback on page 347

Revision question for study session 13

In negotiations, failure to plan properly often leads to poorly formulated objectives, and the use of inappropriate negotiating styles or tactics. Describe what planning should take place if negotiations are to be successful.

Feedback on page 347

Revision question for study session 14

Describe the role that ethics plays in purchasing decisions.

Feedback on page 348

Revision question for study session 15

Explain to what extent the theories surrounding transactional analysis, game theory and body language enhance the skills of a negotiator.

Feedback on page 348

Revision question for study session 16

Discuss whether closer, cross-functional relationships are the future of buying.

Feedback on page 348

Revision question for study session 17

Disputes will arise with suppliers because of the inherent conflict within the relationship, if each party to the agreement is seeking to maximise their return on the contract in pursuit of higher margins. Describe and evaluate these disputes.

Feedback on page 348

Revision question for study session 18

Explain how e-technology has contributed to more efficient information flows between the buyer and supplier.

Feedback on page 348

Revision question for study session 19

Explain the contribution made by total quality management to the competitive position of an organisation.

Feedback on page 348

Revision question for study session 20

Consider the view that all organisations need a web-based strategy for commercial success.

Feedback on page 349

Feedback on revision questions

Feedback on revision question for study session 1

The strategy of an organisation is important for the direction and purpose of that organisation in the future. All successful organisations have a strategy whether planned or emergent and as part of that strategy goals are translated into policies and objectives which flow down the organisation into the various functions that make up the value chain. The competitive position of the organisation and the margin achieved is dependent upon each of the functions contributing to the final outcomes.

Feedback on revision question for study session 2

The 5Rs still have merits as they are at the core of supplier selection. Carter's 10Cs, however, deal with the increasing complexity of supply selection and the importance of aligning the supplier more closely with the buyer's organisational needs, building the supplier's competences into the buyer's own. The supplier base will be reduced.

The question of the supplier role needs to be considered. For example, if the supplier has world-class credentials then they should be involved so far as is reasonable in the process of design and development of new products. The question of supplier development should also be considered.

Feedback on revision question for study session 3

The purchasing function needs to establish some form of quantitative or qualitative measurement of supplier performance. KPIs focus on the most important measurable performance aspects. The former are those that are measured against set performance standards such as price reduction or reduction in lead times, whereas the latter will look at some of the broader strategic issues and are therefore more difficult to assess. KPIs must be achievable and sustainable and be closely linked to the strategic direction of the business.

Feedback on revision question for study session 4

There are many reasons for supplier assessment, e.g. selection, motivation, development, reduction of risk, measuring against standards. The process of assessment should also be discussed to examine whether it is credible, consistent and accurate. In addition there should be some discussion concerning the wider issues of supplier performance such as agility and responsiveness.

Feedback on revision question for study session 5

Effective vendor rating systems if properly constructed and implemented will provide the basis for assessing supplier performance against established metrics and business criteria. Some discussion of the relationship life cycle should be included. Also the nature of the competitive market and the need to reduce the supplier base to more efficient levels, and the introduction of tiering.

Feedback on revision question for study session 6

This question requires a review of the PESTEL or DEEPLIST methods of tracking the environment and the importance of identifying factors beyond the organisation's control that might impact on the business.

Feedback on revision question for study session 7

Organisations have for many years sought to reduce their supplier base as they seek to implement a lean supply regime. By segmenting the chosen supply base into tiers, it gives a measure of prioritisation in the management of the supply chain. The first tier is reserved for the immediate and direct suppliers of assemblies and other final stage components whereas other layers involving second tier suppliers are reserved for component suppliers who supply the first tier suppliers, thus removing them from direct involvement with the manufacturer.

This enables more comprehensive integration of the supply base for the benefit of the buyer.

Feedback on revision question for study session 8

This involves an understanding of the basic communication tools and the possibility of distortion and noise. In addition there has to be requisite knowledge to make an effective communication, and lastly the communicator should have essential skills, for example an ability to perceive how a message may be received is an important skill, as is precision. A professional buyer learns to be succinct in their communications, gaining credibility for that precision and relevance.

Feedback on revision question for study session 9

An understanding of the importance strategically of lowering costs and beating the competition. Strategies for cost reduction include positioning within the product life cycle, the usual discounts for volume, the impact of technology, and the establishment of a more competitive buying system. Suppliers should be encouraged to have their own cost reduction systems.

Feedback on revision question for study session 10

At the fundamental level the impact of a supply-based event should be assessed and managed. Some consideration should be given to the development of a tried and trusted supply base. There should also be a discussion of the need for a contingency plan in the event of a disaster beyond the control of the organisation.

Feedback on revision question for study session 11

Research is about gathering intelligence concerning competitors and suppliers, and to build up a market intelligence system. It is also about the deeper investigation of processes such as JIT, so as to understand how best to take advantage of such processes.

Feedback on revision question for study session 12

There are several examples of e-business which can be discussed to show how organisations have improved their competitive position:

- intranet portals which allow employees to access all the information they need to do their job via a desktop application
- email
- data exchange including EDI
- transportation product tracking
- supply chain management
- exchange platforms to share information and trade with supply chain partners
- databases.

Feedback on revision question for study session 13

As well as the make-up of the negotiation team and the skills required, there should be some consideration of the supply market context in terms of growth: is this a new market, a growing market, a mature market, a retracting market? What is the impact of new technology on this market? Geography: is this a global market, a distributed market, a rural market? Is distance an issue? And also the power of the supplier in terms of turnover and market position.

The procurement decision should be considered in terms of (1) Risk: what is the nature of the purchase that is being made in terms of its level of risk, and level of expenditure? (2) Complexity: how complex is the good or service that is being purchased?

Also the relationship between the parties in terms of history and timeline: how much time is available for the negotiation?

Feedback on revision question for study session 14

Lysons lists the importance of ethics for purchasing:

- Purchasing staff are the representatives of the organisation in its dealings with suppliers
- Sound ethical conduct in dealing with suppliers is essential to the creation of long-term relationships and the establishment of supplier goodwill
- Purchasing staff are probably more exposed to the temptation to act unethically than most other employees
- It is impossible to claim professional status for purchasing without reference to a consideration of its ethical aspects.

There should also be some discussion of the CIPS code on ethics.

Feedback on revision question for study session 15

The value of these theoretical techniques is dependent upon the essential skills of a negotiator. They are also culturally centred, and at times may be of limited use, especially if the other negotiators are also fully aware of the techniques. They may be of some value in pressurised situations where negotiators are under stress.

Feedback on revision question for study session 16

The question calls for the consideration of the benefits of long-term relationships and if possible the opportunity for first tier suppliers to become working partners with the buyer. Partnership models and forms should be considered and the advantages and disadvantages.

Feedback on revision question for study session 17

This question requires the consideration of conflict as an issue within the procurement function and the techniques to resolve it successfully. There should be some discussion of the disruptive elements of conflict but also, in the right context, the benefits it brings to the relationship.

Feedback on revision question for study session 18

The increasing use of software to assist with the supplier relationship side of business as well as the range of e-procurement techniques has streamlined the trading aspect of business, added further supply dimensions in the global market and assisted in lowering the cost of procurement.

Feedback on revision question for study session 19

The contribution of TQM is attested by its success in Japanese manufacturing industries. Any strategy that looks for increasing quality has the potential to deliver a competitive advantage. TQM is a philosophy, however, that needs to be supported and driven by senior management.

Feedback on revision question for study session 20

Many view extranets as the next era in web development. While other business-to-business communications, such as electronic data interchange (EDI), are out there, an extranet is more user-friendly because of its web interface and allows for less regimented and more ad-hoc inquiries. The benefits of extranets, such as reduced time to market and cost of doing business, and faster access to partner information, may be outweighed by the costs: security, web servers and development, legacy systems integration, ongoing support and maintenance. Extranets require a large amount of time and energy, much more than what it takes to get an intranet or website up and running.

References and bibliography

This section contains a complete A-Z listing of all publications, materials or websites referred to in this course book. Books, articles and research are listed under the first author's (or in some cases the editor's) surname. Where no author name has been given, the publication is listed under the name of the organisation that published it. Websites are listed under the name of the organisation providing the website.

Andrews, K (1971) *The Concept of Corporate Strategy*. Homewood, IL: Irwin.

Armstrong, M, K Gallagher and G Watson (2005) *Managing for Results*. London: Chartered Institute of Personnel and Development.

Baily, P, D Farmer and D Jessop (2004) *Purchasing, Principles and Management*. Harlow: FT Prentice Hall.

Bendell, T (1991) *The Quality Gurus*. London: DTI.

Berne, E (1970) *Games People Play: The Psychology of Human Relationships*. London: Penguin Books.

Blair, G and S Meadows (1996) *A Real-Life Guide to Organizational Change*. Aldershot: Gower Press.

Blake, RR and JS Mouton (1964) *The Managerial Grid*. Houston, Texas: Gulf.

Blake, RR and JS Mouton (1978) *The New Managerial Grid*. Houston, Texas: Gulf.

Boddy, D (2005) *Management: An Introduction*, 3rd edition. Harlow: FT Prentice Hall.

British Quality Foundation: http://www.quality-foundation.co.uk

BSI Quality Assurance: http://www.bsi.org.uk

Business Listening: http://www.businesslistening.com

Calvi, R, MA Le-Dain, Harbis and MV Bonotta (2001) 'How to manage early supplier involvement into the new product development process'. *Proceedings of the 10th International Annual IPSERA Conference 2001*, pp158–62.

Carter, R (1995) 'The 7Cs of Effective Supplier Evaluation', *Purchasing and Supply Chain Management*, April, pp44–5.

Crosby, PB (1979) *Quality is Free*. McGraw-Hill.

Crosby, PB (1984) *Quality Without Tears*. McGraw-Hill.

David, JS, Y Hwang, KW Buck and H Rencou (1999) *The Impact of Purchasing on Financial Performance*. Tempe, AZ: Arizona State University Press.

Day, M (ed) (2002) *Gower Handbook of Purchasing Management*, 3rd edition. Aldershot: Gower Publishing.

Deming, WE (1986) *Out of the Crisis*. MIT.

Dobler, DW, L Lee and DN Burt (1990) in *Purchasing and Materials Management*. London: McGraw-Hill Education.

Doole, R and I Lowe (2005) *Strategic Marketing Decisions*. Oxford: Butterworth-Heinemann Ltd.

Drucker, P (1985) *Managing in Turbulent Times*. London: Harper Collins.

DTI (1991) *Total Quality Management and Effective Leadership*. London: DTI.

European Foundation for Quality Management: http://www.efqm.org

Evans, JR (1993) *Applied Production and Operations Management*, 4th edition. Minneapolis, MN: West Publishing Co.

Evans, JR and WM Lindsay (2005) *The Management and Control of Quality*, 6th edition. London: Thomson.

Feigenbaum, AV (1951) *Quality Control Principles, Practice and Administration*. McGraw-Hill.

Finlay, P (2000) *Strategic Management: An Introduction to Business and Corporate Strategy*. Harlow: FT Prentice Hall.

Forsyth, DR (1993) 'Building a bridge between basic social psychology and the study of mental health', *Contemporary Psychology*, 38, pp931–2.

French, JPR, Jr and B Raven (1960) 'The bases of social power.' In: D Cartwright and A Zander (eds) *Group Dynamics*. New York: Harper & Row.

Geert Hofstede personal website: http://www.geert-hofstede.com

Goffman, E (1981) *Forms of Talk*. Philadelphia, PA: University of Pennsylvania Press.

Hamel, G and CK Prahalad (1994) *Competing for the Future*. Boston, MA: Harvard Business Press.

Hammer, M and J Champy (2001) *Reengineering the Corporation: A Manifesto for Business Revolution*. London: Brealey Publishing.

Hannagan, T (2005) *Management, Concepts and Practices*, 4th edition. Harlow: FT Prentice Hall.

Harrison, J (1994) 'The role and practice of benchmarking', *Knight Wendling Newsletter*, 12, p9.

Heltriegel, D and JW Slocum (1988) *Management*, 5th edition. Reading, MA: Addison-Wesley.

Hines, P (1993) 'Integrated materials management: the value chain redefined', *International Journal of Logistics Management*, 4(1), pp13–22.

House, RJ and TR Mitchell (1974) 'Path-goal theory of leadership', *Contemporary Business*, 3(2), pp81–98.

Huczynski, A (2004) *Influencing Within Organizations*. London: Routledge.

Hughes, J, M Ralf and B Michels (1999) *Transform Your Supply Chain*. London: International Thomson Business Press.

Institute of Quality Assurance: http://www.iqa.org

Jaeger: http://www.jaeger.com

Johnson, G and K Scholes (2002) *Exploring Corporate Strategy*, 6th edition. Harlow: FT Prentice Hall.

Jones, DT and JP Womack (2005) *Lean Solutions: How Companies and Customers Can Create Value and Wealth Together*. New York: Simon & Schuster.

Juran, J (1951) *Quality Control Handbook*. McGraw-Hill.

Kaplan, RS and DP Norton (1992) 'The balanced scorecard: measures that drive performance', *Harvard Business Review*, Jan-Feb, 134–47.

Kipnis, K (1986) *Legal Ethics*. Harlow: Prentice Hall.

Lamming, R (1998) *Beyond Partnership: Strategies for Innovation and Supply*. Harlow: Prentice Hall.

Lawrence, P and JW Lorsch (1967) *Organization and Environment*. Boston, MA: Harvard Business School Press.

Lee, R and P Lawrence (1991) *Organisational Behaviour: Politics at Work*. Cheltenham: Nelson Thornes.

Lewicki, R, D Saunders, B Barry and John Minton (2003) *Essentials of Negotiation*, 3rd edition. London: McGraw Hill.

Lynch, R (2000) *Corporate Strategy*, 2nd edition. Harlow: Pearson.

Lysons, K and B Farrington (2006) *Purchasing and Supply Chain Management*, 7th edition. Harlow: FT Prentice Hall.

McDaniel, CD and RH Gates (1999) *Contemporary Market Research*. London: International Thomson Publishing.

McDonald, M (2000) *Marketing Plans*. London: Butterworth-Heinemann.

McDonald, M and M Christopher (2003) *Marketing: A Complete Guide*. Basingstoke: Palgrave Macmillan.

ManagementFirst website: http://www.managementfirst.com/knowledge_management/articles/knowledge_assets.php

Melaville, AI (with MJ Blank) (1991) *What It Takes: Structuring interagency partnerships to connect children and families with comprehensive services*. Washington, DC: Education and Human Services Consortium.

Mentzer, J (2001) *Supply Chain Management*. London: Sage Publications.

Moller, C (1988) *Personal Quality: The Basis of All Other Quality*. Hillerod, Denmark: Time Manager International.

Mullins, L (2002) *Management and Organisational Behaviour*, 5th edition. London: FT Pitman Publishing.

National Statistics Online: http://www.statistics.gov.uk

Neely, A, C Adams and M Kennerley (2002) *The Performance Prism*. Harlow: Pearson.

Oakland, JS and LJ Porter (2004) *TQM: Text with Cases*. Oxford: Butterworth-Heinemann Ltd.

Palmer, R and R Brookes (2004) *Contemporary Global Marketing*. Basingstoke: Palgrave Macmillan.

Parasuraman, A, VA Zethami and LL Berry (1990) 'A conceptual model of service quality and the implications for future research', *Journal of Marketing*, 49(4), pp41–50.

Peters, T and N Austin (1985) *A Passion for Excellence: The Leadership Difference*. London: Collins.

Porter, ME (1985) *Competitive Advantage*. New York: Free Press

Porter, ME (1998a) *Competitive Strategy*. London: Free Press.

Porter, ME (1998b) *Competitive Advantage*. London: Simon & Schuster.

Pryor, LS (1989) 'Benchmarking: A self-improvement strategy', *Journal of Business Strategy*, 10(6), pp28–32.

Robbins, SP and DA DeCenzo (2005) *Fundamentals of Management*, 5th edition. London: Pearson Prentice Hall.

Ross, DF (2003) *Distribution Planning and Control: Managing in the Era of Supply Chain Management*. London: Kluwer Academic Publishers.

Senge, P (2006) *The Fifth Discipline*. London: Random House Business Books.

Shannon, CE and W Weaver (1949) *The Mathematical Theory of Communication*. Urbana, IL: University of Illinois Press.

Simchi-Levi, D, P Kaminsky and E Simchi-Levi (2003) *Managing the Supply Chain*. New York: McGraw-Hill.

Smith, A (1996) *The Wealth of Nations* (K Sutherland (ed) 1998). Oxford: Oxford University Press.

Stogdill, RM (1974) *A Handbook of Leadership*. New York: Free Press.

Supply Chain Online: http://www.supplychainonline.com

Thomas, KW (1976) 'Conflict and conflict management.' In: MD Dunette (ed) *Handbook of Industrial and Organizational Psychology*. Chicago, IL: Rand McNally.

Thompson, DM and GR Homer (2001) 'Internet searchable supplier database in the automotive industry', *Proceedings of the 10th annual IPSERA Conference*, pp815–25.

Vollman, DC, WL Berry, DB Whybark and FR Jacobs (2004) *Manufacturing Planning and Control Systems*, 4th edition. New York: McGraw-Hill Publishing.

von Neumann, J and O Morgenstern (1947) The Theory of Games and Economic Behavior, 2nd edition. Princeton, NJ: Princeton University Press.

Weber, M (1947) *The Theory of Social and Economic Organisation*. Glencoe, IL: Free Press.

Womack, JP, DT Jones and D Roos (1990) *The Machine that Changed the World*. Oxford: Maxwell Macmillan.

World News: http://www.worldnews.com

Wynstra, JP, A Van Weele and B Axelsson (1999) 'Management Supplier Involvement in New Product Development', *European Journal of Purchasing*, 5, pp129–41.

Yuki, G (2001) *Leadership in Organizations*, 5th edition. Englewood Cliffs, NJ: Prentice Hall.

Index